BOOK TWO

COVERT OPERATIONS
IN THE WAR ON DRUGS
A TRUE STORY

NICK JACOBELLIS, SENIOR SPECIAL AGENT
U.S. CUSTOMS SERVICE, RETIRED

Controlled Delivery, Book II

Copyright ©2018 by Nick Jacobellis

ISBN 978-0-9982956-6-4 (print)
ISBN 978-0-9982956-7-1 (ebook)

Book design by www.StoriesToTellBooks.com

Email: badgepublishing@gmail.com

Website: www.badgepublishing.com

CONTROLLED DELIVERY

FOREWORD

A controlled delivery is the ultimate sting operation. In the 1980s and 1990s, undercover operations known as a controlled delivery became an effective tactic to use to dismantle Colombian based smuggling organizations.

The story *Controlled Delivery* is not your ordinary police procedural and depicts the actions of one of the most unique undercover operations ever mounted by the United States Customs Service. In addition to being the author of this book, I am also the U.S. Customs Agent who initiated, directed and participated in the undercover operation that is the main focus of this two-part true story.

While serving in an undercover capacity, my colleagues and I waged a secret war on the drug merchants who threatened our borders on a regular basis. Whenever we went operational, we became the portable front lines of The Drug War and achieved a victory for our side. The undercover personnel featured in this book were The Dirty Dozen With Wings, a group of self trained covert operators, who performed a mission that most people of sound mind would shy away from.

In order to understand how this true story came about, I need to take you back in time, to when I was a kid growing up in the Flatbush section of Brooklyn. It was during this period of time, that I had two dreams in life. One was to become a federal agent and the other was to learn how to fly. To be more specific, whenever I thought about the future, I always imagined myself wearing a military style flight suit and being involved in a law enforcement aviation pursuit of some kind.

After years of wondering how this vision of the future would materialize, I knew exactly how I was going to achieve my goals, when I read a magazine article about the missions that were performed by the U.S. Customs Service. The more I learned how this federal agency used uniformed officers, a special agent force and a fleet of vessels and aircraft to combat acts of smuggling, I knew exactly what I wanted to do for a career. After getting a college degree and working in city and state law enforcement positions, the day finally came when I was hired by the U.S. Customs Service.

After being assigned to the Resident Agent in Charge (RAC) Office at JFK Airport and the RAC Long Island, I requested a transfer to the front lines of The Drug War in South Florida. While the main focus of our efforts were in the ports of entry and along our borders, some of us also aggressively pursued smugglers beyond our shores.

My first assignment when I arrived in Miami was to serve as a member of the Freighter Intelligence Search Team aka FIST. FIST was the unit that interdicted acts of smuggling along the Miami River, as well as in the Port of Miami. On certain occasions, we also conducted vessel boarding operations in Customs Waters (within 12 miles of the shoreline).

After serving in the Miami Freighter Intelligence Team, I experienced deja vous in megaton proportions when I received my wings and I became a U.S. Customs Air Officer. As an Air Officer, I flew interdiction missions throughout the Caribbean, in search of smugglers who used private aircraft and high speed "go fast" boats, to smuggle drug contraband into the United States.

While residents and tourists enjoyed South Florida beaches and nightlife, an armada of U.S. interdiction assets engaged drug smugglers on a daily basis throughout the Caribbean. In time, the blue and green water of the Bahamas became littered with the rusting hulks of smuggling aircraft that didn't make it to their intended destination. Contraband occasionally washed up on the beach and the thunder of high-speed boats could always be heard rumbling off shore throughout the night.

After being promoted to the rank of Special Agent, I was assigned to the newly formed Miami Air Smuggling Investigations Group 7. Group 7 was located in a trailer complex behind the Miami Air Branch facility at Homestead Air Force Base. After a successful run at making several significant cases, I set my sights on more elusive targets.

During the period that I refer to as The Miami Vice Era of The Drug War, smugglers used various methods to penetrate our Southeast border at all hours of the day and night. While their goal was to "shotgun" as many drug shipments as possible into the United States, our mission was to stop them from doing so.

By the late 1980s and early 1990s, U.S. and Bahamian drug interdiction forces were very effective in forcing air and marine smugglers to operate further away from our shores. At the same time, it became more challenging for U.S. interdiction forces to operate farther away from their bases. Before our success in the Caribbean, the smugglers came to us, sometimes in droves. In fact, the smugglers seemed to subscribe to the theory, "If you throw enough shit against the wall, some of it was bound to stick."

During the period of time that it took to drive the smugglers away from South Florida and various locations in the Bahamas, smuggling organizations suffered significant losses of planes, vessels and crews. This was a serious blow to their operations, because transportation is the key element in any act of smuggling. As a result, without transportation, the smugglers were unable to bring their products to market.

While serving in this successful interdiction effort, I saw an opportunity for a group of undercover operatives to offer their services to unsuspecting violators (criminals). In order to conduct a successful infiltration operation, we had to convince our "clients" that we had ability to smuggle drug shipments into the CONUS (Continental United States), while avoiding U.S. interdiction assets. However, this plan would only work, if we utilized private aircraft that could carry large shipments of drug contraband. These planes also had to be capable of flying long distances without needing to be refueled.

In the last two decades of the 20th Century, South Florida was a labyrinth of intrigue that included a large number of informants, domestic drug traffickers, smugglers and law enforcement officers in the local population. As a result, my colleagues and I were in the right place at the right time to put our feelers out and draw attention to ourselves. Our targets were Colombian based smuggling organizations and their stateside representatives / receivers. My plan was to strike deep into the heart of the enemy through the effective use of covert operations.

In order to fund this operation, I intended to use the "front money" aka the expense money that was given to us by our Colombian "clients." This money would be used to pay the expenses that we incurred, when we provided the transportation services to "smuggle" drug shipments from Colombia to the United States. Once we were "hired" by a smuggling organization and we picked up a drug shipment in Colombia, we would maintain complete "control" over the contraband at all times. This included when we executed the "delivery" phase of every operation. It is also important to note, that whenever we went operational, my colleagues and I had to act like real smugglers without breaking the law.

Once an undercover aircraft and crew returned to the CONUS, my plan was to use the drug shipment as bait, to lure out as many drug smugglers and stateside receivers as possible. To add insult to injury, my colleagues and I would wait until we were paid a sizable amount of drug money for services rendered, before we agreed to deliver any of the contraband. Once the delivery was made, a small army of U.S. Customs Agents and other law enforcement officers would move in and arrest the subjects of our investigation. If everything went according to plan, the undercover operatives would ride off into the sunset, devise a new cover story, get introduced to another group of unsuspecting smugglers and repeat the same process as many times as possible.

Because we could not confide in the Colombian government, it was imperative for us to utilize the services of contract aircrews and sources of information to operate covertly on foreign soil. To be more specific, due to the risks involved, sworn law enforcement officers were not allowed to operate in an undercover capacity in places like Colombia. This policy necessitated the use of non-sworn civilian personnel, who were formally documented as confidential sources of information and contract employees.

In order to make my idea a reality, I turned to my most trusted network of airport contacts and documented sources of information. Up until this time in my career, my sources of information had helped me make a number of cases and seizures. The day I approached my private aviation contacts, they all agreed to serve and provide me with planes, crews, hangars, mechanics and office space. All I needed now was authorization from my superiors and we would be in business.

In October of 1988, I requested permission to form an undercover air unit that would be responsible to infiltrate smuggling organizations, for the purpose of executing as many controlled deliveries as possible. After presenting my plan to the Special Agent in Charge (SAC) in Miami and the Regional Commissioner, my "Trojan Horse" operation was approved. Clearly, at that time, the U.S. Customs Service was an agency that encouraged individual initiative.

With no prior military experience and an expired student pilot's license in hand, I became the ad hoc commanding officer of my very own undercover air unit. Looking back, I was probably the last person who should have been put in charge of a covert air operation, considering the fact that I only had about a dozen hours of flight training and three solo flights under my belt in single engine aircraft. The simple truth is, I got this job because it was my idea and no one else apparently wanted to assume the responsibility.

Having authorization to do anything in federal service was more important than anything else. Fortunately, a recent change in federal law allowed federal law enforcement agencies to establish proprietary corporations and create phony bank accounts, in the same way that intelligence agencies are known to operate. In addition, this new law authorized agencies to use trafficker directed funds, or money that was provided by violators (criminals) during undercover sting operations, as expense money to conduct undercover operations. This meant, that we could react to situations without delay, because we did not have to apply for traditional government funding through normal channels. While conducting these high risk undercover operations, every penny that we recovered from our drug smuggling "clients" would be deposited in a certified undercover bank account and would be strictly controlled.

In order to go operational, I recruited a cadre of contract personnel who were willing to play by the rules, despite the fact that on the surface we had to act like the smugglers we were targeting. Our contract crews included, war heroes, convicted felons, three defendant informants, a former Colombian drug cartel pilot, experienced private pilots, commercial airline pilots and a smuggler who never got caught.

While mounting these highly specialized covert operations, we assembled an impressive fleet of undercover aircraft that were "leased" to the U.S. Customs Service on a case-by-case basis. Because some of my contacts were aircraft brokers, we were able to rent any aircraft that we needed that we did not have in "inventory."

Officially, we were assigned to the U.S. Customs Service Miami Air Smuggling Investigations Group 7. After we completed our first mission, we became known as The Blade Runner Squadron, a nickname that we adopted because we flew on the edge. The original logo for this operation depicted an undercover aircraft taking off on the edge of a knife blade; the same knife that would be used to execute our crews, if their real identities became known to our adversaries.

When I wasn't working alone, I had at least one special agent, sometimes two or three, assigned to help me run this rather unorthodox covert air operation. When we went operational, we teamed up with other special agents from Group 7, from other Customs units in Miami, as well as with special agents from other agencies and from other Customs offices throughout the country.

In the process of executing a succession of transportation cases aka controlled deliveries, we made history on a number of occasions. The stakes were always very high and despite what one of our critics had to say, we took calculated risks because we were in a risky business, but we never took chances and believe me there's a difference between the two. Everyone who worked for us also proved to be incredibly trustworthy. This is evident by the fact, that we transported tons of cocaine and handled millions in untraceable cash without experiencing any integrity problems.

As you can imagine, participating in undercover operations involving multi-hundred and multi-thousand kilogram shipments of cocaine would prove to be a very dangerous and demanding experience. What was even more bizarre was that none of us were specially trained to do what we did. You see, despite the fact that controlled deliveries were the "meat and potatoes" of the U.S. Customs Service, there was no formal training available, that prepared us to mount safe and successful covert operations using undercover aircraft.

To be more specific, there was no specialized training program entitled Controlled Delivery 101. The undercover school that did exist provided very basic training at best. Worse yet, a number of special agents who were stationed in South Florida, weren't sent to undercover school in a timely fashion. As an example, I wasn't sent to undercover school until September of 1991. This meant that my colleagues and I were largely self-taught and learned our trade in the field. We learned how smugglers conducted business and how they behaved, by investigating acts of smuggling and interdicting smugglers in the act of violating

the law. Working with reliable informants and documented sources of informa-

tion also helped us to hone our skills as undercover operatives. The next hurdle

was to learn how to negotiate smuggling ventures and drive hard bargains with

Colombian based smugglers and their stateside representatives.

In order to learn the business of directing undercover air operations, I relied

on my experience as a U.S. Customs Air Officer and what little training and

experience that I had as a student pilot. Just like I was a self-taught undercover

agent, I was a self-taught director of flight operations as well. Since no school

existed that could train me to serve in this capacity, I spent my spare time devour-

ing flight manuals and talking to U.S. Customs Pilots and private pilots, to learn

about the flying characteristics of different types of aircraft. In doing so, I learned

how far different aircraft could fly, while carrying the required crew compliment

and various amounts of fuel and cargo.

I also became well versed on the capabilities of different types of aircraft,

to safely land and take off on different kinds of runways. This included while

taking off with a "full bag" of fuel and a cargo bay bulging with drug contraband.

I also had to become familiar with seaplane operations. In addition, I learned

how to navigate and plot courses on a map/air chart so I could plan operations

down the last gallon of aviation fuel. Last but not least, I also learned about

the weather and other factors that related to the safe operation of aircraft. This

included learning how to successfully penetrate Colombian airspace undetected.

Luckily, I was a people person. This made it easy for me to recruit, direct and control an eclectic group of the informants, sources of information and contract personnel. Even though there were times when I felt like the headmaster of a school for wayward boys, I accepted the antics of our "hired hands" as a way to let their hair down before going in harm's way.

While directing and participating in this undercover operation, I came to believe that pilots are a special breed, because each and every time they got airborne they defied gravity. I also believe that because I tried my hand at flying, I elevated my standing a notch or two with the experienced pilots that I recruited to serve in our UC OP.

Looking back, this dream of mine was only a success because I had the best people imaginable working by my side. In time, I saw us gel into an effective undercover force that never compromised its integrity and was able to fly under the most adverse conditions imaginable without experiencing the loss of life. We had close calls, but fortunately for us, being close only counts while playing horseshoes and throwing hand-grenades.

Everyone who agreed to work with us was treated with respect, regardless of their past mistakes and crimes against society. The special agents who were involved in this operation received a few quality step increases and monetary awards amounting to a few thousand dollars. A few of the Group 7 Special Agents who were actively involved in this certified undercover operation were eventually promoted and became Senior Special Agents. None of us asked for, or received any medals and none were handed out, even though many of the things that we did warranted being formally decorated.

In order to receive substantial monetary payments, a person had to be directly responsible for helping U.S. Customs Agents arrest major violators and seize significant amounts of contraband, drug money and valuable assets. If necessary, sources of information and contract personnel also had to be prepared to testify, if that's what it took to prosecute a case in federal court.

From the time that I started investigating acts of smuggling in South Florida until our undercover operation was disbanded, I was authorized to pay my sources of information and contract aircrews approximately $2.5 million dollars for services rendered. That figure alone should give you some idea of how successful we were. I say this, because the federal government does not authorize this amount of money to be paid to informants, sources of information and contract personnel unless they provide a very valuable service.

During this undercover operation, my colleagues and I provided the specialized assistance necessary that enabled U.S. Customs Agents, FBI Agents and DEA Agents, to arrest dozens of major violators and seize a number of multi-hundred and multi-thousand kilogram shipments of cocaine, thousands of pounds of marijuana and large quantities of drug money. In addition to helping me seize a number of drug smuggling aircraft, my cadre of informants and sources of information also made it possible for me and other agents to seize over thirty vehicles, two go fast vessels, dozens of firearms and other drug assets valued in the millions of dollars. Clearly, whatever amount of money we paid our "hired hands" was only a fraction of what they enabled the government to seize. In fact, in some respects, it is difficult to put a price on certain aspects of our success.

When these operations were being conducted, we never released any information that explained how these major drug seizures and arrests were actually made. When the media wanted to know more, our response was, "No comment." To their credit, the reporters who covered our press conferences didn't push for more clarification.

After reading this true story, some of you might ask why I never walked away from this incredibly stressful and dangerous assignment, in order to become a so-called "regular agent." One reason is because this operation was my idea. I should also mention that this operation didn't happen overnight. As you will read, it took several years of participating in interdiction missions and conducting different types of smuggling investigations, before I requested permission to form an undercover unit that specialized in executing controlled deliveries using private aircraft. By the time we completed our first high risk controlled delivery, I was hooked and wanted to stay in the game as long as possible. Quite frankly, I always believed that I would know when it was time to move on. Until that day came, I had every intention of honing my own skills and developing the capabilities of The Blade Runner Squadron.

One of the reasons I was drawn to covert operations, was because every controlled delivery required a great deal of "Yankee" ingenuity. I was also seduced by the taste of the hunt and the challenge of participating in the ultimate sting operation. I also enjoyed the adrenaline rush that was always present while working in high risk drug enforcement operations.

To give you an idea of where I am coming from, consider that one of my favorite movies is The Dirty Dozen. The theme of this unusual war movie should give you a better idea of what makes me tick as a human being. The idea of taking a dozen misfits, eccentrics and social outcasts and grooming them to become a force to be reckoned with, was something that got my creative juices flowing and made it worthwhile for me to get out of bed in the morning.

As a result of my Catholic upbringing, I also believed in forgiveness. Having this mindset enabled me to treat the informants, sources of information and contract personnel who had a "tainted" past with respect, providing they followed the rules and served with distinction. In fact, one of my sources of information who was a convicted felon, performed so admirably, I would have gladly given this guy a full pardon, if I had the authority to do so. I also worked with certain defendant informants, who I thought deserved to be formally pardoned.

From a professional standpoint, running the undercover operation that is the main subject matter of this book was the high point of my entire law enforcement career. In fact, nothing that I did before was as exciting and nothing I would ever do in the future, would peg my intrigue meter more, than being involved in covert air and marine operations.

There was also a bit of the rebel in me, who hated wearing suits and ties and working 9 to 5 as a "regular" agent. Call me crazy, but I preferred to make my own hours and work 12 to 18 hours days, instead of working 8 hours a day in an office pushing paper. If maintaining this level of activity meant that I had to work with little or no quality time off, then so be it. I was also a bit of an eccentric, who preferred working with other eccentrics.

I also liked the idea of cultivating my own cases, instead of being handed a stack of cases to investigate. In this regard I loved being proactive. I also like being creative and what was more creative than concocting cover stories and invading Colombia. I was also very loyal to the U.S. Customs Service and saw my involvement in cutting edge undercover operations, as a way to help keep my agency on the front page of the national news. In this regard, I was no different than any other professional, who did his best to make his team look good.

In order for us to get to the point where we were ready to go operational, my colleagues and I spent many days and nights learning the ropes of running successful undercover operations. We also learned early on, that failure to cover some small detail could result in the loss of life and a variety of other problems.

Any federal agent, who needed an undercover crew to infiltrate a smuggling organization and successfully transport a shipment of drug contraband, had to believe in our capabilities. In order to develop and maintain a favorable reputation, we had to execute every mission without making any mistakes, or causing an international incident. This was critically important, because making mistakes and creating international incidents were not tolerated. In this regard, only time would tell if my colleagues and I would always have the so called "right stuff."

In the late 1980s and the early 1990s, the U.S. Customs Service was evolving into an agency that was heavily involved in certified undercover operations. High ranking Customs managers liked having investigative groups under their command involved in successful covert operations for two main reasons. As I briefly mentioned before, one reason for this, was because successful UC ops generated the money aka trafficker funds that enabled agents to pay for a variety of legitimate expenses. In our case, this included rental fees for undercover vehicles, aircraft and vessels, as well as paying fuel bills, cell phone bills and travel expenses. In order to document every legitimate expense that we made, my colleagues and I obtained receipts whenever possible. In fact, we became so judicious about documenting our legitimate expenses, our unofficial motto became, "GET A RECEIPT!"

Having access to this outside source of revenue made local SAC and RAC Offices less dependent on headquarters for funding. Because the U.S. Customs Service had a knack for running successful undercover operations or special ops, annual cash awards and Quality Step Increases (QSI Awards), that were mini promotions, were handed out to the most active agents, as well as to their superiors. Naturally, the bosses received the larger cash awards, while the smaller amounts went to the worker bees.

It is also important to note, that in my opinion, the statistics generated during The Drug War should be viewed as being even more impressive, when you consider that a smaller number of agents were actually responsible for initiating the most significant cases. The bulk of the remaining agents provided valuable support, with some agents doing as little as possible. In other words, the heaviest load was actually carried by a smaller number of agents than you are aware of. I say this because, when a major case breaks on the local or national news and you hear that fifty federal agents were involved in an enforcement action, this case was probably made by one or two hard charging special agents, but forty eight others were needed to conduct surveillance's and execute search and arrest warrants. Like it or not, that's the way it was.

INTRODUCTION

I started writing this book in February of 1989. From the inception of this rather unusual undercover operation, I documented our adventures, trials and tribulations as they occurred, with the hope of one day sharing these events with the general public. With the exception of periodic editing, I wrote this true story while I was actively involved in directing and participating in drug interdiction missions, smuggling investigations and undercover operations. One reason why it took so long for me to publish Controlled Delivery Book I and II, is because this is not an easy story for me to tell.

Whether boarding tall ships in New York Harbor during the early days of our country, or preventing the smuggling of different types of contraband in more modern times, the agency known as the U.S. Customs Service had an outstanding reputation for protecting the revenue and the national security of the United States. After the terrorist attacks on 9/11/01, the U.S. Customs Service that I worked for was merged with the Immigration and Naturalization Service (INS) and transferred from the Treasury Department to the newly formed Department of Homeland Security. Today, an agency called

U.S. Customs and Border Protection (CBP) represents the uniformed side of the original or "Legacy" U.S. Customs Service and the "Legacy" INS. An agency called Homeland Security Investigations (HSI) and U.S. Immigration and Customs Enforcement (ICE) are the entities that perform a combined Customs/Immigration and DHS enforcement and investigative mission. This is strictly my opinion, but I hope the day comes when ICE/HSI are merged into CBP. Doing so, would enable us to have ONE federal agency that performs every Customs and Immigration mission.

For the purposes of contributing to the amazing history of the "Legacy" U.S. Customs Service, I will keep things as they once were and use the agency name that dates back to 1789 when I tell this true story. Putting the present situation aside, the U.S. Customs Service is often the last agency to capture the mind of the average person, when one considers the contribution made by the federal government in undercover drug enforcement operations. Far too many people believe that Customs "Agents" are the folks who go through your luggage at the airport when you return from a trip overseas. Although uniformed Customs Inspectors (now called CBP Officers) perform a necessary and at times a dangerous job, they are not part of the investigative side of the house. Only Special Agents and certain Customs Officers conducted criminal investigations and worked undercover. Hopefully, this book will shed some light, on one of the missions of the "Legacy" U.S. Customs Service that very few people are aware of.

The story *Controlled Delivery* takes you through several years of adventure and intrigue as seen through my eyes, while performing the duties of a U.S. Customs Patrol Officer, Air Officer, Special Agent and Senior Special Agent. In the beginning of this true story, I'll take you on the same journey that I took, when I graduated from the ranks of being a more traditional law enforcement officer and I became an undercover agent.

For security reasons, this story could not be told when these undercover operations were being conducted. After waiting over two decades to tell this story, the time has come to let the world know, how a relatively small group of undercover operatives executed a number of highly successful controlled delivery operations, that resulted in the seizure of over 22,000 pounds of cocaine, 11,000 pounds of marijuana, the arrest of dozens of major violators and the recovery of approximately $3 million dollars in trafficker directed funds (drug money). Of all the individuals who were arrested and sentenced as a result of our sting operations, two major violators received life sentences in federal prison for their "Drug War" crimes. I decided to go with a figure of 22,000 plus pounds of cocaine, because this is the amount that was transported in our undercover aircraft. An additional quantity of cocaine was air dropped to an undercover vessel, by the Colombian based targets of a Miami Group 7 investigation. This airdrop occurred after one of our undercover aircraft picked up an initial shipment of 500 kilos. This case is included in *Controlled Delivery Book I*.

While working in an undercover capacity, my colleagues and I made record-breaking drug seizures in different locations and broke our own record four times in the New England area alone. As you will read, our efforts were not without sacrifice. The question is, why have so many law enforcement officers given so much, for what at times seems to be such a hopeless cause? First, I think that we all respectively love our jobs. Our strong work ethic and upbringing molded us into people who are not afraid of a little hard work, even when the odds are against us. Second, I believe that we live in a world of extremes and are attracted to a combative existence when the cause is noble and just.

Law enforcement officers also enjoy protecting society from harm. In fact, one of the most gratifying aspects of our job was to seize a large drug shipment, or a significant amount of drug money. To put things in a more modern perspective, law enforcement officers from my generation considered drug smugglers to be no different than the terrorists that we are fighting today. Simply put, drug smugglers were the enemy and we engaged them to the best of our ability on a daily basis. As a result, we enjoyed being in a profession where we could bring major violators to justice and make them trade their Rolex watches, for an inexpensive pair of Smith & Wesson handcuffs.

All good things come to an end and as such, our operation did not last forever. The sanctioned undercover operation that was unofficially known as The Blade Runner Squadron was disbanded on May 12, 1993. Looking back, there was never a dull moment. I also have to state for the record, that I was actually grateful when I was transferred to other duties. I felt this way, because I had no more to give and I needed a change in scenery.

During my law enforcement career I was a chain-smoking workaholic, who would have preferred to work twenty-four hours a day if such a thing was possible. I guess you can say that I was an adrenaline junkie, who eagerly ran into harm's way each and every time an opportunity presented itself. By the time I joined the U.S. Customs Service and transferred to Miami, I lived by the motto that was made famous by Operation Greenback Agents (a money laundering operation in Miami); "So many Colombians, so little time."

As a result of my involvement in covert operations, I learned that being an undercover agent is a lot like being a stand-up comic, in a place where the audience gets to kill you if your jokes aren't funny. I also learned that working undercover can make the Grand Canyon look more like a shallow grave than a National Treasure.

Even after my line of duty spinal injuries got worse, I pushed myself as hard as humanly possible. I knew plenty of other law enforcement officers who would have gladly traded places with me and retired early, until the first time they were unable to walk right, or were in excruciating pain. After I turned down the first offer to medically retire, I used prescription medication and a cane to help me stay on the job and get around when my injuries flared up. In the process, a bad situation made worse, when I was re-injured for a third time in the line of duty.

After a long and very successful law enforcement career, I was forced to medically retire after I failed a medical fitness for duty examination. Since I had no say in the matter, I graciously accepted the set of retired special agent's credentials that came in the mail to my home. It was time for me to move on to the next phase of my life.

Once I retired, I went from doing 100 miles an hour in a 25 mile an hour speed limit, to a crawl. While it took some time to get used to a much slower pace, I eventually saw my situation as a blessing in disguise instead of a curse. As a retired agent, I used my free time to immerse myself in the lives of my family members. You might say that I made up for lost time, even though time is something that you can never really make up.

The first step that I took to accomplish this was to apologize to my two sons for being away so much. Even when I was technically off duty and at home, all of our lives were constantly interrupted by phone calls and emergencies that caused me to return to work. The day I made this apology, my youngest son Michael, who was 10 years old at the time, responded with all of the innocence of a child when he looked up at me and said, "Don't worry, Dad. You were fighting for our country." I still get choked up to this day whenever I think of my youngest son's kind words.

The story *Controlled Delivery* takes you back to a time when a relatively small number of U.S. Customs Agents and private contractors took the fight to the enemy through covert means. Whether my colleagues and I were very lucky, or good at what we did, is up to you to decide. Personally, I believe that God was our Co Pilot and that my colleagues and I were protected by a higher authority whenever we went operational. If you doubt this is true, I suggest you read on.

I also sincerely hope that you will find the information in this book to be even more interesting, because it was written by a special agent and not by a journalist who tagged along and documented these events through inexperienced eyes. It is also my hope, that after reading *Controlled Delivery*, you will have a greater insight into the efforts that were made by a few good men to successfully engage a very elusive enemy. Enjoy!

A NOTE FROM THE AUTHOR

Due to the volume of information that I received written authorization to publish, I decided to divide the true story *Controlled Delivery* into two parts. Doing so enabled me to include some additional information, that provides a more detailed description of what it was like to serve during The Miami Vice Era of The Drug War.

In order to conceal the identities of the government personnel that I worked with, I used their first name, followed by the first letter of their last name to identify them. I also used nicknames to identify the contract pilots, crew chiefs, informants and sources of information who helped us accomplish our mission. The bad guy's identities have also been changed, as are some of the details of certain events to protect trade craft.

When I decided to write this book, I sought immediate direction from the Office of Regional Counsel in 1988, regarding the publication of written material by a U.S. Customs Officer/Agent. In order to comply with agency policy and obtain written permission to publish the story *Controlled Delivery*, manuscripts that contained additional information were provided to the U.S. Customs Service for official review. The first letter of authorization that I received from an agency administrator is dated March 19, 1991, the second is dated July 15, 1994 and the third letter is dated June 10, 1996.

The photographs that are included in Book I and II were taken by various agents and undercover operatives in the field and were provided to me over the course of several years. *Copies of documents that authenticate the information in this book will be posted on my website: badgepublishing.com.

The story *Controlled Delivery* was written from my perspective and is based on what I did, what I observed, what I was told and what I documented when these events occurred. This includes, when I performed certain duties on my own and with other law enforcement officers, as well as when I recruited, debriefed, directed and worked with various informants, sources of information and contract personnel. I also made sure to give credit where credit was due, by acknowledging the contribution that was made by the law enforcement officers, contract personnel and sources of information, who served with great distinction during various enforcement actions, investigations and sanctioned undercover operations. When it was appropriate to do so, I also included my opinion and some personal information. I also left a few things out of this story, in order to comply with certain instructions that were relayed to me by the U.S. Customs Service. Regardless, I promise you won't be disappointed.

I should also mention, that documenting what we did was easy, compared to the process of editing the mountain of raw material that I was given authorization to publish. While I continued to prepare this story for publication, I also sanitized the contents well beyond what was required. This process included deleting and sanitizing certain information that I was previously authorized to publish.

In the years that I waited to publish Book I and Book II, I further developed my skills as a freelance writer, by publishing over 170 magazine articles and two historical fiction books; *The Frontline Fugitives Book I, The Khaki Cops* and *The Frontline Fugitives Book II, Cops In A Combat Zone.* Currently, *The Frontline Fugitives Book III and The Frontline Fugitives Book IV* are in their final stages and will be published in 2018.

Contents

ACKNOWLEDGMENTS

Controlled Delivery Book I and Book II are dedicated to my wife, my sons, the members of The Blade Runner Squadron, as well as to the U.S. Customs Agents, U.S. Customs Pilots, U.S. Customs Officers, FBI Agents, DEA Agents, police officers, sheriff's department detectives, federal prosecutors and U.S. military personnel who participated in the investigations, enforcement actions and undercover operations described in this true story.

THE BLADE RUNNER SQUADRON MOTTO

We fly at night if the price is right, no load too great, no distance too far, I'm the man for your contraband, one plane in, one plane out, last call!

CHAPTER 1

MANO DE NORTHE & CAMMORONES

I don't know if this is true, but according to my Cuban informant Hombre de la Calle, the Colombians called U.S. Agents Mano de Northe or Men from the North and Cammorones, which means shrimp. The designation of Mano de Northe was given to American federal agents because the United States is geographically located in North America. The designation Cammorones or "shrimp" had nothing to do with the physical stature of U.S. Federal Agents, but rather the fair complexion of our skin, because many American agents are Caucasian.

ANOTHER BOAT TRIP TO COLOMBIA

The most recent weather report called for a tropical storm to hit the Windward Passage, at the same time that my colleagues and I were traveling to the coast of Colombia on another undercover mission. As we traveled deeper into the storm, the roaring ocean began to build in ferocity, until we were completely surrounded by an angry sea of white capped waves. It was an awesome sight to behold.

While I held on for dear life, I couldn't help but think of the circumstances that led to me to participate in another undercover marine operation. Once again, the inability to secure country clearance and use an undercover aircraft to fly into Colombia, prompted us to become resourceful. Even though I generally preferred air operations, there was something very alluring about going to sea, that made me understand why some folks were drawn to a mariner's life. Clearly, traveling on the open ocean, while being protected by the deck of a relatively small vessel, was an exhilarating experience.

For those who consider themselves "sunshine" sailors, the ocean is a fun place to be. This is the case, when the weather is fully compliant and the conditions at sea are on the calm side. For U.S. Customs Agents in route to the Colombian coast in hurricane season, this journey was no day at the beach.

Despite the obvious risks involved, my colleagues and I volunteered to go on this mission in a rented 100 foot work boat, that looked large enough at the dock, but got a lot smaller once we put to sea. As we traveled deeper into the Windward Passage, the weather started to get progressively worse. In fact, the ocean was one big growling mess all the way to the horizon. Wave after wave crashed over our bow and occasionally sent foamy salt water cascading over the top of the wheelhouse. Even a novice sailor like me, could tell by the ferocity of the conditions, that this was the tropical storm that the weathermen warned us about. Tropical storm or not, in order to reach the first pick up point off the coast of Colombia, we had no choice but to forge ahead.

As soon as we entered the storm, the 16 foot waves were coming on fast and furious. In no time at all, the ocean around us was filled with huge mountains of dark green water that were topped off with frothy white caps. A low overcast sky made the storm seem even more ominous. The deeper we ventured into the storm, the angrier the ocean got. Soon, the 16 footers were followed by much larger waves, until finally the ocean was licking the top of the radar mast that towered over our vessel.

One of the most awesome sights in the world is to observe a giant wave pass right over your head. From my position at the helm, I could see the larger waves rolling up and down in the distance and coming our way, long before they actually made contact with our vessel. As the undercover vessel crashed through giant walls of seawater, the sound of her hull bending and being stretched to its limits, became an eerie reminder of the perils we would face, if our ship broke apart.

Waves are the heartbeat of the ocean. Nothing and I mean nothing on this earth, is more exciting, or potentially more dangerous, than coming face to face with one of the ocean's largest offspring. I know that there are sailors out there who have been through a great deal more than I have, but for a guy from the Flatbush section of Brooklyn, I can assure you, that this particular tropical storm had my undivided attention.

Each and every time we crashed into a giant wall of seawater, our boat would rise up as high as it could go, before gravity and the suction of the wave action would force us back down. The scariest part of the ride, was when our boat reached the very bottom of the trough of the wave and the entire vessel was surrounded by a giant wall of green seawater. As our boat made the climb back to the top of the angry ocean, I celebrated the fact that we were still alive and making headway. The fact that there was no place to go, made me feel like I was part of a captive audience to the greatest show on earth.

The longer I stood at the helm and steered the undercover boat through the stormy sea, the more I was in total awe of the immense power that controlled our destiny. At this point in our journey, I was feeling very strange as I came face to face with the intense power of nature. Clearly, something had come over me and it wasn't seasickness.

As I steered the undercover vessel through such a powerful storm, I was drawn to the force that commanded its fury. I guess you can say that I saw God's handy work on each and every wave. All it took, was a ride through an angry ocean, for me to realize how insignificant my land locked problems were. In other words, the bureaucratic bullshit and inter agency mumbo jumbo didn't mean a damn thing out here.

Things got a little dicey for me, when I tried to go below to retrieve something for me and Agent Joe G. to drink. While I did my best to hold on, a giant wave picked the boat out of the water and suspended it in mid air, causing the deck to be sucked out from under my feet. The second this happened, I was thrown backwards against the steel bulkhead of the undercover vessel.

The last thing that I needed, was to re-injure myself, after wrecking my back and neck in the plane crash landing incident a few weeks earlier. (The fact that I repeatedly smashed my spine against the steel bulkhead on the same vessel, during the first boat trip to Colombia also didn't help my situation.) Things got even worse, when I made the mistake of trying to get up, as another huge wave molested our vessel and threw me backwards at full speed into the steel bulkhead. A split second later, I was thrown forward into the railing that led to the wheelhouse. After being bashed around by the cruel sea, I was unable to stand or climb the ladder to the upper deck. Fortunately, I managed to get to my cabin and take some prescription pain medication.

That day we traveled 180 miles through a tropical storm and managed to make an average speed of 6 knots. Once we passed through the eye of the storm, the ocean around us began to settle down to a more sedate sea state. The fact that we survived this ordeal, was a tribute to our vessel's seaworthiness and a credit to the ability of our crew to hang in there. I'm also convinced that Almighty God personally authorized our safe passage. If you don't believe that Divine Intervention had anything to do with our survival, I suggest you go to sea during a violent storm and see how long you last before you start praying.

After spending several long days at sea, we finally arrived on station. Off in the distance I could see a coastal city near Point Galinas, that was partially illuminated by a few white lights. The Mano de Northe aka Cammarones had arrived.

There's not much sense in writing about the week we spent cruising up and down the Colombian coast and never picking up so much as a gram of coke. Unfortunately, things weren't meant to be on this trip. After a night of us not moving in and the Colombians not coming out to meet us, the radio crackled to life and we heard an agent back in Miami relay the following order; "Withdraw, ASAP, repeat, by authority of the SAC, withdraw and RTB (Return to Base) immediately!" The only response to that order was, "Roger." The Special Agent in Charge was the closest thing to a god with a small g in federal service. When the SAC said return to base, you did not question the order. It was that sense of discipline that separated a good agent from a slob.

We knew things were serious, when we were notified over the radio of a potential trap that made it unsafe for us to be in the area any longer. As we would later learn, our mission was compromised, when the violators involved were told, that the Men from the North were trolling off the Colombian coast in a vessel, that matched the description of our vessel to a T. Fortunately, an undercover agent from another federal agency, was able to learn about the leaked information that obviously spelled trouble for our crew. As soon as this undercover agent was able to brief our superiors in Miami, the emergency message instructing us to "Return to Base ASAP" was transmitted over the radio in the clear.

As we pulled away from the country where the national pastime was drug smuggling, we headed back to the U.S. Navy Base at Guantanamo Bay, Cuba. As I mentioned in CD Book I, during the height of the Drug War, the U.S. Navy

Base known as GITMO was a safe haven in the Caribbean for us to operate from; a place with like minded government personnel, clean sheets, decent food, plenty of desalinized water to wash in and pay phones for us to call home on.

Once again, we were tested by a series of events that were beyond our control. We played by the rules and followed our orders. In the process, we picked up a great deal of experience and even managed to further one case just by us being there. More importantly, we survived and lived to fight another day.

Unfortunately, my sea going adventures ended, after my third undercover boat trip to the Colombian coast. In fact, when I was scheduled to participate in a fourth undercover marine operation, I had no choice but to refuse to go along. The reason I did so, was because repeatedly smashing my spine against the steel bulkhead of our undercover vessel, took its toll on my line of duty injuries. This became especially obvious, when we were at sea and it became incredibly painful and almost impossible for me to stand. After we rendezvoused with a U.S. Navy surface warfare vessel, a Pharmacist Mate boarded our boat to render assistance.

The medication that this Pharmacist Mate gave me knocked me out for several days. All I remember is waking up in a daze and looking around before I passed out again. This experience was especially eerie at night, when I would wake up and feel the ocean tossing our vessel around, while the hull sounded like it was being stretched to its limits. A few seconds later, I would pass out and fall back to sleep.

I knew I was in bad shape, when I forced myself to try and climb the ladder to the upper deck and I was unable to do so. As I laid back down, I knew that if our boat boat sank or broke apart in rough seas, that I would likely go down with the ship. After this experience, I had no choice but to refrain from participating in any more long range undercover marine operations. Even though this was the case, next to crash landing a 27,000 pound undercover aircraft without seat belt protection, the three undercover boat trips that I made to the Colombian coast, were some of the most exciting and rewarding experiences of my entire law enforcement career.

CHAPTER 2

THE BLADE RUNNER SQUADRON STRIKES AGAIN

O n October 19, 1990 Special Agent Jim S. contacted us to report that he and The Salesman successfully managed to infiltrate another Colombian based smuggling organization. This particular smuggling organization agreed to provide The Salesman with $30,000 in front money, to pay the initial expenses to transport 500 kilos of cocaine from Colombia to the United States. The case I refer to as the Albuquerque CD II was now catapulted to the front burner.

JOSE

Jose was a Colombian businessman who was in a position to broker a transportation service for 500 kilos of cocaine; a service that required him to enter into an agreement with a group of gringo smugglers, who were properly equipped to handle this job. Fortunately for us, a friend of a friend recommended The Salesman to Jose. Initially, The Salesman's contact with Jose was through intermediaries. Every time we had the right answer to a question, or we made the proper representations, we moved one notch closer to meeting Jose and being able to pull this deal off. Naturally, the violator who recommended The Salesman asked not to be forgotten when the big bucks came in. Once again The Greed Factor was working in our favor.

The night The Salesman picked up $25,000 in front money from a violator named Oscar, they met at the Holiday Inn on Collins Avenue and 167th Street in North Miami Beach. During this meeting, I remained in the vicinity of the hotel with Special Agent Eric M. and several agents from Group 7. (Eric worked with Jim S. in the RAC Office in Albuquerque) Even though Oscar was five grand short on his end, The Salesman agreed to do the deal and pick up the 500 kilos of cocaine from Jose and his people in Colombia. (What's five grand among friends?)

Once we followed Oscar to his hotel and made sure there were no bad guys in the area conducting counter surveillance, Eric M. and I debriefed The Salesman in the undercover hotel room and took possession of the trafficker funds. As soon as Captain Video joined us, we planned the next phase of the operation. Once we agreed on a game plan, Captain Video and I took The Salesman and Eric M. out for a drink.

After joining the guys for one drink, I called it a night and headed home. As much as I loved driving my government issued Chevrolet IROC Camaro, this wasn't the undercover car that someone with a bad back should be driving. After taking some time to painfully slip down into the driver's seat, I started the car, put it in gear and did my best to avoid bumps in the road as I drove home.

By the time I got home I was in worse shape and had a very difficult time getting out of my G ride (government car). As I limped into my house after midnight, I wondered if I was asking for too much, when all I wanted was one more mission and maybe one more after that, before I transferred to less demanding duties, or I medically retired.

It was also at this time, that Rob K. assigned Special Agent Kip H. to be my new partner. Kip was a former U.S. State Department Diplomatic Security Service Special Agent, who joined the U.S. Customs Service the year before we ended up working together. Even though I was sorry to see Mike R. go to a Marine Unit, I was grateful that Kip was willing to help me run our undercover operation.

From October 19th until November 2, 1990, Kip H. and I worked on operational plans and prepared our crew and plane for the Albuquerque II deal AKA Operation Tequila. Three days before we launched I had a nightmare in living color that scared the hell out me. After another sixteen hour day, I began to dream that I was sitting in the co pilot's seat of one of our undercover seaplanes, as the aircraft picked up speed and prepared to take off on a very short runway. I woke up just as the plane ran off the end of the runway and started to crash down the side of a very steep mountain.

As I sat up in bed, I was rattled beyond belief and couldn't shake the feeling of sheer terror from my thoughts. I didn't have to be Sigmund Freud to know that I was still suffering from the side effects of the plane crash landing incident that I survived back in June. Personally, I was afraid that if I said anything about the nightmares I was having, I would be posted to other duties. Since that was

the last thing I wanted, I decided to keep things to myself. I was also hoping,

that if I could hold onto Kip for a while, I would be able to take a break, as soon

as he was able to handle things on his own. In the meantime, I did the best I

could to hang in there, despite the fact that I needed some time on the beach.

On November 5, 1990, Kip and I along with Captain Video, The Salesman

and The Colonel departed South Florida in another one of our rented ex military

seaplanes and flew to the U.S. Navy Base at Guantanamo Bay, Cuba. After

waiting seven days in GITMO for the signal to launch, Kip and I had The

Salesman tell the Colombians, that he was heading home, but that he would

leave his crew and plane stashed at the forward area; a place they suspected was

either in Aruba or Puerto Rico. Our plan was to return to Florida and ask the

Colombians for more expense money to support our crew during the delay.

Once again, our knowledge of the enemy paid off. Immediately after we

returned to the states, the Colombians proved that they were as committed as we

were to get the job done, when they wire transferred an additional $10,000 to our

UC Agents in New Mexico. As soon as The Salesman returned to Miami with

Customs Pilot Steve S and Jay R., we made the final preparations to make the

pickup. Rather than rush and make the pickup on Monday morning November

19, we had to delay the deal for at least 24 hours. Once again, country clearance

was the problem.

According to DEA, due to the presence of the Colombian military on the

Guajira Peninsula, the area where we needed to land was too hot for us to operate in. As a result, our orders were to wait until the Colombian military was finished with their special operation. The next day we assembled at the Group 7 office to wait for the clearance to launch. During this delay we had to be very careful how we dealt with the Colombians. On one hand, we had to massage the deal forward, so our "clients" would be ready to load our plane when we secured the clearance to go operational. On the other hand, we couldn't push the bad guys too much.

After another day of preparing to fly this mission and working on other matters, we received the call that we were waiting for at 1710 hours or 5:10 PM. As soon as I heard my ASAC say, "Nick, I've got bad news," I listened intently as I braced myself for another letdown. When I asked my ASAC when we could expect to fly into Colombia, he said maybe by Tuesday of the following week.

As soon as my ASAC finished filling me in, I heard another telephone extension ring in his office. After excusing himself to take the other call, I stood in Rob K's office and gave Kip H. the thumbs down sign, while I waited to finish my conversation with our ASAC.

When our ASAC came back on the line, he wasted no time in saying, "Nick, you're not gonna believe this," before he continued and explained that DEA just called to say, that due to a breakdown in Colombian military equipment we were clear to launch, but we had to move fast. As I looked at my watch and started making calculations in my head, I asked our ASAC when we should go. His advice was not to wait and to get in by morning, because we could not take the chance that DEA would shut us down on Thursday. That meant that we had to be in GITMO and ready to launch by 3 AM, or we had to stand down and wait for another window to open before we could go operational.

It is also important to note, that when my colleagues and I conducted these operations we launched on a verbal order. While it's true that we had to submit numerous Reports of Investigation, written requests for foreign travel authorization and operational plans in advance, the actual order to violate the sovereignty of a foreign nation like Colombia was always given verbally. In other words, at no time did any supervisor, or high ranking government official relay the authorization to execute a covert operation on foreign soil in the form of a written order. I mention this, because my colleagues and I were used to carrying out highly sensitive verbal orders. In other words, when someone told us to do something, we did it and WE NEVER GOT IT WRONG!

After accepting these terms, I said goodbye to our ASAC and handed the phone to Rob K. before I returned to the squad room to brief the others. Fortunately, we had the capability to make this pickup off shore in the open ocean, where the sea state was suitable for a water landing. If we didn't have this capability, we would never have been able to make this case at this time. Having access to different types of aircraft, including seaplanes, as well as the right crews, made us a force to be reckoned. This was especially the case, when we had to comply with very strict rules that governed how we conducted undercover operations on foreign soil.

As soon as I entered the main squad room, the guys perked right up when I told them that we were in business, even if we had some constraints on how we had to execute this mission. In less than three hours Larry K., an Aviation Group Supervisor from the Miami Air Branch, who once served as a Special Agent in Group 7, came through for us and put a U.S. Customs aircraft our disposal to transport us to GITMO.

RACING AGAINST THE CLOCK

Once we landed in GITMO, we took the crew to the Bachelor Officer Quarters (BOQ) to get some sleep before they were scheduled to launch. As soon as we began to prepare the plane for this mission, our ace crew chief, Johnny Walker, noticed that the right landing gear was in need of a blast of nitrogen. The nitrogen was needed to push the strut back up into the proper position. Unless we fixed this problem we would have to scrub the mission. Once again, we were forced to deal with a situation that special agents were not officially trained to deal with.

The moment Johnny Walker said, "Nick, we need a nitro cart," I said, "No sweat, I'll be right back." As soon as I jumped into the gray World War II era U.S. Navy Jeep, that the U.S. Customs Service kept on GITMO, I could see that my new partner was somewhat perplexed when I remarked, "Somehow I don't remember them covering any of this shit at FLETC," referring of course, to the Federal Law Enforcement Training Center. "No good buddy, they sure didn't," responded Kip as we drove along the flight line in search of a nitrogen cart.

After driving to the main terminal at the Guantanamo Bay Naval Air Station, we found a Petty Officer who assisted us by calling a Navy mechanic into work after hours. Fifteen minutes later, we had a nitrogen canister hooked up to the right landing gear strut and had the repair made. Once we sterilized the undercover aircraft and put ice in the coolers, Johnny Walker cranked up both engines and checked the systems. After a brief run up, Johnny Walker shut the engines off and gave me the thumbs up signal, an indication that all was well.

It was almost 1 AM by the time that Kip, Johnny Walker and I stumbled into Room 114 at the Bachelor Officers Quarters. We had an hour and fifteen minutes before we had to wake up our crew, for an all hands briefing at 0230 hours (2:30 AM). Rather than fall asleep, we made a pot of coffee and prepared two bags of microwave popcorn for a late night snack. So far we had done everything possible to prepare for this mission and insure the integrity of our operation. The only thing left to do was to wake up our crew, brief them one more time and wish them luck before they took off.

RISE AND SHINE

Because everyone involved in this case had put in some long hours, I let our crew sleep as long as possible before I woke them up. Moments later, our contract pilots emerged from their rooms, along with the U.S. Customs Pilots from New Mexico and Jacksonville, Florida who were providing air support for this mission.

After getting into a huddle in the empty day room, some of us sipped cold sodas or hot cups of incredibly strong U.S. Navy coffee, while I went over the operational plan again. Once I finished the briefing, we made our way down the coast road to the airport in our dilapidated fleet of Mad Max vehicles. As I shifted gears on the old U.S. Navy Willy's Jeep, I wondered how many men before me used this same vehicle, to take combat aircrews to their planes during previous conflicts.

As usual, no one said much on the way to the plane. When we arrived at the airfield, some of us inspected the exterior of the aircraft, while others sanitized the interior again. This was done to make sure that nothing was accidentally left on board, that could identify the crew as being affiliated with the U.S. government. Just before the crew went to board the undercover aircraft, I gave my usual last minute briefing of the most critical points of the operational plan. Once I was confident that everyone knew the game plan, I said adios and wished them luck. One by one the crew shook our hands and cracked a few jokes, as they climbed into the undercover seaplane.

CLEAR!

Just as I had done many times in the past, I watched our crew for as long as I could until the cargo door was closed. While Johnny Walker, Special Agent Kip H. and I stepped away from the aircraft, Captain Video leaned out of the pilot's side window and yelled, "Clear!" before he cranked up the number one, then the number two engine. Once I finished my prayer, I gave the crew a quick salute and off they went.

As I stood on the tarmac while our plane taxied to the active runway, I felt exceptionally bad that my request to go along on this flight was denied by DEA. I rationalized this letdown, by deciding that my job was to run this operation from our command post in the Customs trailer on GITMO. Besides, the U.S. Government did not want a special agent killed or taken hostage in Colombia. Like it or not, contract aircrews and sources of information were as they say, expendable.

Even though the departure of our undercover aircraft was not as spectacular as being catapulted from the deck of an aircraft carrier, there was something very nostalgic about every take off that I witnessed. As the undercover plane rumbled down the runway, the roar of her radial engines echoed across the entire base.

Once the UC plane was airborne, the landing gear was retraced while the aircraft climbed to a cruising altitude and evaporated from sight. Moments later, Customs Pilot Steve S. and Customs Pilot Jay R. applied full power to the U.S. Customs-Albuquerque Air Branch twin engine King Air C12 aircraft and took off right behind our undercover plane. Following the Albuquerque based C12, was the Jacksonville Air Branch's Cheyenne (Chet) high endurance tracking and surveillance aircraft. This long range mini AWAC aircraft was a TDY bird detailed to GITMO by Harry B., the Branch Chief of U.S. Customs Puerto Rico Air Unit. (Harry B. was a former Miami Group 7 Special Agent who transferred to air operations and was one of our greatest supporters.)

When we could no longer see or hear our planes, Kip, Johnny and I jumped in the jeep and headed back to the BOQ. As I shifted gears on the old Willies' Jeep, my stomach was turning as I looked at Kip and noticed that it looked as if he changed since we first met. By the time our undercover seaplane took off into the night's sky, Special Agent Kip H. had become a Blade Runner.

CHAPTER 3

FLYING THE MISSION

T he ocean below was as black as ever as our crew leveled off at 5000 feet and flew straight for the Colombian coast. Thanks to the U.S. Customs escort aircraft, the undercover seaplane was given excellent navigational assistance and pointed right to the x that marked the spot in the ocean where the pickup was supposed to be made.

While Captain Video never left his position in the cockpit, The Salesman and The Colonel took turns filling in as co-pilots. Knowing our contract pilots like I did, I imagined them joking around rather than being concerned about the dangerous nature of their mission. Regardless of the risks involved, our crew pressed on and flew lights out in the stealth mode toward the set of coordinates that Jose gave to The Salesman.

WAITING OUT THE NIGHT IN GITMO

After watching some TV, Kip and I left the Bachelor Officers Quarters for the U.S. Customs trailer that was closer to the airfield. Our contract mechanic Johnny Walker was so wiped out, we let him crash in the BOQ while we went to man the phone in our "command post." As the sun came up over Cuba, I looked at my watch and saw that it was 0600 or 6 AM. If my calculations were correct, our undercover seaplane was within striking distance of the Colombian coast.

AN EARLY MORNING CLOSE CALL

As I mention throughout CD Book I and II, all air surveillance activities to support undercover operations were coordinated through the U.S. Customs Air Operations unit known as C3I. At that time, Joe B. was the No. 2 man at C3I. Joe B. was a veteran U.S. Customs Air Officer, who miraculously survived the Black Hawk helicopter crash that cost the life of Customs Pilot George Saenz.

In my first call to C3I I was told, "They're" coming back to GITMO." While I began to pace back and forth with the phone firmly planted against my ear, I responded by saying, "Which "they" are you referring too? Who's coming back? We have three planes out there; maybe it's the Customs C12 from the Albuquerque Air Branch, or the surveillance aircraft from our Jacksonville Air Branch?" By this time I was wearing out the carpet in front of Kip, who was starting to look like me and every other special agent, who sent one of our crews to Colombia to pick up a shipment of cocaine.

Under the circumstances, I could tell that C3I was very busy by the amount of radio chatter in the background. When the Radar Detection Specialist said, "I'll call you right back," I decided it was time to light a cigarette while I waited for more information.

*Even though I was officially cleared to include additional details in this chapter, I decided to further sanitize certain events that occurred and limit my remarks by saying the following: The second the phone rang and I answered it on the first ring, I was not prepared to hear the Detection Specialist report, that Colombian Air Force fighter aircraft were on patrol and were heading toward the area where the undercover seaplane was scheduled to operate. Because this area was now deemed to be "too hot to operate in," the U.S. Customs aircraft were ordered to RTB (Return To Base). When the undercover seaplane wasn't recalled, I had words with the C3I Detection Specialist and ended up slamming the phone down, after I directed him to get my plane out of the area as well.

THE POINT OF NO RETURN

As the sun came up over the Guajira Peninsula, Captain Video was at the controls as the undercover aircraft maintained a low level approach to the pickup point. Fortunately, the U.S. Customs Jacksonville Air Branch crew had the balls to take their sweat time leaving the area. They accomplished this, by making wide circular turns instead of returning to GITMO in a straight line. Doing so, made it possible for the Jacksonville, Florida based U.S. Customs aircrew, to use their high powered long range radar to scan the area for any approaching Colombian fighters. By taking their mission seriously, while also "following orders," the Jacksonville crew maintained contact with our contract pilots, during THE MOST crucial phase of this particular mission. As usual, U.S. Customs Air Operations personnel, went above and beyond the call of duty in order to support our undercover operations.

While the undercover seaplane was flying toward the pickup point, the Customs Pilots from the Jacksonville Air Branch notified our crew that they were ordered to RTB, because the area was too hot to operate in. Based on what I was later told, our undercover seaplane crew was also told, "You're on your own if you stay."

Unfortunately, by this time in the operation, the undercover seaplane was approaching the location off shore where it was scheduled to land. As a result, our contract pilots decided that they were too close to the pickup point to RTB. After receiving the thumbs up from his two co pilots, Captain Video continued to fly toward the open ocean LZ (Landing Zone). Regardless of the potential risks involved, our crew did what any other Blade Runner would do. They went in!

THE OPEN OCEAN PICKUP

As soon as the undercover seaplane landed near the Colombian vessel, our crew picked up twenty five duffel bags that contained 1251 pounds of high quality cocaine. During the loading process, Jose was present and was gleaming with pride. As far as his amigos were concerned, Jose looked like a man who could make things happen.

When the cocaine shipment was being loaded into the seaplane, Captain Video wore a baseball cap and Wayfarer Sunglasses, while he remained in the cockpit ready to take off at any sign of trouble. Outside of one armed Colombian, who was wearing a pistol on his belt, the rest of the boat crew appeared to be unarmed.

"Why didn't you come yesterday?" yelled Jose over the sound of the turning engines.

"Couldn't chance it. Today's a better day," yelled The Salesman as he passed a 25 kilo package to The Colonel. The Salesman then told Jose that he would speak to him in 20 hours.

As soon as the transfer was complete, The Salesman closed the cargo door, while The Colonel ran back to join Captain Video in the cockpit. While The Salesman finished securing the load in the cargo bay of the aircraft, Captain Video applied power to the engines. Once the seaplane was skimming along the surface of the ocean, Captain Video pulled the controls back toward his chest and rotated the undercover aircraft into the air.

WAITING AT THE COMMAND POST

As soon as the phone rang inside the U.S. Customs trailer, I jumped out of bed and stumbled half asleep into the living room to see who was calling. "Yea," I said in a very sleepy tone of voice. "Nick, it's so and so from C3I. Your bird is airborne and on the way back."

When I asked, "What's the count on board," the technician asked me to hold on while he checked. While I waited, I could hear the radios in the background, as the C3I technician contacted the Jacksonville Air Branch crew, that was escorting the undercover seaplane back to GITMO. Before the C3I operator could get back on the phone, I heard one of Jacksonville pilots relay that the load was picked up and we had a count of three on board. The other good news was that the Colombian Air Force aircraft never got close enough to observe what was taking place off shore. At 11:15 AM or 1115 hours, exactly as scheduled, I saw the long wings of our undercover seaplane bank to the left, as our crew came off the base leg and onto the final approach to the runway at GITMO. The Blade Runner Squadron did it again!

ROAD TRIP

By 1 PM Special Agent Kip H, Captain Video, The Colonel, The Salesman, Johnny Walker and I climbed into the undercover plane and departed GITMO to return to Homestead Air Force Base. As I sat on a cooler full of ice cold beer and soda, I ate some fried chicken and admired the shipment of cocaine that filled the cargo bay of the seaplane. No matter how many times we completed one of these missions, I always marveled over the sight of a large cache of drug contraband in one of our aircraft.

On November 20th and 21st, 1990, The Blade Runners logged another 1200 miles of fancy flying after several months of painstaking investigative activities. As happy and grateful as we were, we still had to play out the rest of this sting operation and see this controlled delivery all the way through to the end.

By the time we landed at Homestead Air Force Base we had been up for almost two days with a miniscule amount of sleep. Our reception committee

included Rob K., a number of special agents from Group 7, Roger G., the Miami
Air Branch Chief and other air operations personnel.

That night we left Homestead Air Force Base filled with a tremendous sense
of accomplishment. When I got home I packed my bag for a long stay out west
and played with my sons, before I helped my wife put them to bed. I was scheduled to leave Homestead Air Force Base on November 22, 1990 on Thanksgiving
morning, to fly in the Albuquerque Air Branch King Air C12 aircraft, to deliver
the cocaine shipment to Special Agents Jim S. and Eric M. in New Mexico. (As
I was told at the time, this was done to please the Special Agent in Charge in El
Paso who covered Albuquerque, New Mexico.)

During the long flight cross country flight, The Salesman turned to me and
said, "Did you ever wonder how what we do affects people?" Of course I did. I
thought about it all the time. Plenty of people were impacted by what we did.
As we continued having a philosophical conversation, I ate a bag of Doritos and
drank a can of warm Diet Pepsi, while we flew across a country that was filled
with people who were feasting on a turkey dinner.

Ever since the plane crash landing in New Mexico and the boat trips to
Colombia, I was beginning to see things from a different perspective. For the first
time in my life, I was starting to think about the consequences of my workaholic
lifestyle. Nothing seemed more distasteful to me than the thought of not seeing
my sons, because my wife and I got divorced. My sons deserved to be raised by
a full time father, more than they needed to have a Blade Runner in the family.

I also realized, that even though I changed as a result of the plane crash and some of my other adventures, I wasn't changing enough to make a real difference in my personal life, at least not yet. It was almost as if I was on a runaway train that was heading for disaster and I had no idea what would kill me first, the train wreck, or jumping off to "save myself." The good news was, that I finally realized that being a workaholic sucked the second after you got that pat on the back for another job well done. The fact that it bothered me that I volunteered to go to New Mexico on a holiday, was another good sign that there was hope for me yet.

While The Salesman and I reflected on the impact of our activities, we had 1251 pounds of cocaine stacked all around us; enough cocaine to destroy thousands of lives. There was simply no escaping the fact, that in every American city that we flew over, there were record numbers of families destroyed, or negatively impacted in some way by the drug problem in our country. The Colombian drug cartels and all of their collaborators throughout the smuggling chain were evil people, who fed off the desperation of weaker souls. Hopefully, the day would come, when the American people would learn that during The Drug War, my colleagues and I put our personal lives on terminal hold, in order to fight back and even the score to some extent.

Just because he started his relationship with us as a defendant informant, didn't mean that The Salesman didn't have a conscience. Initially, his devotion to our cause was to save his own skin. While in the process of paying his debt to society, The Salesman evolved and became a member of our rather unorthodox undercover operation. In doing so, The Salesman made the transition from being a bad guy to a good guy.

HILLS & VALLEYS

As soon as we arrived in Albuquerque, we unloaded the Customs aircraft and secured the contraband in the Customs office at the airport. After congratulating Eric M., Jim S and Group Supervisor Ward O., I was told that the Special Agent in Charge did not want any Miami agents involved in this case. All I could think about when I heard this news was, "When will I learn?"

Despite the wishes of the local SAC, the New Mexico agents encouraged me to ignore their boss and remain involved in this investigation. Since I had no intention of doing otherwise, I unpacked my bags and made plans to stay in Albuquerque to see this operation through to the end. Once again, life was filled with hills and valleys.

While I grabbed something to eat in a local diner, a small army of agents used bolt cutters to open the locks on the 25 duffel bags that were filled with a total of 1251 pounds of cocaine. Once the load was photograph and field tested for a second time, each 2.2 kilo brick was individually weighed and logged into evidence.

At this stage in the controlled delivery process our negotiations were conducted by phone, usually two calls a day. During these calls, Eric M, Jim S, The Salesman and I would stand around a pay phone at a prescribed time and hook up our tape recorder and wait. Jose was rarely late and with some exceptions the phone always rang whenever it was supposed to.

Originally, Jose moaned and groaned about not having any money to give us, as partial payment for our services at the time of the delivery. It didn't take long before we got extremely tired of hearing, "My freng, it is impossible. I need some merchandise to work with first, then I promise to pay you." Then we heard, "You can keep say 100 and give me 400." A firm, "NO!" was always our answer, as if we would ever agree to turn over any part of this load without being able to take down some cash and every violator involved. We used the tactics that we did, because we knew it hurt the bad guys to lose a large amount of money, more than it did to lose a load of cocaine.

During the negotiations on December 11 and 12, Jose agreed to exchange the first 200 kilos for $200,000 in cold hard cash. After numerous conversations, we finally managed to get the bad guys to commit to paying us a specific amount. If they tried to give us less, we told Jose there would be no delivery. By December 13th we were all packed and ready to travel cross country.

When Jose asked us to deliver the first part of his shipment to the New York Metropolitan Area we agreed, providing that he told his people that they had to come to us. The reason for this move was two fold. First, if Jose picked the city, then we would pick the location for the exchange. Even though The Salesman and Jim S. were from out west, the fact that I was a native New Yorker, let the Colombians know that we would not be lured into a location that gave them the upper hand. Naturally, our concern was to choose a location that made it as easy as possible for our backup teams to protect us, when The Salesman, Jim S. and I received payment and relayed the take down signal. There was also no way that we intended to operate in Queens, New York, since this was the home away from home for a large Colombian population. So, for various reasons, we decided to draw the Colombians into Newark, New Jersey.

The U.S. Customs SAC Office in Newark, New Jersey proved to be immediately cooperative and in one phone call we had thirteen hotel rooms, a handful of rental cars, mobile phones, radios and lots of local support lined up by Special Agent Tony M.. Unfortunately, just as things were beginning to percolate, I received the bad news that Special Agent Kip H. was being transferred to Miami Group 6. This meant that I had no partner to help me run the operation.

CHAPTER 4

PUTTING THE CONTROL IN A CONTROLLED DELIVERY

O n Saturday morning at 4 A.M. New Mexico time I was wide awake and packed. By 7:30 AM The Salesman, Ward O., Eric M., Jim S., Customs Pilot Jay R., Customs Pilot Steve S. and I looked like the Colombian Olympic duffel bag throwing team, as we tossed each of the nine yellow sports bags containing $30 million dollars of cocaine into the Customs C12. Once we loaded our luggage and our weapons on board, we took our seats and strapped in.

After flying cross country in a U.S. Customs C12, we landed at Teteboro Airport in northern New Jersey, where we were met by a contingent of special agents from the SAC Newark office. Once the cocaine was unloaded from the unmarked Customs aircraft, we were transported to the local Customs SAC Office, where we were introduced to Special Agent Eddie C., the case agent representing SAC Newark.

Eddie could not have been a more cordial host. In no time, we had our cowboys from New Mexico saying things like, "Hey, you know who asked about you the other day? Naturally, the response was, "No fucking body." Trying to teach our brother agents from out west to say pitza instead of peeetzer and computa instead of computer was a task in and of itself.

Aside from our East Coast grammar lessons we had a job to do in Newark. Once we got settled, we set up our tape recorder and used an undercover phone in the SAC Office to place a call to Jose. The first call was just to let Jose know that we were en route to the New York area. After checking in with the main violator, we agreed to call him back on Monday morning at 10 AM. Once we finished for the day, fourteen of us headed out to dinner.

So far we had been working on this deal almost non stop for several weeks. The fatigue factor had started to catch up with many of us, especially when you have to constantly listen to the Colombians whine about money. After a while, you get real tired of listening to someone who sounds like Tony Montana (the Al Pacino character from the movie Scarface) calling you, "My freng." Weeks go by and all you want to do is deliver the cocaine shipment and start arresting people.

LIVING TO FIGHT ANOTHER DAY

When it came time to do the deal, I was handed a small transmitter to wear on my belt under my leather flight jacket. I gave my U.S. Customs credentials and my 9mm pistol to Senior Special Agent Pat R. to hold for me, while I tucked my five shot .38 caliber Smith & Wesson Model 49 revolver in my waistband. Jim S., Tony M. and our tech agent would man the surveillance van, while Eddie C., Eric M, Pat R. and the other agents encircled the area in a very discreet fashion. Special Agent Tom H. and Customs Pilot Jay R. set up a position in a tractor trailer, while four state troopers led by their sergeant covered the exits and entrances to the New Jersey Turnpike. Everyone wished us well and The Salesman and I were off to do the deal.

According to the game plan, we agreed to meet the Colombians from Queens, New York in the rear lobby of the Holiday Inn, on Route 1 & 9 South near the Anheiser Bush beer plant. The deal was simple. The Colombians would flash our $200,000 in cold hard cash. As I covered The Salesman, he would quickly check each bundle to make sure that we were not being stiffed (cheated). If the count looked good, we agreed to leave the money in the trunk of a parked car that we held the keys for. We would then drive another vehicle (known as the load vehicle) that they provided, to pick up "their" coke shipment. To prevent being ripped off, or found out, a convoy of federal agents would screen our trip back to the location where the cocaine was secured. Once we were ready, we would call the Colombians on their mobile phone and tell them where to meet us.

As soon as we returned with the load car, I would give the keys to their driver, pick up our cash and ride off into the sunset with The Salesman. If all went well, we would drop the load car off, get our money and be leaving the area, just about the time that an army of U.S. Customs Agents and police officers moved in to arrest every violator involved. Unfortunately, that day it wasn't meant to be. After waiting an hour for the Colombians to show up, we called them on their mobile phone. They complained of heavy traffic, then another problem, then a request for us to wait.

Things got a little dicey, when The Salesman and I became a bit concerned about our safety and wondered if the enemy had us under surveillance. Our surveillance teams confirmed our suspicions, when they spotted a car that matched the description of the vehicle that the Colombians said they would be using circling the block. All of a sudden my skin began to crawl. Both The Salesman and I saw an opportunity for us to escape, so we took it.

"This is bullshit. I don't like it," yelled The Salesman as he put in a call to our Colombian "clients."

"Listen, my freng, we had problems. I only have a hundred," (meaning a hundred thousand dollars) responded one of the Colombians.

"This is a fucking set up," answered The Salesman, as I ushered him toward the rear parking lot door of our hotel.

"No, my freng, listen we are almost...."click.

As soon as The Salesman hung up the mobile phone, I remarked, "Let's get out of here," as I hit the automatic door locks on our rented white Dodge and took off. I then spoke out loud figuring our backup teams would hear my voice over the transmitter that I was wearing. "If you guys can hear me, cover us. We're breaking this off."

A split second our UC mobile phone rang. Only our agents had the number. When The Salesman said hello, he was greeted by the voice of Senior Special Agent Pat R. Apparently our backup team picked up enough from by belt transmitter to formulate the same plan as we did. Pat R., Eric M., Jim S. and Eddie

C. were all in agreement. It was time to screw with our Colombian "clients," the part of the job that we liked the most, next to picking up a drug shipment in Colombia and arresting the players involved.

HEY NICK, SHOW HIM YOUR NUTS

As soon as we returned to the Newark SAC office, we made a bee line for the undercover telephone. Before we called the main Colombian violator that we were dealing with, we had a detailed discussion about the best way to proceed. I can't emphasize enough that we never did anything on the fly, or without a great deal of planning. Every move we made was usually well choreographed in advance to insure our safety and our success. This meant that before every UC meeting, or phone call, we would have a think tank session and explore every and I mean every, possible option and situation that could possibly come up. This way, instead of the smugglers dealing with one undercover agent and one case agent, they were really going up against several experienced undercover operatives and field agents. You might say that this was our version of community policing.

Naturally, there were times when an undercover agent had to be prepared to act without the benefit of consulting others. Since our mission in life was to remain in control, we took the time to plan our moves whenever it was appropriate to do so. This case was no different.

All it took was for the phone to ring twice, before Jose answered our call in a desperate tone of voice. The Salesman was furious and in a typical academy award performance he lashed into the Colombian drug broker like there was no tomorrow. "If you ever want to see your 500 again (referring to Mr. J's 500 plus kilograms of cocaine) you call us when you've got a big bag of money." Then I chimed in and lashed out at Jose from the other side of the room. "You hear my people in the background, they're going nuts over this," yelled The Salesman.

The Salesman brought the house down when he covered the phone for a split second, looked at me and said, "Show him your nuts, Nick." Naturally, my response was to quickly simulate pulling my pant's zipper down. The Salesman quickly recovered from our little inside joke and after the look of determination returned to his face, he slammed the undercover phone down onto the receiver with a loud bang.

The die was cast. We had to make a stand, or we would look like easy prey and in a dope deal, being easy prey is the kiss of death. Our only course of action was to sit tight and let destiny take over. We had 500 kilos of "their" cocaine, that as far as they knew, was safely smuggled into the U.S. by The Salesman and his people. If they ever suspected us of being the police, they certainly didn't feel that way anymore.

There was also the issue of Jose to contend with. Even though it was important to arrest errand boys or couriers, we were in business to dismantle smuggling organizations from top to bottom. This meant, that we had to lure the brokers, the money men and the stateside receivers into our traps, as often as circumstances allowed us to do so.

We played things a certain way to insure that we maintained the "control" in the controlled delivery at all times. We also knew that the bad guys would call us back. After all, no one walks away from 500 kilos of cocaine.

THE RETURN OF THE DIRTY DOZEN PLUS ONE

On Sunday morning January 13th, 1991 at 11 AM, I returned to Newark, New Jersey to meet with Jose and his people. When I stepped off the plane Special Agent Eddie C was waiting for me.

From the moment I met Special Agent Eddie C. I liked him a lot. When we first started working together, Eddie was an 18 year veteran of the U.S. Customs Service with a reputation for being a feisty, hard charging, former U.S. Marine, who served with just as much distinction during The Drug War, as he did when he served in Vietnam. Eddie was a dedicated agent who didn't tolerate losers and would circumvent the chain of command, if that's what it took to get the job done. Simply put, Special Agent Eddie C. was a Blade Runner.

Once Special Agent Eric M., Jim S., The Salesman and Miami Group 7 Special Agent Jim Z. arrived, we set up camp in the Golden Eagle, a Portuguese bar restaurant that was located near the Newark SAC Office to discuss our plan of action. (This joint had an outstanding pork chop dinner on their menu.) Our first objective was to meet with Jose, who had recently traveled to the New York City Metropolitan area from Colombia to personally oversee this deal.

The next day Eddie used his contacts in a nearby hotel, to secure a suite of adjoining rooms that we would use for the face to face meetings with the

Colombians. Once again, we used the drug money that the Colombian smugglers

paid us to pick up the tab.

Our next phone contact with Jose went well, even though he did not like the

fact that we raised the anti and said we wanted $400,000 before we would turn

over any merchandise. As far as we were concerned, the Colombians caused a

delay that resulted in us incurring additional expenses in "guarding" their cocaine

longer than we expected. Even though this wasn't true, it sounded like something

a real smuggler would say.

As a result of the delay that we caused, by refusing to go through with the

delivery, Jose had problems back home and was feeling pressure from the source

of supply in Colombia to move the deal along. From what we were privy to,

Jose desperately needed to receive delivery of the first 200 kilos, or he would

be held personally responsible for failing to perform as promised. As you can

imagine, when a drug cartel holds you personally accountable for your actions,

you better get your affairs in order, because your next stop is the Gates of Hell

if you fail to produce.

No one loved screwing with Colombian smugglers and drug traffickers

more than we did. Our sting operations were nothing more than mind games

personified. We knew Jose spread his bullshit a little too deep, when he con-

vinced the owners of the load, to let "his" contacts handle the transportation for a multi-hundred kilogram shipment of cocaine to the Estados Unidos (U.S.). As a result, when we failed to fold like a deck of cards and accept peanuts to deliver a sizable portion of the shipment, Mr. Big down south made plans to have a heart to heart talk with Jose. To put it another way, it was time for Jose to come clean.

COMING CLEAN

When Jose traveled back to Colombia to meet the owner of the load, he had a legitimate reason to be concerned about the outcome of his visit. According to what I was told, Jose faced the music like a man and admitted that we were promised a sizable portion of our transportation fee on delivery. To his credit, Mr. Big in Colombia honored the terms of our agreement. He did so, because the way we conducted our end of the negotiations, compelled Jose to tell this man the truth. In other words, my colleagues and I were merely demanding what was promised to us, when we were given the contract to "smuggle" this particular 500 kilogram shipment of cocaine into the U.S.

As a result of Jose's coming clean, the big man down south authorized Jose to pay us $400,000 when he received delivery of the first 200 kilos of cocaine. Their plan would be to sell the 200 kilos and re-contact us again. Another meeting would be scheduled and we would exchange full payment for the remaining 300 kilos. All this was bullshit as far as we were concerned, because there would be no second delivery. Still, we had to play the game a certain way.

In the remote chance that the first load could be taken down without raising suspicions, the Colombians could come back for the rest of the load, providing they were willing to pay us $1.1 million dollars, plus a bonus, to cover some additional expenses due to the delay in finalizing the deal. If these two deliveries went well for them, we expected to be asked to finalize plans to pick up three different shipments that totaled about 10,000 kilos of cocaine. Naturally, once they found out who we really were, we would not be welcomed in Colombia by Jose's contacts.

"JOSE, CAN YOU SEE....THIS IS A CONTROLLED DELIVERY"

On Thursday morning we assembled at 0800 in the Newark SAC Office conference room for a briefing. I do not know why, but we always scheduled these briefings at the crack of dawn, knowing full well that the deal would be delayed.

All total there were around twenty federal agents and New York Port Authority Police Officers involved in the final phase of this operation. Special Agent Eric M. kicked things off and introduced Jim S., The Salesman and me to the members of our back up teams. Once the briefing was over, we drove over to the Sheraton Hotel near Newark Airport to join the technical officer while he wired our room.

By 10 AM everyone was in place and anxiously awaiting the arrival of our Colombian "clients." We expected at least three would show, but felt that it was possible that they might be real smart and have more bad guys backing them up. The hotel manager was a gracious host and asked that we do everything possible not to take anyone down inside the hotel lobby.

Waiting was always the hardest part of the job. As best as we could determine, our Colombian "clients" were leaving New York City by 10 AM, which meant that we should start expecting company in one hour and fifteen minutes. While we waited in our hotel room, we joked around, knowing full well that our back up team was monitoring our actions with the help of a hidden camera.

As the minutes passed by, I tried to run scenario after scenario through my mind in anticipation of the arrival of our "clients." While I did so, The Salesman was watching Star Trek, "The Wrath of Kahn on the cable TV. Throughout the next hour I began to fidget and get very anxious. While I waited, a collage of thoughts raced through my mind, as I relived a host of memorable moments that took years off the tail end of my life.

"There they are!" were the first words that broke the silence in our room, when UC Agent Jim S. spotted two of Jose's associates in the rear parking lot of our hotel. As soon as I joined the others by the window, I spoke up and said, "There's the shooter," when I spotted the younger Colombian cowboy type walk towards the rear entrance of the Sheraton Hotel.

The bad guy I call Senior S. was a 27 year old native born Colombian, who emigrated to the U.S. as a child and never contributed a damn thing of any substance to this country. Fortunately, Mr. S. parked his Chevy Monte Carlo in a parking space that was right under the window of our hotel room. Another Colombian I called Pistol Pedro, parked the load vehicle (a Ford van) on the other side of the parking lot.

If there is one thing that an undercover agent needs to develop, it's the ability to interpret the body language of the criminals that they come in contact with. All human beings possess a powerful force that can be used to save your life in any emergency or a survival situation. This force is called your instincts. While it's true that knowledge is power, relying on your instincts can also enable you to make the right decisions whenever you are exposed to danger.

When I first saw Pistol Pedro I instinctively knew that he was the shooter. In other words, if any of these guys were carrying a gun, it had to be him. Don't ask me how I knew, but I could almost picture a gun resting comfortably under his zippered leather jacket, even though I saw no bulge in his clothing. As soon as I alerted our backup teams, that I thought Pistol Pedro was armed, Jose and Mr. S headed to our room to join us.

By 12 noon we received a call from Jose that he was on his way up to our room. Moments later there was a knock at the door and it was show time. "I'll get it," I said in a low voice as I got up to greet our guests.

As I said before, being an undercover agent is like being a stand up comic in a place where the audience gets to kill you if the jokes aren't funny. The script that you use is in your head and not on a TelePrompTer or on a set of cue cards. From the moment that you go into your song and dance, the words seem to leap out of your mouth, as if everything you have to say comes from the heart. Your body language is also critical. You must appear comfortable and confident, even when you are coiled up inside and ready to strike at a moments notice to defend yourself. At the same time, you must be on guard not to slip up and say something that will queer the deal, or expose who you really are. You also learn from experience, that life is full of surprises and you have to be prepared for the unexpected. In other words, if you can't go with the flow, you should never work undercover.

It also doesn't take long to learn, that the operational plan that everyone went over a dozen times, makes great toilet paper when the shit hits the fan. Most important, is the take down signal. Never forget, the take down signal. When you slam the car trunk, or take your baseball cap off and throw it on the ground, you want an army of federal agents and cops to pour out of every crevice in creation to come to your rescue.

As soon as I opened the door, I put on a friendly face when I greeted the man who hired us to smuggle a cocaine shipment into the United States. If Jose was concerned about conducting this transaction, he didn't look it. In fact, Jose appeared to be in good spirits, when he accepted my invitation to enter the room.

Being the showman that he was, Jose turned to face me after making eye contact with Jim S. and The Salesman and said, "Yes, the beard, I remember that day," referring to the bearded pilot of the seaplane that he spotted sitting in the cockpit, when he and his boat crew placed the 568 kilos of cocaine on board the undercover seaplane. Naturally, we lucked out and Jose never actually got on board to meet Captain Video. Instead, all Jose saw was a scruffy faced drug smuggling pilot, who wore a baseball cap and pair of black Wayfarer sunglasses. Today, I was Captain Video and so far Jose appeared to be buying my act without reservation.

"And you're the reason why it's getting gray," I said with a smile, while I stroked my beard and looked directly at Jose. "

"And this, my friend, is because of you," he responded, as he showed me the bald spot on the top of his head.

Everyone laughed. Then, almost as if a whip was cracked, a deafening silence fell on the room, as Jose switched gears and got down to business. What an actor.

According to Jose, he had $400,000 in cash waiting for us, once we filled his van with the 200 kilos of cocaine. Jose then told us how he and his associates came in three cars and that our cash was secured in the trunk of the Monte Carlo. When Jose's young companion Mr. S. removed two sets of keys from his jacket pocket, I got the distinct impression that the Colombians also took the time to put an operational plan together.

"Here are the keys to the van and the keys to the Monte Carlo," said Mr. S. as he handed me the keys to two of their vehicles. We had a plan of our own, one that had Jose remain in our hotel room with UC Agent Jim S. and the money, while I loaded their van with the cocaine and called the Colombian cowboys when it was time to make the exchange.

We weren't in the room with the bad guys for five minutes, when you could put a match to the first page of our operational plan. In order to allow our cover team in the adjoining room, to get a better idea of the game plan that was being presented by our Colombian "clients," I began asking Jose and his companion a few direct questions. My first question was to ask where the Monte Carlo was parked. "Out there," said Mr. S. in a polite tone, as he pointed to the silver Chevy that parked just below our hotel room's eight floor window. Then, Jose jumped in and told us to keep the car keys and go with Mr. S. to check on the cash that was secured in the trunk of the car inside a suitcase.

I thought quickly and said to myself, if he's going to change our operational plan, then we're going to change his. "Sure, you come with us," I said to Mr. S. "We have a nice safe place for you to wait while we load your van."

"But we were going to wait around here," Mr. S. said trying to appear nonchalant.

"It won't be long... you come and show us the cash," I said to Mr. S.

"And we can hold the keys right?" added The Salesman, as he dangled the GM car keys out in front of himself, as if to tantalize our Colombian associates. The Colombians agreed and off we went.

CHAPTER 5

CASH ON DELIVERY

While Jim S. and Jose stayed in the room, our cover team waited in the adjacent room to protect Jim and arrest Jose, when the time came to shut this operation down. Our cover team on the 8th floor was also supposed to be in a position to keep an eye on the hotel parking lot as well. As I said before, The Salesman and I were responsible to make a quick count of the money before we went anywhere.

Mr. S. seemed friendly, but cautious, as we rode the elevator down to the lobby. Once outside, the Colombian led the way as if he had been in this hotel before. Our first stop was the northwest side of the hotel parking lot, where Mr. S. pointed to a gold colored Ford Astro van that was parked at the end of the lot. "Yea, I see it," I said as I followed his directions and spotted the vehicle parked where he said it would be located.

As soon as I said, "OK, show us the Monte Carlo," Mr. S. led the way around to the southwest side of the hotel's rear parking lot. After walking up to the vehicle, The Salesman inserted the key and opened the trunk. Resting inside was the biggest piece of luggage I ever saw. "Check it out," I said as The Salesman opened the suitcase and flipped back the top flap exposing layer after layer of bundled U.S. currency.

In order to make sure that that we were not given tissue paper stuffed in between large bills, The Salesman checked bundle after bundle of cash in the suitcase. This group swore to us that there was $400,000 in that luggage. The bag was huge and no doubt filled with a lot of cash, but $400 grand, who could tell? Even though there was a large percentage of bills in small denominations in every bundle, this was no time to haggle over money.

As if it mattered, I asked Mr. S. if it was all there. Of course he said yes. In our last trip to Newark, New Jersey, we called the deal off because things did not feel right. Whatever we did worked to our advantage and we were now looking at $300,000 dollars more than the Colombians initially offered to pay us. The other benefit of waiting, was that we were also in a position to take Jose and his "helpers" into custody when the time was right to do so.

As we stood by the open trunk of the money car, Mr. S. anxiously waited to hear our decision. "OK, let's go, we'll make the exchange," I said before The Salesman slammed the trunk. "You follow us," I said as The Salesman placed the Chevy keys into his coat pocket. Fortunately, it didn't take long for us to walk across the parking lot to the Ford van. Once inside, The Salesman and I remained cautious not to say anything that might give us away, in case our Colombian friends had placed a monitor inside their load vehicle.

By this time I managed to secretly flip on the small transmitter that I wore on my belt. As usual, we had tested this alleged hi-tech transmitter in the office.

Unfortunately, just because this transmitter worked in the office, didn't mean that it would always work in the field. Clearly, the mobile phone that we carried, was the most reliable link to the agents who were backing us up.

As soon as I got the van going, I pulled it around the rear of the parking lot past some very well hidden surveillance units and headed for the hotel exit. Just as we expected, Mr. S. and Pistol Pedro were sitting in their blue four door Buick, waiting with the engine running near the front entrance to the hotel. As I drove by, I gave them a nod to signal Mr. S. to follow us.

After driving the route that we practiced a dozen times before, I pulled the van into a nearby Holiday Inn parking lot. Once I exited the Ford van, Mr. S. and Pistol Pedro pulled the Buick into a nearby parking space and followed us into the rear entrance of the Holiday Inn. While all this was going on, one of our helicopter crews and two ground units kept an eye on the back parking lot of the hotel. Once inside, I directed the two Colombians to remain by the bank of pay phones and said, "Stay here and wait for our call. It won't be long, OK."

They both acknowledged and agreed to wait for further instructions. So far so good. Now we were off on our own. I was as positive as one could be, that there was only one car of

Colombians that followed us from the Sheraton hotel. Nevertheless, I drove through a maze of streets and eventually made my way to another safe location where the coke load was stashed under heavy guard. We had teams on the first hotel, teams on the Holiday Inn and several teams back at another location waiting to load the van.

As I drove the van to our stash site, the load vehicle started to buck and jump like a rodeo bull. "What's wrong?" asked The Salesman.

While I re-started the engine in the middle of a New Jersey highway, I couldn't believe my eyes, when I looked at the fuel gauge and remarked, "I don't frickin believe these guys. There's no gas in this thing."

At this point, my only concern was being able to make it back to the location where we had the cocaine stashed, without getting stranded on Route 1&9 North in New Jersey. Behind me I had Special Agent Dan H. from the Newark SAC office and Customs Pilot George P. from our New York Air Unit following me in their unmarked Chevy Impala. After lurching around for almost four miles, I managed to bring the van to a complete halt, at the location were the load was being guarded by another team of agents.

When I jumped out of the van Special Agent Eddie C. ran over to tell me that my transmitter wasn't working and they were not picking me up. That meant that the small transmitter that I wore on my belt was a useless piece of crap. I remember feeling somewhat annoyed that our equipment, which was at times our only lifeline to safety, often failed to operate. Another reason we relied on our technical equipment, was because we used these recorded conversations as evidence. Since stress and fatigue could cause memory problems, it was in our best interest to write numerous reports, take copious notes and gather as much evidence as possible to make sure that nothing fell through the cracks.

READY OR NOT HERE WE COME

In a matter of minutes, nine duffel bags filled with cocaine were loaded in the rear of the beat up van. While a contingent of heavily armed U.S. Customs Agents and Port Authority Police Officers loaded the last of the bags, I replaced my five shot .38 caliber revolver with a 9mm pistol that I put in the back of Eddie C.'s government car. After I slipped my 9mm inside my waistband, I hung my gold Special Agent's badge on a chain around my neck and stuffed it under my Corona Beer sweatshirt.

Just as we were getting ready to leave to make the delivery, Agent Eric M. said that Jose decided to leave the room and go down to the lobby of the Sheraton Hotel. We all previously agreed, that if Jose attempted to leave the room, that our backup team would move in. Just as planned, Jim S. stepped into the bathroom, as Rob K. and Ward O. led a party of five agents and raided the undercover hotel room.

While the RAC Albuquerque Group Supervisor Ward O. provided back up, Miami Group 7 Supervisor Rob K. patted Jose down and took him into custody. Without wasting any time, UC Agent Jim S. then ran down to the lobby to pick up one of Jose's other associates. The Colombian known as Mr. L. was a real fashion statement. His thick pin stripped green suit was loud enough to put this character on the front cover of Bogota's version of GQ Magazine. Looking as if he just got off the pickle boat, the Colombian version of "Palyachi" was easy to pick out of the crowd, especially since he wore those high water pants and white sweat socks. I'm not joking, this guy looked like a real asshole.

Now it was time to play out the rest of the delivery, with the two Colombians that remained. As soon as the van was fully loaded, I waved to Eddie C. and Eric M. then jumped behind the steering wheel. After making eye contact with The Salesman and exchanging smiles, I started the van and drove off with a contingent of unmarked government cars positioned all around us.

Our main concern was putting our hands on the money, before we made it look like we were going to hand over any cocaine. If any remaining Colombians got wind of the arrest of their friends, they might try to hop in the money car and split. Even though we held onto the car keys, there was always a chance that they had another set. As a result, we decided to move quickly, once we rounded the corner and arrived in the vicinity of the rear of the Sheraton Hotel.

Fortunately, I positioned our rental car in a spot that would allow me to park the load vehicle close to the curb, so it would be blocked in by two other parked cars. As soon as The Salesman jumped out of the van, he got into the rental car and pulled the four door red `91 Buick over to the space where the Chevy Monte Carlo was parked. While The Salesman was straining to pull the 100 pound bag of money from the trunk, I quickly put the van into the space formerly occupied by the rented Buick. As soon as we were ready, we made the call and had Senior S. and Pistol Pedro meet us behind the Sheraton Hotel.

While I waited by the rear entrance to the hotel, The Salesman put the money into the trunk of our rental car and parked the vehicle on the other side of the parking lot, under the watchful eyes of a small army of surveillance agents. As I paced back and forth on the chilly January afternoon, I spotted two special agents positioned nearby, while I waited for the two young Colombians to arrive. (I told Mr. S. earlier, that during the final transaction, I would personally hand him the keys to the van.) Rather than have The Salesman risk his life any more than he had too, I told our favorite contract pilot from New Mexico to wait in the safety of the command post until this was over. When The Salesman refused to leave my side, I had to order him to do so.

After what seemed like an eternity, I spotted Mr. S. walking my way. Under the circumstances, I forced myself to smile as I approached the stateside receiver on the sidewalk and I asked where his sidekick (Pistol Pedro) was located. When Mr. S. answered, "He's out front," I decided to go through with the delivery.

As I pointed to the "load vehicle" that was parked nearby, I tried to sound as friendly as possible when I said, "The keys are in the ashtray." I made the decision to keep the van keys out of the ignition, to make it more difficult for anyone to get in the vehicle and drive away. By forcing Mr. S. to get inside the van and lean over to remove the keys from the ash tray, I was buying time and setting the stage for the safest take down possible. Again, this wasn't taught to us in any of our formal training.

While I escorted Mr. S. to the van, I acted as if I was going out of my way to show him exactly where the keys were located. The presence of two special agents standing inside the rear lobby of the hotel reassured me that help was close by. I also knew that a small army of special agents and Port Authority Police Officers were waiting for the signal to move in.

As I rounded the rear fender and stepped into the street, I waited until I was one step behind Mr. S., before I removed my black baseball hat and tossed it to the ground to relay the take down signal. Needless to say, I couldn't believe it, when not one agent moved in. All I could think about was the Colombian called Mr. S. getting into the load vehicle and driving off with 200 keys of cocaine. Even if he didn't get very far, Mr. S. could still hurt someone when our back up teams moved in to arrest him.

Under the circumstances, I was so pissed, I actually considered picking my hat off the ground, so I could put the hat back on my head and repeat the process over again. Instead, I looked up to the eighth floor of the Sheraton Hotel, in the hope that someone in the command post could read my fucking lips.

Just as Mr. S. opened the door to the van and began to enter the cab of the load vehicle, I removed my gold badge that was hanging on a chain around my neck under my sweatshirt with one hand, while I used my free hand to draw my 9mm pistol from under my jacket as I yelled, "U.S. Customs! Don't move!" When Mr. S. ignored my command to get down on the ground, I grabbed the major violator by the nape of his neck and flipped him face down onto the pavement. As soon as the cover team agents, who were closest to my position, FINALLY arrived by my side, I told them to let the other units know, that Pistol Pedro was out front and to remind them that I thought he was carrying a gun.

By the time the message was relayed, the Colombian I called Pistol Pedro was taken into custody at gunpoint. My instincts were proven to be correct, when the cocaine cowboy was ripped from his car and found to be armed with a fully loaded fourteen shot Beretta .380 caliber pistol that was cocked and ready to fire.

When Eddie C. ran up to me, he gave me a big hug and said, "I love the way you put him down." Under the circumstances, I found it difficult to enjoy the fact that Eddie liked my impression of Chuck Norris, because I was pissed off to no end, that the two agents who were positioned closest to me, were slow as molasses when it came time to back me up. I'm purposely not mentioning any names, because my mission and purpose in life is not to embarrass anyone. Still, these guys were standing close enough to get to me a lot faster than they did. That's my opinion and I am entitled to it.

We had prisoners to move, 200 kilos to put back in the safe and a ton of follow up work to do. Congratulations were in order and once we settled down from the adrenaline rush, we raced back to the SAC Office to put the finishing touches to this case. Throughout the rest of the night we kept a hectic pace, while we dispatched several teams to places as far away as Flushing, Queens, to check on various leads that were uncovered as a result of our four arrests. About halfway through the long night, one tiny shred of paper led us to capture our fifth member of Jose's organization.

Thanks to our agents in Pennsylvania, a seven digit phone number identified the location where Oscar the middle man/broker could be found. In order to round up Oscar, Agent Jim S. traveled to Pennsylvania to identify the deal maker from Colombia, who loved to spend his time in American shopping in malls. In order to get Agent Jim S. to Pennsylvania ASAP, Customs Pilots Steve S. and Gary G. cranked up the U.S. Customs C12 aircraft and flew the case agent/lead UC agent from New Mexico to Philadelphia a lost faster than he could have gotten there by car.

Jim S. could not have timed it more perfectly. When Jim arrived at the multiple dwelling where Oscar was taking up temporary residence, our Philly agents were leading the Colombian broker out of his apartment in handcuffs. As soon as Jim S. said "That's him," Oscar was led away by the local agents. All five subjects faced removal hearings and would stand trial in New Mexico, for their involvement in violating Rule # 1 of the official code of conduct for drug smugglers. Don't get caught!

As a result of this joint operation, a big pile of trafficker directed funds (drug money) was shared between the SAC Miami Group 7 undercover operation and our office in New Mexico. The bad news was, that when I returned to Miami I confirmed that I had no chance of getting Kip H. reassigned to Group 7. Luckily for me, there was one agent in Group 7 who wanted to help me run our undercover operation.

Senior Special Agent Pat R. made my day when he approached me and said that he wanted to be my partner. Even though another agent I know, thought Pat was a super laid back clean cut guy, who wasn't exactly cut out for undercover work, I knew otherwise. I felt this way, because I never forgot how impressed I

was, with the way Pat handled himself out on the street, when we were assigned

to work together to make a few arrests. This particular enforcement action

involved an attempt to smuggle hand grenades and explosives on a cargo plane to

a Banana Republic. Since first impressions count, I knew that day after working

with Pat, that he was one hell of a fearless street agent. As a result, I felt truly

blessed the day we shook hands and Senior Special Agent Pat R. became my

partner.

THE BRAVEST LITTLE MAN I KNOW

When I finally came in for a landing after completing another controlled

delivery and I tried to make up for lost time with my family, I found out the

hard way, that time is something that you really can't make up. I also realized,

that it must have been both exciting and scary, for my sons to have an action

figure for a father.

When I first put pen to paper and wrote this chapter, my oldest son was

approaching nine years of age and my youngest son was five. Today, our oldest

son is a 36 year old police detective and our youngest son is serving our country

in foreign lands. Both of my sons were also just as positively influenced as I was,

by the actors who portrayed good guys on TV shows and in the movies. Who

knows, maybe I even had something to do with their development as well.

Like most kids his age, my oldest son Nick would occasionally come up with something that was really profound when we spent time together. (My son Nick was named after my paternal grandfather, not me.) As a parent, I knew that whenever my son Nick asked me certain questions, he was taking a step closer to manhood. An example of what I am talking about, happened one day when I found Nick watching the film *Predator*. The moment my son Nick looked at me and said, "Dad, are those men brave?" I knew he was well on his way to becoming a young man.

When I answered his question, I told my oldest son that there were many kinds of bravery. I also let Nick know, that most of the time, the people around you will think that you did something special, while you will probably be wondering what all the fuss was about.

In an effort to answer his question in the most comprehensive fashion possible, I told Nick that being brave is not being scared until it's all over. I also told my oldest son, that being brave means never giving up. Even if he makes the same mistake over and over again, he should keep plugging away until he gets it right.

That day Nick and I talked a great deal about bravery. In order to teach Nick that bravery is not always attached to a physical act of courage, I told him about his mother and how brave she was when she survived a bout with cancer. I also let Nick know, that he should never allow his fears and concerns to paralyze his ability to move forward and survive.

After my discussion with my oldest son, I stopped to consider what it must be like for him and his brother to observe my life through their young and inexperienced eyes. Before I had this discussion with my son Nick, I never realized just how scary it must be for my sons to see me charge out of the house carrying all sorts of weapons just because the office called. Then it hit me, children have no idea that when you go in harms way, that you have complete confidence that everything will be all right. In other words, how can your children begin to feel your sense of confidence, when they can't even spell the word. They also have no idea, that the politics of The Drug War, incidents of back stabbing jealousy and the overall demanding nature of working in the drug enforcement field, will negatively impact your health, long before you have to be concerned about getting injured or killed in the line of duty.

After we had this discussion, I decided that if I published this true story when my sons were still young boys, I would autograph the copies that I presented to them with the following inscription: "To the bravest little man I know. Love always, Dad." Since both of my sons are now grown men, I will autograph their copies of CD Book I and CD Book II with a few additional sentiments.

As the saying goes, a lot of water has passed under the bridge since I originally wrote CD Book I and II. Both of my sons have grown up to become fine young men and for that I am extremely grateful. The one person I have to thank, for helping me to pay more attention to what really mattered in life, is my wife. Approximately two years before the undercover operation shut down, my wife warned me that the day would come when I would retire and I would wonder where the kids went. Hearing her comment was like being hit in the face with a bucket of ice water. She was right. Our sons were still young at the time, but they were growing up fast.

Chasing smugglers and working undercover was a very adventurous and seductive way to earn a living. While I can't speak for anyone else, in my case, being successful was just as much of a blessing as a curse. I say that because good cases didn't grown on trees. Since it was impossible to know in advance which cases would end in success and which ones would fizzle out, you had to take every lead seriously. As a result, when an informant called or when another agent called with a potential case, you either responded or you didn't. When you had several informants and sources of information working for you and you had other agents calling to ask for help, you can see how it became difficult to be in two places at once. In my case, I always believed, that my family would be right where I left them, when I returned from another adventure. Needless to say, I risked EVERYTHING by having that mindset.

Although others might think that my evolution from being a workaholic to a semi "regular person" took too long, I saw an immediate change in my way of thinking, even if I had a way to go, before I made a more complete transformation. I fully admit that even though my wife made perfect sense, it wasn't easy for me to change. Luckily, I listened to her wisdom and I began to spend time more time bonding with our sons.

Without question, our bonding time together was THE BEST experience I had in my life as a father. Every weekend I was off I tried to take the boys out for lunch. I taught them how to build models and we even went on a few boy scout outings. One of our greatest road trips, was when we drove to Virginia Beach for the 50th Anniversary of the D Day landings in Normandy, France. The historical and educational value of this trip was beyond description. Seeing such an impressive number of of World War II re-enactors "hit the beach" and recreate the Invasion of France was an incredible experience.

Before we left on this road trip, both of my sons had some idea of the significance of this moment in history. However, sitting right behind the mock German defensive positions, while the guns were blazing away with blank ammunition and the battle unfolded, was an amazing experience that had a very powerful positive affect on all of us. Both of my sons left Virginia Beach with a much better understanding of the definition of bravery and had a greater respect for those who serve our country in a worthwhile cause.

Don't wait as long as I did to change, if you're not enjoying enough quality time with your loved ones. Remember, time is something that you can never get back.

CHAPTER 6

ANOTHER ROUND IN BOSTON

When Group Supervisor Jimmy S. from the Boston SAC Office called me earlier in the year, I agreed to help Special Agent Russ P. set up a controlled delivery on a case that had tremendous merit but lacked only one ingredient, front money. As soon as the Colombian violators in this case finally agreed to come up with $60,000 in cash, they wanted us to meet certain demands before they delivered the money to Boston.

Our adversaries on this deal tested us on a few occasions, to see how we reacted to their rather unusual requests. When they asked for copies of everyone's passport, we politely refused to comply with their request. Then they asked for the name of one of the pilot's and his picture, our answer was, "What's in a name." As far as pictures were concerned, we said, "While we're at it, how about sending us yours? When they asked us for a copy of our flight plan, I said no problem and provided them with one that I put together with the help of Major Tom and a contract pilot called Ricky Ricardo. (As soon as I recruited this contract pilot to fly for us, I called him Ricky Ricardo, because whenever he got excited he sounded just like the Cuban American actor and band leader Desi Arnez from the I Love Lucy Show.)

In addition to supplying a copy of the phony flight plan, that we would use to "punch the border" undetected, I also provided the bad guys with a color photograph of the aircraft that we intended to use on this deal.

As much as I'd like to write about the undercover story that we used, I must bite my tongue and classify this story as a very top secret piece of work. Suffice it to say, our bullshit story worked and the Colombians we were dealing with took the bait, hook, line and sinker. Now all we needed was the front money and we would be ready to pick up their load in a week or so.

When Jimmy S. called again, I initially assumed that it was in regards to the case Russ P. was working on. As soon as Jimmy said, "Can you get up here right away?" I could tell by the sense of urgency in his voice that he needed help on something very important. Without wasting any time, Jimmy said he had another mission for us to fly and asked me if we could pick up 1500 kilos on a joint FBI/Customs controlled delivery. It was also at this time, that I learned that the U.S. Customs case agent on this deal was a young agent by the name of Bob C.

According to Jimmy, when the FBI Agents in Boston came to him for help and asked how they were going to pull this case off, he smiled and said, "I'll call the Air Czar." When one of the FBI agents asked Jimmy who he was referring to, the Boston Office Customs Group Supervisor said, "Nick Danger and The Blade Runners!"

As tired and run down as I was, I agreed to help the Boston agents because good controlled deliveries didn't grow on trees. As a result, you had to take them whenever you could get them. I also agreed to go to Boston, because I could never turn down a request to help a fellow agent, especially a friend like Jimmy S.

A BIRTHDAY IN BOSTON WITH NO CAKE AND NO CANDLES

The day I was preparing to travel to Boston, Special Agent Bob C. called me at home with some disturbing news. It seemed that Jimmy S. wanted me to stand by and not leave for the airport. Let the games begin was all I could say to myself, as I tried not to get frustrated with my colleagues in Boston, when they asked me to go into a holding pattern, until they got things worked out with the FBI. When I told Jimmy that I would miss my flight if I didn't leave right away, I was told that the problem was with FBI headquarters, not the FBI Agents in Boston. Instead of looking forward to going up to Boston, I was now dreading it. Finally, Jimmy asked me to come up, even though things had not been resolved yet.

On February 22, 1991, Ricky Ricardo and I traveled to Boston. From what I was told when I arrived in Boston, FBI Headquarters did not want our Miami based undercover operation involved in their investigation. As a result, FBI (Bureau) Headquarters instructed the Boston FBI office to call their Miami office and have their own people in Florida carry out this covert air operation. Based on what I was told, in an effort to please his superiors, the FBI supervisor in Boston called the Miami FBI office for help. The last thing that FBI

Headquarters wanted to hear, was that their agents in Miami recommended, that the FBI Agents in Boston call the U.S. Customs Service Group 7 in Miami, if they wanted a cocaine shipment picked up in Colombia by plane.

I later learned from an FBI Agent I knew in Miami, that his (narcotics) group was aware of our capabilities and advised their superiors in Washington to let the Boston FBI agents work with us, if they wanted a drug shipment successfully transported from Colombia to the U.S. by private aircraft. I made it a point to include this story in this book, to acknowledge the professionalism of the street agents and the supervisors in the FBI Office in Boston and Miami. Clearly, their interest was in getting the job done.

As I soon as I arrived in New England, I was briefed in more detail about this joint effort between the Boston based Customs Agents and the Boston based FBI Agents. During this briefing session, I was told that the agents in Boston spent a large sum of money to get some Colombians to deliver a cocaine shipment to Massachusetts. Needless to say, this chapter wouldn't be in this book, if the Colombians used the undercover seed money they received from the Boston Agents to actually deliver a drug shipment to Massachusetts. Even though their initial plan didn't work, the FBI Agents in Boston had one thing going for them; they successfully infiltrated a Colombian based smuggling organization. To their credit, the FBI Agents in Boston were also a very determined lot. Whether the tactics they initially used worked or not, they never gave up.

After spending my 38th birthday in a hotel room in Boston with no candles to blow out and no cake to eat, I came to the conclusion that the joint FBI/Customs investigation needed some work, before this case would result in a successful controlled delivery. After doing all I could do to help the agents in Boston, I headed back to Florida to pick up where I left off.

THE GROUP 7 THINK TANK

In March of 1991, I felt like a Hollywood screenwriter, who constantly concocted new scenarios and cover stories that would be used in future undercover operations. I knew what was successfully tried and used in the past and what would not work and the reasons why. I also knew what ideas were used in the past and how well each was received. In the process, I developed a sixth sense and learned how drug smugglers operated and conducted business. I also got into the mind of the enemy and learned how they viewed the smuggling business from their perspective. In addition, I knew their weaknesses and strong points, but most of all I knew ours. Because the men I worked were just as knowledgeable, we were a force to recon with, when we planned each and every move that we made to further an investigation.

My colleagues and I also knew from experience, that we had to juggle several cases at the same time, because we might have to work ten deals before one would come to fruition. Sometimes, the deal that looked the most promising would fizzle out and a deal that had some start up problems ended up as a successful controlled delivery. This aspect of the job proved to be as much of a physical and mental drain as it was a proving ground. I say this, because we learned just as much from the deals that fizzled out, as we did from the ones that ended in success.

When I wasn't working on my own cases, I was helping other agents on their investigations. It was a fairly common occurrence for agents to approach me and say, Nick I need a way to convince some bad guys that I can successfully smuggle a load in for them. I'd ask a few questions and come up with a game plan that fit the case at hand. Other agents would call me after hours to run ideas by me and discuss their cases. I should also mention that I wasn't the only one with an overactive imagination. All of my colleagues were brilliant undercover tacticians. As a result, when we put our heads together, we made magic.

By this time in 1991, I was still having some really scary nightmares and difficulty sleeping. I was also experiencing more bad days when I could barely walk and had to use a cane to get around. Clearly, my line of duty injuries were getting progressively worse. This point was driven home to me, when my doctor explained the nature of my injuries and my long term prognosis. Hearing him use words like degenerative disc disease and "crippling" got my attention. I also didn't like hearing that I would only make a bad situation worse if I was re-injured again.

It was also about this time in 1991, that I was beginning to accelerate my transformation from workaholic to semi normal human being. Clearly, the plane crash landing incident and my seagoing adventures to the Colombian coast had a great deal to do with my evolution. In fact, I knew I was changing for the better, when I began to ask myself more and more, if the juice was worth the squeeze?

I first heard this expression from a veteran U.S. Customs Agent, Mr Bob G. from the RAC Office in Ft. Lauderdale. Simply put, this particular expression was meant to do more than remind us of the time consuming and messy process involved in making freshly squeezed orange juice. The expression "Is the juice worth the squeeze," was a clever way to get you to evaluate, whether or not anything that you did was worth it, when you considered the various factors involved. Naturally, this included, the investment of time, the problems encountered and the outcome in terms of risks versus rewards. The trick in life, was to learn when "the juice was worth the squeeze" and when it was more appropriate to settle for drinking OJ from a container.

Last but not least, I continued to be concerned, that one of our crews would be captured and killed because I forgot to think of something, or because someone in the system was corrupt and provided information about our operation to the enemy. All things considered, there was never a dull moment.

CHAPTER 7

CAPTAIN TROJAN

A t 28 years of age our newest recruit was one of our most colorful contract pilots. The Gambler had initially hired the contract pilot I would
later call Captain Trojan to fly a cargo plane for one of his companies. After
taking a few months to check him out, Pat R. and I decided that it was time
to bring this young man with a commercial pilot's license into the fold. Our
first meeting went well and the youngest pilot who ever flew with us, agreed to
become a documented source of information and a contract pilot for the U.S.
Customs Service.

To his credit, the former airline pilot turned free-lance private pilot had plenty
of time behind the controls of everything from commuter style multi-engine
turbo prop aircraft to 727's. He was polite and courteous, if anything, maybe
too polite to be a Blade Runner. Captain Trojan was also unlike anyone else
that we recruited into our operation. I say that because he looked like a guy who
wore monogrammed pajamas and called his mother "mummy" instead of mom.

In addition to being very intelligent and clean cut, our new recruit gave us
the impression that he was born with a silver spoon in his mouth, because he
didn't drink or smoke and dressed like a rich kid from a preppy New England

boarding school. Captain Trojan was also the most unlikely person you would ever expect to find drinking milk out of a dirty glass, in the kind of bars where our informants and contract personnel hung out. Even though on the surface he didn't seem to fit in, there was something about Captain Trojan that made Pat R. and I say let's give him a chance. Once we welcomed him into the unit, he was instantly accepted by the others.

THE FASTEST CONTROLLED DELIVERY IN HISTORY

After returning from another trip to New Mexico in early April, I was asked to help Special Agent Scott D. put a transportation case/controlled delivery together. In an effort to help SAC Miami Group 8 Special Agents make their case, I made arrangements to rent a suitable undercover plane from The Gambler. The aircraft that we selected was capable of transporting our crew from South Florida to Colombia, via our base in GITMO, then back to South Florida with 300 kilos on board.

To round out our crew, I asked Ricky Ricardo to go undercover and negotiate with the main violator in Miami. In addition, I asked our longest serving crew chief, Johnny Walker, to go along just in case any last minute repairs needed to be made on the UC plane. Just as I expected, Ricky Ricardo did an amazing job when he went UC and met with the bad guy I nicknamed Romeo, a Class 1 violator with a criminal history a mile long. During the initial phase of the infiltration process, Ricky Ricardo managed to strike a deal with Romeo, that enabled us to do business with him according to our rather strict rules of engagement.

By this time in our operation, Ricky Ricardo had an excellent reputation as a contract pilot and source of information. Ricky Ricardo was also a pleasure to work with. In addition to being very eager, Ricky was easily directed in the field. Between his talents as a pilot and his ability to go undercover as a smuggler, Ricky Ricardo was a tremendous asset to our unit.

A new record was set, when we were given the coordinates in Colombia where we had to make the pickup and $50,000 dollars in front money, all within four days of entering the case.

When it came time to select a crew for this mission, Pat and I decided to have Captain Trojan fly as the Contract Pilot in Command, in a turbo prop ex commuter plane that The Gambler and Johnny Walker just finished refurbishing to like new condition. In order to repay The Salesman for the good times that we had on the cases that he generated, we asked him to fly right seat (co pilot), while Ricky Ricardo rode in the back and dealt with the natives once the plane landed in Colombia. In order to insure that everything went well, I asked the The Salesman and Ricky Ricardo to help our new recruit get through his first mission in one piece.

This time, the load was to be picked up on a 1000 meter dirt strip near Port Estrella, Colombia. In one of the last phone calls Ricky Ricardo made to Romeo, I told him to ask for a primary and an alternate airstrip. I also told Ricky to find out everything there is to know about the conditions on both strips. As far as runways were concerned, one thousand meters or 3300 feet was more than enough for our crew to land and take off on. What concerned me wasn't the length of the airstrip, but the consistency and the condition of the runway.

Just like the smugglers, we had to pick the right plane and the right crew for each mission. We also knew from experience, that the conditions on the runways in certain parts of Colombia left an awful lot to be desired. Landing a plane on a dirt strip, that was in need of repair or washed out by heavy rains, could prove to be a disaster. Rumor also had it that airstrips in Colombia were being bombed, to prevent the smugglers from operating with impunity. This was an aspect of The Drug War that was never discussed on the evening news. So, for various reasons, I decided not to take any unnecessary chances and instructed Ricky Ricardo to ask Romeo to provide us with coordinates for an alternate strip. By asking for an alternate strip, we increased our chances of making the extraction, if the primary runway proved to be unsafe for our crew to use.

Unlike the old days, our relationship with DEA had changed for the better and we were now receiving country clearance in as little as four days. As soon as Agent Scott D. said that we were good to go, we prepared to fly to GITMO on Thursday April 4, 1991 at 1600 hours (4 PM) so we could make a Friday morning pickup. After fielding all sorts of phone calls, I arrived at the airport in time to make our scheduled departure. As soon as Johnny Walker finished refueling the UC plane, we took our seats inside the nicely refurbished commuter aircraft and blasted off for GITMO.

Once we landed at GITMO, we were greeted by a contingent of U.S. Navy Police Officers. Since we had no ground transportation, we asked the Navy cops to give us a lift to the BOQ, while Johnny Walker got the plane ready for the mission. After we registered the crew at the Bachelor Officers Quarters and got them settled in their rooms, I ordered steak dinners for everyone from Danny's Hideaway.

While everyone except our crew chief ate a late supper at 2220 hours (10 PM), I conducted a quick briefing. As soon as we were finished, I took Johnny Walker his dinner and watched him devour his meal while he stood by the side of the plane. While our crew got some sleep, Johnny Walker refueled the aircraft. Even though we were all part of the same government, we had to pay the U.S. Navy for the fuel. Once we returned to the BOQ, Scott D. and I stayed up, while Johnny Walker crashed on a nearby couch.

I had been through this ritual before, so I knew how being responsible for sending a crew to Colombia could affect all parties involved. I also knew from experience, that it helped a great deal to be with someone you respected and worked well with, when you went through one of these ordeals. In this case, I was fortunate to be with U.S. Customs Agent Scott D.

Whenever we prepared to launch one of crews on an undercover operation, it was quite common for the agents who were responsible for the people who were going in harms way, to feel "the weight of the world" on their shoulders. It became even harder to send a crew anywhere near Colombia, when you developed a very close working relationship with your contract personnel and sources of information. Even though Scott D. didn't really know the men that Pat R. and I selected to fly this mission, he looked like he was starting to become concerned about their safety and they hadn't even left yet. Scott D. didn't know it at the time, but in addition to being a dedicated U.S. Customs Agent, he was in the process of becoming a member of The Blade Runner Squadron.

At 3:15 AM on Friday, April 5th, 1991, I walked down the quiet hallway of the Bachelor Officer Quarters (BOQ) on the Leeward Island side of the U.S. Naval Air Station at Guantanamo Bay, Cuba and woke up our crew. Fortunately, our crew made my job easy and immediately got out of bed.

The flight from GITMO to the pick up point near Port Estrella was expected to take 1.9 hours. The main reason for the short flight time, was because the undercover aircraft that we were using for this mission, was a lot faster than some of the other propeller driven planes that we used.

Despite the fact that we had no way of controlling the actions of the Colombians, our superiors in Miami expected our plane and crew to be loaded and out of Colombian airspace at a certain time. Even though it was impossible for us to control what happened on the ground in Colombia, we accepted the operational restrictions rather than be told that we couldn't go.

As soon as everyone assembled in the lobby of the BOQ at 0400 hours (4 AM), young Captain Trojan appeared to be as happy as a kid at summer camp. When our new recruit smiled wide and remarked, "The rooms are nice at this hotel," I shook my head, while the others snickered and I informed Captain Trojan that the BOQ is not called a hotel, even though it served the same purpose. (The first time I was stationed at GITMO on a TDY (Temporary Detail), the BOQ was rather dingy and very dated in appearance. After being renovated and remodeled, the new BOQ was a very nice place to stay.)

Before we left for the flight line I conducted another briefing. After going over the nuts and bolts of the operational plan, I told our crew what to do and how to act if they were forced to remain in Colombia because of a crash or a mechanical problem. (I am not at liberty to discuss what I told our crew, because these tactics and techniques can still be used by other undercover personnel who become stranded in a dangerous location. The bottom line, is that we had contingency plans for everything and anything that could possibly happen.) When I was finished, I turned to the U.S. Navy Police Officer who was standing by to give us a ride to the flight line and said, "We're ready."

TIME TO GO

As we left the building, I hesitated to wake up Johnny Walker. Since I knew that Johnny wanted to be there when our crew took off, I didn't feel bad when I shook him by the arm, until the Vietnam veteran turned Blade Runner Squadron crew chief and mechanic woke up.

While the U.S. Navy Police Officer drove us to the flight line, I had a good feeling about this mission. In fact, this deal happened so fast, we were unable to arrange our usual air surveillance coverage for the UC aircraft when it headed south.

Once we arrived at the airfield, I conducted another quick briefing session, while Johnny Walker removed the wooden chocks from the wheels. Immediately after Captain Trojan and The Salesman completed their pre-flight inspection of the aircraft, there was nothing else to do but fly the mission.

At 0415 hours, Customs Agent Scott D., Johnny Walker and I said goodbye to the crew and watched them board the undercover plane. Once the cabin door was secured by Ricky Ricardo and checked by Johnny Walker, we stepped back while the cockpit crew prepared to take off. With the exception of our new contract pilot we had been through a great deal together. Even though there was supposed to be some distance kept between us, it was impossible to have a cavalier attitude about sending our hired hands in harms way.

It is also important to note, that by the time it came time to launch one of our crews, everyone involved in the operation knew everything about the investigation, including who the main violators were and who the undercover personnel were supposed to be. In my opinion, this made everyone feel like they were an integral part of the team. In fact, operating in this fashion, insured the success of every case that we worked and every mission we flew. I was also very lucky that our crews always made it easy for me to get through the departures, by being upbeat and confident. Tonight was no different.

From where I was standing on the tarmac, I could see The Salesman put his head set on, while Captain Trojan strapped into the pilot's seat. I knew Captain Trojan was a Blade Runner when he held up a box of Trojan condoms and smiled wide, as he let me know that he understood the hazing we gave him when he was recruited into the fold.

As our youngest CPIC (Contract Pilot in Command) put the box of condoms down and began speaking to the control tower, I smiled for the first time that night. While I couldn't see him from where I was standing, I knew from the operational plan, that Ricky Ricardo was assigned to work the radios and deal with the Colombians when they reached their destination.

The moment Captain Trojan applied power to the engines and taxied the plane to the active runway, I saluted the crew as they rolled by. As the undercover aircraft prepared for takeoff, I stood off to the side and asked Almighty God to protect our crew on their mission and bless us with victory over the forces of evil. When I was finished with my prayer, I was joined by Scott D. and Johnny Walker. As the three of us stood there in silence, we watched the undercover plane take off and climb into the darkness. The time was 0430 hours.

Since the issue of sleep was out of the question, we stopped at the base police station for some super strong U.S. Navy coffee, before we made our way to the BOQ to wait out the night. After getting as comfortable as possible, Scott and I picked up where we had left off and did the best we could to pass the time, while our crew made their way to Colombia.

KNOCK, KNOCK, NOBODY'S HOME

The Salesman was on the controls when the undercover aircraft went feet dry at 225 knots and headed inland at precisely the right time. As soon as our crew reached the first landing zone, they followed my advice and circled the area a few times to size up the terrain. The more pressing problem was not the condition of the poorly maintained crater filled runway, but that nobody was around. (So much for landing at the primary airstrip.) Once Ricky Ricardo managed to finally raise someone on the radio, he learned that the Colombians got the runways confused and had the alternate as the primary. Once everything got worked out, our crew headed over to the alternate strip.

As soon as The Salesman and Captain Trojan found the right airstrip, they continued circling, while they waited for Ricky Ricardo to be given the signal to land. After the third pass The Salesman checked his watch and saw that they had ten minutes to land, get loaded and RTB (Return to Base), in order to comply with our orders to be clear of Colombian airspace by a certain time. Even the route our crew flew into and out of Colombia was selected to help them avoid detection.

As our crew circled the field, they spotted four trucks arrive one right after the next near the edge of the airstrip. Once the Colombians on the ground and Ricky Ricardo exchanged the proper code words, our crew was invited to land and make the pickup. While our cockpit crew reduced power settings, applied the appropriate degrees of flap and lowered the landing gear, they visually inspected the runway before they made their final descent.

THE POINT OF NO RETURN

There comes that point in every undercover operation, when the only thing left to do, is suck it up and go for it. That's exactly what our crew did, when they landed the refurbished turbo prop former commuter airliner on a runway in Colombia to pick up 330 kilos of cocaine. With no time to waste, Captain Trojan turned the plane around to put it in the position to get loaded and take off. While our young Contract Pilot in Command taxied the UC aircraft over to our "clients," Ricky Ricardo moved to the rear of the cargo bay and opened the cargo door hatch to handle the loading.

Up front Captain Trojan could feel every bump and depression in the field as he taxied toward an array of vehicles. While the newest member of The Blade Runner Squadron continued to handle the controls, The Salesman talked the young pilot through his first undercover deal. When a surprised Captain Trojan remarked, "They have machine guns," The Salesman turned to the young pilot and calmly but sarcastically remarked, "They must be with airport security." Both men laughed and used the joke to break the tension. A split second later, a yell to stop came from the back of the aircraft.

While Captain Trojan kept the engines tuning, Ricky Ricardo accepted the shipment of cocaine from the local natives. It took less than one minute for the Colombians to load 330 kilograms of cocaine that were neatly packaged in heavy plastic sacks into the plane.

After hearing Ricky yell, "Go," Captain Trojan applied power to the engines, just as the crowd that stood nearby stepped aside to allow the undercover plane to pass. Light on fuel by 150 gallons The Salesman took over the controls and fire walled the throttles, to get full power into the engines. It took only a short distance of traveling at full power, to get the former commuter plane off the ground and into the air. Once again The Blade Runner Squadron acted like a thief in the night and tricked our adversaries on their own turf.

BRINGING HOME THE BACON

After staying up all night, I grabbed a quick shower and changed into some fresh clothes, before I joined Scott D. in the lobby of the BOQ and waited for a base police officer to pick us up. As soon as the Navy cop arrived at 0700 hours sharp, we headed over to the flight line to wait for the return of our crew. While I paced back and forth and chain smoked cigarettes, Scott stood on the tarmac next to a U.S. Customs Citation Jet from the Miami Air Branch, that just arrived for a TDY in GITMO.

Even though we didn't have any dedicated air surveillance aircraft covering the UC plane on this trip to Colombia, U.S. Customs air assets were available at daybreak. While a U.S. Customs aircraft from the Jacksonville Air Branch on TDY status to GITMO patrolled the area between Cuba and Colombia, I said a silent prayer, while I waited with Scott D. for our crew to return.

While using a radio in another Customs aircraft, that was based at GITMO to contact our crew, I smiled from ear to ear, when I heard The Salesman respond to my transmission and report that they would be landing in a few minutes. Right on schedule, our plane and crew arrived safely after successfully completing their mission. Not bad for a bunch of misfits, eccentrics and social outcasts.

Once we departed GITMO, we traveled to Homestead Air Force Base and delivered the 330 kilos of cocaine to Rob K. and other agents who were waiting for us. We then took off and returned the plane to the private airport where The Gambler's hangar was located.

With our mission accomplished it was time to celebrate. After being joined by Captain Kilo and Major Tom, we put two tables together in one of our favorite hangouts and ordered several buckets of chicken wings and a round of drinks, that included a shot of tequila in a dirty glass for the newest member of our unit. As soon as The Gambler heard that we were back, he raced over and joined us. (Even though The Gambler aka Mr. Lucky was a hardcore businessman, who at times had the disposition of the Don Rickles character Crap Game (from the movie Kelly's Heroes), he truly cared about everyone in our rather unorthodox unit, especially when we went operational.)

That night we experienced the best part of this job, the camaraderie. After reminiscing and joking around for several hours, we decided to call it a night at 11PM. Tomorrow was another day and we had plenty of work to do.

CHAPTER 8

DO NOT PASS GO, DO NOT COLLECT $200 BUT GO DIRECTLY TO JAIL

When it came time to execute the final phase of this transportation case, I volunteered to drive the load car and make the delivery. Between my long hair and my beard I looked a lot like the Good Lord himself as I listened to the briefing.

After giving my badge and credentials, as well as my 9mm SIG P228 pistol, to my partner Pat R., I tucked my five shot .38 caliber S&W revolver in my waistband and sat behind the wheel of the faded green Oldsmobile that was being used as the load vehicle. As I drove the load car to a Mc Donald's Restaurant in a south Dade County strip mall, I wondered how many of these deals I had left in me. My job was to play the pilot who who picked up the load in Colombia and assist Ricky Ricardo make the delivery. To his credit, Ricky Ricardo acted like a real pro when he demanded that we be paid a half million dollars as a partial payment for our transport services.

As I sat at a window seat inside a Mc Donald's fast food restaurant, I kept an eye on the 200 kilos of cocaine that were secured in the trunk of the load car. Fortunately, Pat R. was nearby. As an extra precaution, I carried a small transmitter that relayed every word and sound that emanated around me to Jim Z. our tech agent. If Jim heard me give the danger signal, he would alert all units to move in and presumably save my life in the process. The fact that our tech equipment didn't always work, made me appreciate having my partner Pat R. sitting a few feet away at another table.

As usual, the stateside receivers that we met that day moaned and groaned about not having enough money to pay us. Short of prying the keys from my dead hand, the bad guys would never know which car in the crowded parking lot contained "their" 200 kilos of cocaine, until we got paid. No money, no honey was the rule of the day. Rather than get ripped off and go tactical, the other undercover operative and I decided to live to fight another day.

"Pull out, Nick," were the first words I heard, when I answered my mobile phone after the negotiations came to an end. Without wasting anytime, I got up and walked outside and headed straight for the load car. If the bad guys intended to rip us off and steal the coke load without paying us for our transportation services, this would be the time when they would make their move. My senses were never more alive, as I made my way to the load vehicle. So far, no one made a move toward me.

The moment I reached the load vehicle I felt relieved, even though I still had to get out of the area, before I would be completely safe. Once I got inside the car, I started the old sedan and drove out of the parking lot at a normal rate of speed. My first concern was to make sure that I wasn't being followed by any of

the bad guys. So far I counted three leased G-rides (government cars) on my

tail, then a fourth, as I turned onto the Florida Turnpike.

After a high speed run down a long stretch of highway, I exited the turnpike

and waited for Rob K., Pat R., Paul G., Brad R. and Scott D. to catch up. As if I

wasn't busy enough, I was receiving non-stop 911 pages from our Boston office.

Jimmy S. and Bob C. had called me at least five times while I was UC. After all

that I had been through in the anxiety department, I was ready to shit can my

obnoxious pager in the closest dumpster, after being contacted so many times

by the agents from Boston. (In all fairness, the Boston agents had no idea that

I was in the middle of another undercover operation.)

As soon as Rob K and the other agents arrived, I called Jimmy S. on a mobile

phone and asked him what the 911 emergency was all about. According to Jimmy,

he was still having some problems on the joint FBI/Customs case.

Ever since Ricky Ricardo and I went to Boston back in February I remained

in periodic contact with the Boston agents. During this period of time, the

Colombian violators promised our Boston agents one thing, then reneged or

failed to produce. As frustrating as it was for me to have to repeat myself, I was

consistent in the advice that I offered. While I fully understood their desire to

make another major drug seizure in New England, I felt that some of the agents

in Boston were far too willing to constantly give in to the Colombians, while

hoping they would comply.

As far as I was concerned, the proof that the Boston agents were pissing up a rope, was plain as day to everyone but them. The fact that they spent a considerable amount of time and money on this case, without making any arrests or seizures, proved that they were using the wrong tactics.

Each and every time I was asked to put in my two cents, I told my colleagues in Boston that they should demand that their Colombian clients pay them some expense money, to cover the delays caused on their end. At the risk of sounding like a broken record, I repeated the same advice whenever we discussed their case. As far as I was concerned, once the bad guys delivered enough cash to pay reasonable expenses, the UC agents would make a suitable cargo plane available, to transport a cocaine shipment from Colombia to New England. As soon as I made these demands, I would tell the bad guys in no uncertain terms that this was my final offer. I would then slam the phone down and go about my business. I also assured my colleagues in Boston, that if the bad guys ever called back, they would have a real deal on their hands, instead of this useless exchange of false promises and bullshit.

Even though Jimmy S. of all people knew how to conduct a "transportation case," he was "in a box" as he liked to say, because he and his agents were working on a joint investigation with the FBI. In a way, this made me the fall guy, or the "man in the middle" who was called to be the bearer of bad news when this case wasn't moving forward. The good news was, the U.S. Customs Agents from SAC Boston had their shit together, as far as their other transportation case was concerned. This was evident by the fact, that the Colombian violators agreed to pay $100,000 and had delivered $50,000 in cold hard cash to solidify the deal.

After I promised Jimmy that I would call him back once I got settled, he wished me luck and hung up. Since the initial negotiations failed to facilitate a successful delivery on the Miami Group 8 case, we knew the bad guys were destined to get in contact with us, because there was no way they were going to let us keep 330 kilos of "their" cocaine.

As soon as the cocaine was secured at the Customs warehouse, we met at one of our favorite watering holes to wait to hear from the bad guys. Ricky Ricardo had his tape recorder standing by his mobile phone, while we waited for a violator called Flaco to call. To kill time, we ordered a few buckets of chicken wings and washed them down with some ice tea and cold beer. Our pagers started going off just as Major Tom and Captain Kilo arrived. Just as The Gambler joined us and filled us in on the case he working with some FBI Agents from Miami, I was contacted on my cell phone by the Boston based U.S. Customs Agents. Meanwhile, Captain Kilo had another Colombian calling him, while Ricky Ricardo was on his cell phone, with the stateside receivers on the transportation case that we were working with Scott D.

As soon as I turned my attentions back to the Group 8 deal, I told Ricky Ricardo to tell our "clients" in the 330 kilo deal to tell their problems to Jesus because the Chaplain went ashore. (An old WWII expression.) "Screw them," I said. "They told us XYZ and we delivered XYZ. They have problems and we have 330 kilos of "their" cocaine. Play it out all the way like a good businessman," was my advice to Ricky. Both Pat R. and Scott D. agreed that we had to play this the right way, if we intended to reach all of our objectives.

The moment the call came in on his undercover mobile phone, all eyes were on Ricky Ricardo. As soon as Ricky answered the phone, he sounded like a sharp tongued dictator from a two bit Banana Republic when he told Flaco exactly how our business was going to be conducted. Under the circumstances, I had no objection when Captain Kilo chimed in and began to direct Ricky from the sidelines. Having an excited Colombian sitting at our table, provided the perfect background noise, as Ricky conducted his negotiations with Flaco over one of our undercover mobile phones.

There were many words in Spanish that I liked the sound of, but if I ever had a favorite it was the word ENTONCES! When said with the right inflection and timed perfectly to the downward swing of the hand and the snapping of fingers, the word that meant "therefore" had a lot more meaning when said in Spanish than in English.

When Ricky hung up the phone I didn't need a translator to tell me that he was hot. Sounding almost exactly like the actor Desi Arnez, my favorite Hispanic contract pilot began to rattle off a translation of the conversation that he just had with the violator known as Flaco. "Nick, they told me to give them 40 kilos for $100,000. I told him, no way. They said, "Oh, yea." I said "Yea." Then they said, "Well then, there's no deal and Flaco hung up."

While everyone at our table had a good laugh at the expense of the enemy, I imagined Flaco sitting back after that last call shaking his head and saying, "What did I just do?" The main violator we were dealing with thought that he was being a real tough guy, when he shot his mouth off, before he realized that we had him by the balls and we weren't about to let go, until he paid us the money we were promised. As long as we held onto "his" cocaine, we called the shots.

Like the predictable adversaries that they were, the bad guys known as state-side receivers would moan and groan for days, until we let them wear us down a bit and we agreed to settle for a few hundred thousand dollars. Even though this wasn't the actual amount that we were originally promised, we knew from experience when it was time to move the deal along.

In the end, the drug traffickers in the SAC Miami Group 8 case agreed to pay us $300,000 for 200 kilos and give us the rest of our money when they received the rest of the shipment. Even though this deal would never get that far, we had to act as if we agreed to the terms and were ready to play ball. The fact that there were only a few ways to conduct these business arrangements, served our purposes whenever we conducted a high risk controlled delivery.

In our case, once we became more experienced, we learned to hold the smugglers we dealt with to the original deal that we negotiated. That meant that we only flew after we received a reasonable amount of expense money and we always expected to be paid before a drug shipment was "delivered." When our "clients" asked us to front them a portion of the coke load, so they could sell some "product" (cocaine) and generate enough cash to pay us what we were previously promised, our position was simple. You contracted with us to pick up your load and deliver it to the U.S. for a certain amount of money per kilo, so why do we have to wait to be paid when our job is already done.

We could also count on the fact, that every drug smuggler we dealt with always gave us more than enough reasons to distrust them. This made it easy for us to stick to our guns and hold out for the cash. Remember, holding out for the cash insured that we we would end up arresting some number of major violators, in addition to some of the lower level violators. This was the case, because lower level violators didn't deliver money to the transportation people. At the very least, the violator who brokered the deal would be made responsible to conduct business with us.

PRACTICE MAKES PERFECT

Once the 200 kilos of cocaine were placed in the trunk, I started the engine in the faded light green Oldsmobile and wondered how this day would end. In addition to being incredibly hot and humid, I was going undercover to deliver a portion of a 330 kilo coke load, in a bad section of Miami; a place where the dope dealers were at home and I was a stranger.

Shortly after I arrived at the location in the Kendal section of Dade County, where the exchange was scheduled to be made, the main violator arrived and exchanged $300,000 for the car keys to the load vehicle. As soon as the state side receiver drove away in the load vehicle, I made sure the coast was clear, before I got into Pat R's undercover car and slumped down to avoid detection. Once Pat handed me my badge and credentials, he accelerated to catch up to the long convoy of Special Agents from Group 7 and Group 8, who were following the load vehicle around Dade County, Florida.

Eventually, the Cuban smuggler parked the load car in front of a huge hacienda, that was located on a side street behind the Florida Turnpike and the S.W. 40th Street Exit. Because it was still daylight, we scurried around the neighborhood, until we found the most advantageous locations to establish a surveillance on the load vehicle. By nightfall everyone was getting anxious.

When a Group 8 surveillance agent spotted a Hispanic male open the trunk and remove a large heavy burlap covered sack, that contained approximately 25 kilos of cocaine, we began to instinctively inch closer to the residence that we were about to raid. The moment the Group 8 surveillance agent reported that someone was carrying the package into the rear of the house, SAC Miami Group 8 Supervisor Wayne R., gave the order to move in and take 'em down. (U.S. Customs extended border search authority authorized any Customs Officer or Special Agent to search any person, location or conveyance anywhere in the United States without a search warrant, as long as we never lost sight of the contraband.)

Between the adrenaline pumping, the darkness and the screams of agents yelling authoritative commands like, "Police, U.S. Customs, Federal Agents,

Adauna, Get Down!, Get Down!" you couldn't cut the excitement in the air with a chain saw. The location we raided was a multiple dwelling, that had once been a large estate and was now broken up into smaller rental units.

As usual, it didn't take long, for our agents to take several violators into custody and recover the 25 kilo package, that was removed from the load vehicle moments before we hit the house. With a total of six arrests, the seizure of 660 pounds of cocaine and the recovery of $300,000 in trafficker funds, this case was all wrapped up in one neat package ready for prosecution. So far, it was looking more and more like 1991 was going to be our best year yet.

CHAPTER 9

MR. ROGERS

T he smuggler I nicknamed Mr. Rogers was a tall thin man with a pale complexion, who was always impeccably dressed and looked more like an accountant than a career criminal. At 52 years of age, Mr. Rogers was trying to make a comeback after serving a stint in state prison. Initially, his goal was to make a big score by smuggling a huge load of marijuana into the U. S. Even though he had the contacts down south (in Colombia), he lacked the ability to smuggle the contraband undetected into Florida. That would soon change.

In early May of 1991, my Cuban CI Hombre de la Calle recruited his brother-in-law into our undercover operation. When Hombre told me that his brother in law had a case for us, I agreed to meet our our new recruit at one of our favorite hangouts; a safe place that was owned by a trustworthy individual, who knew who we were and always gave us the best seat in the house to conduct our business in private. The minute we met Hombre and his brother in law, I knew they were a winning team.

As you know by now, Hombre de la Calle was a seasoned veteran of many campaigns with the U.S. Customs Service Miami Air Smuggling Group 7. In addition to the fact that he was a very active confidential informant, who was constantly providing reliable intelligence information and assistance, Hombre

knew how we needed to operate in order to make a case. I mention this because

some informants had difficulty doing business our way, but not Hombre.

In addition to having a great sense of humor, Hombre was quite personable,

even though I knew he had a dark side. Fortunately for us, Hombre impressed

his brother in law when he "went straight" and started working as a highly paid

confidential source of information for the U.S. Customs Service. When his

brother in law saw that Hombre was making large sums of money without

getting into trouble, he wanted in.

Hombre's brother-in-law was a person that I ended up calling Chain Gang

due to a stint he once did in a rural prison that used chain gangs in the old days.

Later on, I would also call Hombre's brother in law Pepe Lorezno, a name we

decided on in the lobby of a Sheraton Hotel in Newark, New Jersey. During

Chain Gang's incarceration, he became friendly with an inmate I call Mr. Rogers.

As Chain Gang aka Pepe Lorenzo tells the story, he and Mr. Rogers spent much

of their time together behind bars walking the prison yard and discussing the

drug trade.

In May of 1991, Mr. Rogers had an opportunity to broker a drug deal and

provide the transportation services for a multi-thousand pound shipment of

marijuana from Belize. To make a long story short, Mr. Rogers immediately

reached out for his friend from the old days in state prison. What Mr. Rogers

did not know, was that Hombre de la Calle recently recruited his brother in law to work for me and my fellow U.S. Customs Agents in Group 7.

Since Mr. Rogers was under the impression that Chain Gang and Hombre were major players in the Miami drug trade, we created a fictional character by the name of Don Ramon to be the titular head of Chain Gang's smuggling organization. Naturally, I became the gringo who was like a son to Don Ramon. Without question, Don Ramon was the best fictional character we ever created out of thin air.

To round out our undercover team, I decided to ask Special Agent Eddie C. from the SAC Newark, New Jersey to serve as my undercover partner during this operation. If I had to do a deal in the New York City area, I wanted to work with someone that I trusted with my life and respected as an undercover agent. Besides, after the outstanding performance that Eddie gave in the Albuquerque II case, I wanted to pay Eddie back for all that he did for us when we worked in New Jersey. I should also add, that with exception of one individual who we didn't get along with, the SAC Office in Newark, New Jersey proved to be a very hospitable place for us to operate from.

In order to get Eddie C. assigned to work with us, SAC Miami Group 7 Supervisor Rob K. asked our ASAC to call Marty F., the ASAC in Newark, New Jersey to work out the details. Once our SAC Office agreed to split the trafficker funds that we intended to recover in this case, with our New Jersey office, the SAC Newark agreed to our request and Eddie C. made plans to travel to Miami. (It's amazing what you can do when you have money.)

Initially, Mr. Rogers wanted us to use a boat to steam down to Belize, to pick up 20,000 pounds of marijuana and smuggle the load into a quiet little west coast town in the Florida Panhandle. Mr. Rogers was a master at planning and logistics and traveled to various source countries to learn the business from both ends. Like many other drug traffickers and smugglers, Mr. Rogers needed a steady, reliable and well equipped transportation network, that could reliably smuggle shipments of contraband to any destination. Naturally, no one did that better than we did.

By mid-May of 1991, Mr. Rogers was hounding Chain Gang to set up a meeting with Don Ramon's people. "Will I be meeting Don Ramon?" Mr. Rogers once asked.

"No one just meets Don Ramon," answered Chain Gang.

Mr. Rogers then made two trips to Colombia to negotiate the terms of the load and the subsequent delivery.

Personally, I had never worked a controlled delivery involving a large load of marijuana and since we were so busy handling cocaine shipments, we weren't really looking for one either. However, if we were going to do a pot load, we had no problem handling 10,000 or 20,000 pounds of weed, because this was a very respectable quantity of contraband to seize.

Rather than jump on the first deal that came our way, I decided to hold back from meeting Mr. Rogers until he was ready to deal with one plan. (Initially,

Mr. Rogers floated a few possible scenarios past Chain Gang.) For almost two months I relayed my feelings, demands and requests to Mr. Rogers via Chain Gang and Hombre de la Calle. My two very colorful sources of information would meet or talk to Mr. Rogers and say, "Nick said this, or asked for that, or "Nick won't do that but he'll do this." I played it this way in the beginning, to establish my character with the main subject of our investigation and let him know where I was coming from. This enabled Mr. Rogers to get to know Nick Franco before we ever met.

As a side note, I should mention, that I selected the name Franco as my undercover last name as a tribute to the character "Victor Franco" also known as Number 11 in the movie The Dirty Dozen. Since it was standard operating procedure for undercover agents to use their real first name, I adopted the name Nick Franco instead of Victor Franco. While this wasn't the only name that I used when I worked undercover, Nick Franco was my personal favorite.

In one of my conversations with my confidential sources, I told Chain Gang and Hombre to tell Mr. Rogers, that once the Colombians heard that he had access to a long-range cargo plane, they will want to put a coke (cocaine) load on board as well. After all, why go all that way to Colombia to pick up 20,000 pounds of lung busting marijuana without tossing a few hundred kilos of cocaine on such a large plane?

I knew the Colombians would jump on the chance to use our plane to smuggle cocaine, because having access to reliable air transportation was like having gold in your portfolio. Personally, I didn't care either way, but why pass up a chance to smuggle a large combo load when you were able to do so. Since Hombre and Chain Gang were team players, they relayed my comments to Mr. Rogers and did their best to represent the pros and cons of using different modes of transportation, while stressing the fact, that a plane deal would be easier to manage and would go a lot faster than a boat deal.

While continuing to work through my intermediaries, I let Mr. Rogers know that I would accept thirty thousand dollars in front money for basic expenses and a reasonable transportation fee. Initially, Hombre and Chain Gang discussed basing our fee on 1 / 3 of the value of the marijuana load when the delivery was made.

To find out exactly what his contacts down south had in mind, Mr. Rogers was planning a reconnaissance trip to Colombia. The purpose of this trip was to determine whether or not the Colombians preferred to deliver the load at sea, or if we could use a plane. My agreement was that we would use our boat to meet a Colombian freighter anywhere except inside Mexico, not near Venezuela and if possible nowhere near the Panama. (According to our cover story, we were originally a very successful pot smuggling organization, that turned to cocaine smuggling and amassed a fortune that was invested wisely.)

By this time in our investigation Mr. Rogers believed Don Ramon gave us his blessing to proceed and would monitor the progress of our business venture from the head of the table where he always sat. I was, of course, the eyes and ears of

Don Ramon and needed only his permission and I could do business with Mr. Rogers. I also let Mr. Rogers know through my intermediaries, that we would charge the same fee to deliver his shipment to the New York Metropolitan area whether we went by boat or plane.

When Mr. Rogers returned from his fact finding tour down south, he met Chain Gang and Hombre de la Calle on a sunny South Florida Sunday afternoon in Broward County. Since I was scheduled to work UC on this deal, stayed behind while Pat R. and Rob K. provided cover for our sources of information and monitored the transmitter, so the conversation could be recorded for evidence purposes. While I waited with The Gambler at a local restaurant, the two amigos drove in Chain Gang's car to the location that Mr. Rogers and his Colombian partner Fernando selected for the meeting.

During this meeting, Mr. Rogers introduced his Colombian partner to Hombre and Chain Gang and wasted no time in telling them that Mr. Nick was right about the plane. According to Mr. Rogers, as soon as he informed his contacts in Colombia that he had access to a large cargo aircraft, that could carry thousands of pounds of product, they agreed to give Mr. Rogers and Fernando the contract to transport 2000 kilos of cocaine to the New York City area. In addition, the Colombians agreed to provide Mr. Rogers and his partner with 14,000 pounds of marijuana. Needless to say, we were all ecstatic after hearing the news.

While all this was going on, I was having the hardest time of my life with the two Boston deals. When Jimmy S. was the case agent we worked well together. Now that Jimmy S. was a Group Supervisor, he was trying to manage these cases from behind his desk, while he ran an entire group of agents. In all of my time working with the Boston based Customs Agents, I had never been called more, sometimes for no reason at all, to go over and over the same subject matter. While I never had a problem being contacted after hours, or on my days off when it was important, it drove me crazy when I talked to the same agent two or three times during the day and was contacted late at night to go over the same stuff.

WORKING UNDERCOVER AND LOVING IT

In late April, Hombre and Chain Gang reported that Mr. Rogers not only agreed with everything that I relayed through my two intermediaries, but he wanted to meet me in person. The first time I met Mr. Rogers we decided to put on a good show for the subject of our investigation.

To prevent anyone from following us after this meeting was concluded, we arrived at Shooters Restaurant in Miami Beach in an undercover go fast boat. Since Eddie C. was expected to land in Miami that afternoon, we timed this meeting to take place, so Eddie would make a grand entrance shortly after we got started. Because I was unable to take off and hang out with my brother Michael, a member of the N.Y.P.D. on vacation in Florida, I issued my brother a 9mm pistol and had him ride in one of the backup cars.

As soon as we arrived at Shooters, we grabbed a table outside with Hombre and Chain Gang and ordered a round of drinks. Once the subject of our investigation arrived and I was introduced, we exchanged some small talk, then got down to the business at hand.

When Eddie arrived it was like old home week, as we greeted each other like good friends do in front of Mr. Rogers. As soon as I introduced Mr. Rogers to the man who was like my right arm up in New Jersey, Eddie reinforced the point that we were lifelong friends, when he mentioned that he sang at my brother's wedding. By his reaction to our antics, it seemed as if Mr. Rogers was buying our combined act hook, line and sinker.

Our first meeting went extremely well and enabled us to document additional evidence that would be used to make a prosecutable case against Mr. Rogers and his associates. During this meeting, Mr. Rogers got the chance to check us out, while we joked around, then got serious and discussed the transportation end of the smuggling business.

At one point in our discussion I mentioned the possibility of making the pickup near the coast of Guatemala. When Mr. Rogers looked at me as if I didn't know what I was talking about, I stuck to my guns and informed him, that there was a very suitable location near the border of Belize and Guatemala where we could make the transfer to a seaplane or a boat.

When the meeting broke up, we agreed to keep in touch and get together when Mr. Rogers was prepared to give us some expense money. After we said goodbye to Mr. Rogers, we stayed behind, until Pat R. called my cell phone to tell me that the subject left the area and the coast looked clear. Once we left the area, we rendezvoused with our cover team.

Even though he was on vacation, my brother Michael was only too happy to help us out. As an experienced narcotics detective, my brother was used to working street level domestic dope deals in some really bad neighborhoods in New York City. Even though my brother knew what my colleagues and I did for a living, this was the first time that he had the chance to observe us negotiate a controlled delivery/transportation case that involved tons of drug contraband.

That night my brother stayed with us while we celebrated at a local watering hole with some other members of our unit, including some of our wacky contract pilots and the colorful Johnny Walker. The fact that my brother Michael was a police detective, who served in a narcotics unit, made him appreciate the job that we were doing. As a city police detective, my brother Michael saw what happened when drug shipments made their way into the U.S. and were distributed by drug dealers on the streets in high crime neighborhoods. Even though his stay with us was brief, my brother Michael served with us long enough to become a member of The Blade Runner Squadron.

It was during our first face to face meeting with Mr. Rogers, that the subject of our investigation got to make the decision to do the deal with us, or take his business elsewhere. If Mr. Rogers suspected anything was wrong, we would have never seen or heard from him again. When he called and said that he was ready to move to the next step, we agreed to meet. Needless to say, my colleagues and I were looking forward to our next meting, because it was at this meeting that we expected to receive the first installment of front money.

SEALING THE DEAL

When Mr. Rogers agreed to meet us at a location of our choosing, we selected a restaurant called Sundays on the Bay. As far as we knew, Mr. Rogers had ten grand as a deposit on our front money and was ready to turn it over to us. After putting a call into his 1-800 pager, we waited only a few short minutes, before Mr. Rogers called my mobile phone, to confirm that he was on the way. All we had to do was now was wait.

It had been a long day, for that matter, a long week. If there was ever a time in an undercover operation when I felt incredibly relaxed, it was when it was time to go into roll as a smuggler. One of the reasons I was so comfortable working UC, was because the men I worked undercover with were consummate professionals, who routinely gave an Academy Award performance, each and every time they worked in a covert capacity.

The day we arrived at Sundays on the Bay was one of those days when I was hungry and thirsty. As a result, I had every intention of enjoying a good meal, knowing that the bad guys were going to pick up the tab. Having a pocket full of trafficker funds came in real handy when you needed to promote a particular undercover operation. Besides, with all of the hours that we put in, you couldn't fault us for enjoying a little life in the fast lane when the opportunity presented itself.

The waiter was pathetically polite and took our order, while we waited to have diner with the subject of our investigation. While we waited for our drinks to arrive, we went over the scenario again and checked our communications equipment with our back up team. As usual, I felt reassured knowing that Pat R. and U.S. Customs Pilot Brooks B. were outside monitoring the recording equipment and were ready to charge in if something went wrong.

While undercover agents are inside enjoying a nice meal, the agents in the cover team are either freezing or sweating in vans and cars that are positioned around the meeting place. Whether you're all alone, or accompanied by a partner, undercover operatives, as well as the members of their cover team, share the pressure of conducting a safe and a successful operation.

When you work with a professional cover team, you don't have to worry about the people who are backing you up getting spotted by the bad guys. This includes having the actions of your Cover Team / Back Up Team observed by aggressive counter surveillance personnel. Even though "shit happens," the chances of a problem occurring will be significantly reduced, when you work with Back Up Team personnel who have their act together.

While pretending to be real smugglers, we had to make the bad guys believe that we were just as capable, greedy and evil as they were, or we would never be able to infiltrate their camp and do business with them. We also had to look, act and think like real smugglers at all times, while never losing sight of who we really were. Even though we had no fear of being arrested, we had to act like we were concerned about being picked up by the police or the feds, when it was appropriate to do so. In other words, you never wanted to seem reckless or unconcerned about the interdiction capabilities of the United States or other countries. All of these factors and more, made working undercover the ultimate acting job, where failure could result in you losing your life and not just getting bad reviews.

After a second round of drinks we ordered dinner, while we discussed paging Mr. Rogers one more time. A split second later, Pat R. called to say, "I think your man just blew past."

Mr. Rogers was a very intelligent person and I was confident that he would find his way to the location where we were supposed to meet. Since we had some extra time, I decided to go over our plan again before Mr. Rogers arrived.

As serious as our mission was, we were all in good spirits when we joked around at the table, knowing that Pat and the other agents outside could hear every word that we said over the transmitter. "Hey, let's send a few trays of food out to the parking lot, like that scene in the movie Beverly Hills Cop. Yea, I'll sneak out and put a banana in the tailpipe of Pat's car." Our laughter was cut short by the sound of my cell phone ringing. A smile crossed my face when I heard Pat say, that as hungry as he was, he would pass on the banana and "Oh, by the way, I think Mr. Rogers just arrived."

I could see by the look on Hombre's face, that our guest just walked through the front door. From where I was sitting I had my back to the wall, so naturally I had to rely on Hombre and Chain Gang to keep me posted, to what was visible to them and not to me. Lights, camera, action was all I thought, when I spotted a smiling Mr. Rogers as he entered the main dining area.

As I have said before, they should pass out Oscars to undercover agents and not medals for moments like this. (We didn't get any medals either.) While acting as if I heard the director of Hollywood movie say, "Action!" I instantly transformed into my role as the leader of an infamous smuggling organization. As usual, Mr. Rogers was polite, friendly, but all business.

As I mentioned before, during our previous meeting with Mr. Rogers, he had no idea that Guatemala had access to a coastline. Most people wouldn't know that either, unless they visited the area or they studied a map. Luckily for me, I was familiar with different locations that would enable us to execute air and marine undercover operations. This included locations in and near countries like Guatemala and Belize.

When you know you're right you can stand up to anything or anyone. It was the little things like knowing some geographical trivia, or being able to talk from experience about the sea conditions in the Windward Passage that gave you credibility with real smugglers. Again, it didn't matter that we were undercover agents when we planned and executed these covert operations. We still had to do everything that the smugglers did in order to carry out a successful sting operation. Between our combined field experience and all that we knew about drug smuggling, we were a formidable force to be reckoned with, especially when it came to knowing what to say, when to say it and how to say it, in order to appear like the real McCoy.

Being the meticulous type that he was, Mr. Rogers brought a series of small maps with him and made it a point to show me that wouldn't you know it but I was right. Guatemala does have ocean access near Belize where we could land a seaplane. After making some small talk, we went over some previously discussed details.

While trying not to act too surprised, I controlled my facial muscles when Mr. Rogers discussed his plan to have us pick up another load by May 25th, just ten days after we were expected to return from the first pickup. Even though the chance of us doing a second deal with this guy was a billion to one, it was entertaining to play along and act interested.

(There were only two ways that we could do another deal with Mr. Rogers. One was if we made a second pickup before we had to deliver the first load. Second, was if circumstances compelled us to arrest Mr. Rogers and he cooperated. This would be difficult to pull off, due to the severity of the charges hanging over his head from the first load. His Colombian partner would also have to cooperate as well.)

Once we finished dinner, we had coffee and relaxed as best as we could under the circumstances. As soon as I finished my coffee, Mr. Rogers leaned over and told me that he had my ten bucks in his car. BINGO! The deposit

on the $30,000 dollars that would seal our business arrangement had arrived

as expected. While my UC colleagues and I at the table remained calm and

businesslike, I was positive that our backup team was happy for all of us.

After paying the check, I walked Mr. Rogers over to his classic two door Buick

Riviera that was spotless and in show room condition. As soon as Mr. Rogers

opened the trunk, he removed a thin leather attache case from which he pulled

out a thick white business envelope. "This is for you, Sir," said Rogers as he slid

the money-filled envelope into my left hand. As I put the money in my pocket,

we said good-bye and agreed to stay in touch.

After making sure we weren't being followed, we rendezvoused with Pat R.

and Brook's B. As soon as I parked next to Pat's car, I ripped the envelope open

and found a healthy pile of $100 bills waiting to be counted. The deposit of

$10,000 toward a total of $30 grand was a decent amount of front money for

us to receive as evidence that our players were serious.

In order to celebrate our little victory, we headed over to one of our favorite

strip joints where we met several other members of our undercover operation.

We needed this down time to have a few laughs and unwind, after a tough couple

of days of gearing up to get our first installment of front money. Now that we

had some cash in hand, we knew it was just a question of time before we went

operational again.

After hanging out with my co workers and several totally nude exotic dancers,

I went home and played with my two sons, as if I had another "normal" day at the office. Clearly, my life was one of extremes. How I managed to perform this juggling act on such a regular basis wasn't always easy.

CHAPTER 10

OPERATION BLACKJACK

Twenty-one days after Eddie C. landed in Ft. Lauderdale we were ready to execute the controlled delivery involving Mr. Rogers and his Colombian partner. As we got closer to actually pulling this case off, I remembered the first time Hombre de la Calle told me that he and his brother in law were going to put a big load together for us. In fact, according to Hombre, the day would come when we would make history. That day came to fruition on May 15, 1991.

The DC-6 was, as Mr. Rogers himself would say, "an intimidating plane." With a cockpit crew of three, plus two in the cargo section as crew chiefs, the five man crew seemed dwarfed inside the huge cargo plane. In fact, between its four large radial engines, its massive wing span, its height off the ground (some 15 feet) and its long airframe, the DC6 looked a bit like a World War II B29 Bomber. The DC 6 was also the largest plane that we ever used in an undercover air operation. Her four piston engines would burn 400 gallons of Avgas an hour and carry enough fuel (over 5000 gallons) to give this particular undercover aircraft a range of approximately 2000 miles. In addition, a DC6 could operate on a 5000 foot runway and carry a useful load of over 20,000 pounds of cargo.

So far Eddie C. and I had several meetings with Mr. Rogers that were supported by a number of recorded telephone calls. Every time we met, either Chain Gang or I wore small transmitter that was monitored by Pat R. from the back seat of his rented undercover Cadillac G-ride. From an evidence standpoint, we were loaded for bear and had a well documented case against Mr. Rogers and his associates.

Even though we were used to working a very hectic pace, it was still mind boggling to deal with the fact, that we had a total of three major controlled deliveries going on at the same time. Despite the fact that the Mr. Rogers case was a full time job for a dozen agents, we learned to handle all three deals with only a handful of special agents working on a full time basis from beginning to end. Naturally, the word "we" usually meant me, Pat R., Eddie C. and one or two case agents and undercover agents from the other Customs offices and agencies that we assisted. The bulk of the help that we received wasn't made available, until we were ready to execute an actual controlled delivery of contraband.

Even though we always received a great deal of help from our sources of information and contract personnel, many of the duties that we had to perform had to be completed by a special agent. Unfortunately, some of the agents that Rob K. sent to help us seemed disinterested and unmotivated. In fact, in some instances, my two young sons seemed more interested in what we did.

A Catch 22 also existed because we needed two kinds of help at different times. Assigning agents to work with us who were not self starters and had no desire to learn was a waste of our time and theirs. To his credit, of all the young agents who ended up working with us, Special Agent Dave T. proved to be the best of the bunch. Not only was Dave a pleasure to work with, but he did his best to lightened our load. Even though he didn't always understand everything that we did at the time, Dave T. remembered enough to evolve into a hard charger in his own right.

When we were gathering intelligence information, cultivating and directing informants and collecting evidence, we needed investigative assistance to handle mountains of paper work, surveillance operations, the endless debriefing sessions and some of our day to day case management and administrative responsibilities. Simply put, special agents who were unable to adapt to our mission were not worth having around, so they were sent back to Group 7.

Once a case developed to the point of actually evolving into a mission to fly and we went operational, we needed technical assistance in addition to investigative assistance. U.S. Customs Pilots like Brooks B. and Air Officers like John M (who later became a Customs Pilot) proved to be an incredible asset to us, because they knew how to provide investigative support, as well as the type of support that we needed, once we started to gear up to fly an actual mission. This included, getting us AWAC (air surveillance) coverage, enabling us to store UC aircraft on an Air Force Base, helping us get to GITMO etc...

In contrast, most agents only flew on commercial aircraft and were often generally unfamiliar with private aircraft. When you consider that we routinely worked a number of cases at the same time, not knowing which ones would come to fruition, you can see why some special agents were not willing to be involved. Clearly, this type of work wasn't for everyone. Group 7 also had other cases to work. In other words, everyone couldn't be assigned to our undercover air operation.

One of the reasons we worked long hours, had to do with the hours the enemy kept. Anyone who has ever worked in the drug enforcement field knows, that mid level and major violators in places like Colombia don't work 9 to 5. Most smugglers are night people and begin their day long after the average federal agent reports for duty. This means, that when the average special agent is off duty and driving home, the average drug agent will still be at work. As a result, it wasn't uncommon for my colleagues and I to start our day in the morning and work into the night, while we debriefed and directed informants and contract personnel, covered and participated in undercover meetings, conducted surveillance operations and placed late night recorded telephone calls to violators in foreign countries. This meant, that we usually spent all day gearing up for everything that we expected to work on at night.

We also used the daytime hours to handle various administrative matters, that included writing reports and briefing superiors, other agents and federal prosecutors. As I state elsewhere in this book, during the day we also recruited new informants/sources of information and contract pilots, directed and debriefed our informants and sources of information, paid our confidential sources of information and contract personnel for previous assistance, lined up new planes to rent, arranged for repairs on aircraft that were scheduled to be used in a pending mission, changed our UC rental cars, qualified at the firing range, picked up technical equipment and participated in various types of enforcement actions. As if we weren't busy enough, we also helped other special agents who needed assistance.

One of the most time consuming and psychologically demanding aspects of our job, involved recording face to face conversations and telephone conversations with the subjects of our investigations. Doing so was draining and time consuming because we routinely recorded numerous telephone and face to face conversations.

One of the reasons recording conversations was draining and time consuming, was because we decided what would be said on our end before a conversation took place. In order to do so, we routinely had "think tank" sessions before contact was made with the subjects of our investigations. During these discussions, we developed various responses to any questions, or proposals that were presented to whoever from our side was serving in an undercover capacity. Nothing and I mean nothing was left to chance. Every possible base was covered and everyone who engaged in conversations with a target of one of our investigations, knew exactly what needed to be accomplished in our contact with our adversaries.

It was also common for us to record conversations in the afternoon and have to wait until the late evening to record followup conversations. This happened, when someone we were dealing with, had to meet with, or call a broker/contact in Colombia, to learn what happened after they met with potential targets, or actual targets of ours. In order to record these late night "followup" conversations, we either camped out in an undercover office, or in another suitable location, to wait until we made contact.

Since we always had plenty to do, we were never bored and put this time to work by handing administrative matters, working on other cases and meeting with our core group of sources of information and contract personnel. In the process, we mixed business with "pleasure" and often ate a late night super with our hired hands. This usually consisted of takeout Chinese food, take out Cuban food, several large pizzas, or buckets of chicken wings. Since we were a tight knit group, our days and nights were also filled with plenty of joking around. Being able to tease each other and joke around was critical to our morale, because we also had more than our fair share of job stress to put up with.

One tactic that proved to be incredibly effective, that I don't mind sharing with you, is how we used recorded conversations to our benefit. In addition to being evidence, we listened to every recorded conversation over and over again, until we evaluated every aspect of every word that was spoken. When we evaluated these recorded conversations, we focused our attention on the tone of voice that was used, as well as the way people responded to specific questions or comments, to include their level of confidence, any signs of hesitation and the specific words they used. In other words, we dissected every conversation from every angle, in order to get into the mind of the enemy. No matter how brief a conversation was, we usually learned something about our adversaries and often picked up a tidbit of worthwhile intelligence information.

Listening to recorded conversations also helped us to identify other major players, to include who was in charge. Because we often dealt with brokers or middle men, we let them sell our services for us. This is when The Greed Factor kicked in and brokers would make representations to the source of supply that weren't always true in order to move the deal along.

As I repeat elsewhere in this book, we also remembered everything the bad guys said to us. In doing so, we held their feet to the fire as the saying goes, when it was time to drive hard bargains, negotiate deals and make demands of our own. If a bad guy promised us something to get us to comply with his wishes, we waited for the right time to verbally pounce on our "clients" and remind them of their previous promises.

THE FINAL INSTALLMENT OF FRONT MONEY

The one thing that motivated us more than anything else was the receipt of "front money." Front money was the down payment / deposit that the bad guy's put up, to guarantee that their intentions to do business with us were genuine. Without front money we didn't budge. At no time did one of our planes ever take off unless we received some cash in advance. If a bad guy was confident enough to give us a decent amount of money, we would agree to go to the next step in the deal, but not before. In other words, we were a "cash and carry" operation.

With $10 grand already turned over to us, we expected to meet soon to receive the outstanding balance of $20,000 dollars. This time, we decided to meet a little further up north than usual. Because it had been a while since I had Mexican food, I decided to hold the next meeting at Carlos and Pepe's on the 17th St. Causeway in Ft. Lauderdale.

Even though Mr. Rogers was running a little late, we knew that he was on the way. Rather than starve, Eddie, Hombre, Chain Gang and I decided to order and eat dinner, our only meal of the day. Just as we were finished eating my mobile phone rang. It was U.S. Customs Pilot Brooks B. calling me from his surveillance vehicle. As soon as Brooks spotted Mr. Rogers entering the restaurant, he called me on my mobile phone to give us a heads up.

"OK, boys, that's our cue. It's show time," I said as we prepared ourselves for Mr. Rogers to finally arrive. Within a matter of seconds, Mr. Rogers found his way to our table. As usual, he was courteous, polite and very friendly. After saying, "Mr. Nick, how are you?" Mr. Rogers greeted everyone else at the table. After some small talk, we recommended the beef fajitas.

Once we got down to business, Mr. Rogers began to fill us in on his recent contacts with the people down south. From what he was telling us, his Colombian associates were in the process of getting ready to receive our DC6. Mr. Rogers then looked at his watch and excused himself to make a phone call. As he rose from the table, he passed me a piece of paper. While Mr. Rogers walked toward the nearby payphone, I unfolded the paper and examined the coordinates, that represented the location where our plane was expected to land in Colombia.

Mr. Rogers took awhile on the phone and once he returned, he found that his food had been delivered and was no longer piping hot. As Mr. Rogers folded his first tortilla around pieces of beef and onions, he told us that he had one more call to make regarding another load. As if we weren't busy enough, Mr. Rogers was planning another load for us to transport for him. I couldn't believe this guy. Here we were still plotting and planning our first smuggling act together and he was lining up our next gig. Was this guy colorful or what?

With dinner and small talk out of the way, Mr. Rogers ordered coffee then excused himself one more time. While he was making his second call for the evening, we waited patiently for his return. In the meantime, we agreed to wrap things up and move on as soon as he re-joined us. Once Mr. Rogers returned to the table, we finished our coffee then quickly went over our schedule. He still hadn't turned the additional twenty grand over to us, but we were confident that we would have it in hand before we parted company that night. As usual, we promised to keep in touch and with no unexpected delays, we planned to make the proposed pickup on Tuesday at 0700 hours.

After I paid the check, we meandered outside and walked Mr. Rogers over to his car. As soon as he opened the door, he reached inside and removed a large brown envelope from the glove box. After handing the package to Eddie, who passed it to me, he said goodbye and left.

Once Mr. Rogers left the area, we got into our undercover car and cleared the area. At first, we thought some guy in a yellow Chevy was paying a little too much attention to us, so we did a little fancy driving, until we were well out of the area. As soon as we were in a safe location, I opened the envelope and found $20,000 in $100 dollar bills all packaged in nice little piles.

Now that we had a decent amount of front money in hand, we began to really start to plan this operation. We drafted our initial ops plan and started to line up our crew and equipment. Days and nights were spent getting a primary and backup undercover plane lined up, all with the help of The Gambler and an old World War II aviator who knew who we were and was happy to help.

CAPTAIN M

Captain M was the oldest pilot we ever recruited into The Blade Runner Squadron. Thanks to The Gambler and our other benefactor, we met the pilot we ended up calling Captain M when we began planning the controlled delivery for the Mr. Rogers case.

Captain M was a very experienced aviator, who had more four engine flight time under his belt than anyone else in our unit. Best yet, Captain M was able to help us locate and rent a suitable aircraft for this mission. After a few crazy days of running around to check out different aircraft, Captain M located a plane up for us to inspect.

Once U.S. Customs Pilot Brooks B. and Captain M were satisfied with the condition of this aircraft, Johnny Walker prepared the rented DC6 for use as an undercover aircraft in our upcoming operation. As soon as some minor repairs were made, Captain M, Captain Video, The Salesman and Johnny Walker would put our new piece of equipment through its paces, before the plane would be secured at Homestead Air Force Base. That's when the fun began for me and my partner Pat R.

As usual, our contract pilots let their hair down a bit the night before the first test flight. They did so because the work leading up to a launch was rather intense. It was also no secret, that what we did for a living was considered very dangerous work, especially when we went operational and sent a contract crew to Colombia. As a result, after long days and nights of planning undercover operations and taking care of our other responsibilities, it wasn't uncommon for us to get together for dinner and beverages.

Before I go any further, I need to emphasize, that even in our so called relaxed mode, we were always working. It was during these informal "social" gatherings, that we would mix business with time to unwind and discuss what everyone was working on. We also used these more relaxed think tank sessions to congratulate someone for a job well done, to brief our hired hands, to plan operations together and motivate a source of information to perform a certain task for us, the way that we needed it to be performed. It was also not uncommon for us to make recorded phone calls to major violators and remain in contact with the other agents, who we were working with during these meetings.

Spending this "down time" with our sources of information and contract pilots also served to make them feel that we were not your typical federal agents. By running things the way we did, there was little or no chance of ANYTHING slipping through the cracks. In other words, our undercover operations were "seamless" and did not require anyone to connect the dots in order to insure success. This was achieved, because for the most part, a very small number of special agents (usually one, two or three), personally handled every assignment that was required to execute safe and successful undercover operations.

The sources of information/contract personnel who worked with us, also paid very close attention to the fact that the same agents they worked with, opened the undercover office in the morning and were the last to leave at night. This meant that whether I worked alone, with one agent, or with a small team of agents, my colleagues and I were solely responsible for the safe and successful execution of every operation that we were involved in. Working in this fashion insured that we never fell victim to the old adage, "too many cooks spoiled the broth."

Naturally, once all the "spade" work was done, to get a case to the point of picking up a load in Colombia, we received support from various field agents, group supervisors and high ranking managers. As I repeat throughout this book, when we sent an undercover aircraft to Colombia, THE MOST IMPORTANT SUPPORT that we received came from U.S. Customs Air Operations and U.S. Military/DOD assets. Whenever we met with major violators (aka bad guys), THE MOST IMPORTANT support that we received came from ground based special agents, Customs Pilots, Customs Air Officers and in some instances, from the local police. This was especially true when we conducted the final phase of a controlled delivery.

Some of the federal prosecutors we worked with were also very involved in certain aspects of our operations. This included, meeting to discuss certain strategies that involved the conversations that we planned to have with certain major violators. Our Boston office had an exceptionally close relationship with the U. S Attorney's Office, as did our SAC Office in Newark, New Jersey. The same was true in Miami, Ft. Lauderdale, New Mexico, New York City and Arizona.

Another point worth repeating, is that the best agent is only as good as the informants/sources of information and contract personnel that they control and direct. Officially, every federal agency will state for the record, that all documented confidential informants/sources of information and contract personnel work for the U.S. Government and not for any individual special agent or agents. While this may be technically true, it's not the whole story. I say this, because based on my experience, informants, sources of information and contract personnel were generally loyal and productive associates of the special agent or agents they worked with in the field. This doesn't meant that informants, sources of information and contract personnel were not loyal to a particular agency. It's also true, that when an informant, or a source of information screwed up, the agency might get embarrassed, but it's the agent or agents who controlled that individual, or worked with that individual, who would likely get in trouble.

A good source of information won't forget the effort that their control agent/agents made to protect their identity. Productive sources of information and contract personnel, especially one with a troubled past, know when you treat them with respect and you mean it. Informants, sources of information and contract personnel also know when you work long hours to make a case and when other agents go home early and pay less attention to the details that can mean the difference between success and failure. A good source of information/contractor also appreciates being paid well for services rendered. As I mention elsewhere in this book, the best street sources and contract personnel will also show up to help out when they are not getting paid to do so.

Recruiting and directing sources of information and contract personnel is a lot like properly raising your children. Simply put, you teach by example. Good informants and contract personnel are showmen and actors, just like undercover agents are. They love the spotlight and the adrenaline rush of being involved in high risk undercover operations.

Because confidential informants, sources of information and contract personnel are human beings, they also appreciate the recognition they receive when they do the right thing and they perform in an exemplary fashion. After all, it is human nature to want to be successful and recognized, or congratulated when you accomplish a task or act appropriately. It's also natural for the average person to want financial security, a sense of self worth and respect. Likewise, it's normal for most people to enjoy being liked, whether they can tell a joke and get a laugh or not.

A good agent can hang out all night long in a bar with his or her sources and never so much as have one drink of alcohol or get intoxicated. A good agent can handle millions of dollars and tons of drug contraband without taking any samples. A good agent can also motivate people to do the right thing, even if some risk taking is involved.

TEST FLIGHT

On the morning we planned to test fly the DC6, none of our crew members except Captain M arrived at Ft. Lauderdale Executive Airport as planned. While Pat and I wondered what the hell happened to Eddie C. and the boys, we watched our distinguished DC6 Pilot in Command periodically check his watch, as he paced back and forth in front of the plane.

As usual, the night before the DC6 was scheduled to be test flown we celebrated at one of our local hangouts. When Pat and I left the before midnight, I knew there was an excellent chance that Captain Video, Johnny Walker (Otis), Hombre de la Calle, Chain Gang, Captain Dakota/Johnny Churchill, Major Tom, The Gambler, Captain Trojan and Ricky Ricardo would stay until last call. Under the circumstances, we couldn't blame them for celebrating. After all, we were on a roll. Naturally, the more cases we made, the more money they earned. As much as I hated to leave before I knew everyone was tucked in for the night, I felt obligated to do so, because as strange as this may sound, I actually had the trappings of a personal life.

When it came time to test fly our new plane, our cockpit crew (with the exception of Captain M) was fast asleep in Eddie's hotel room. As soon as Pat R. called Eddie's room, our colleague from the SAC Newark Office got everyone assigned to the DC6 up and moving in light speed. Since Captain Dakota aka Johnny Churchill was scheduled to fly a DC3 on an upcoming Boston deal with Major Tom, Eddie let him sleep. (More about Johnny Churchill aka Captain Dakota to follow.)

Even though Pat, Captain M and I would have preferred to see Eddie and our contract crew arrive on time, deep down inside I knew that Eddie was living away from home and was putting in the same long hours as the rest of us. The fact that Eddie was exhausted enough to oversleep was understandable. I also knew that Eddie remained with our sources of information and contract personnel to keep and eye on them. I should also mention, that no one who worked with us ever got in trouble when they went out on the town.

As soon as our crew of misfits and eccentrics piled out of Eddy's undercover car, they sheepishly entered the U.S. Customs Private Aircraft Reporting Station at Ft. Lauderdale Executive Airport. Even though it was nearly lunchtime for the rest of us, I gave up on the idea of grabbing something to eat until the test flight was conducted.

While Pat and I stood nearby, a stern looking Captain M conducted the test flight briefing, while our "crackerjack" crew drank coffee and did their best to pay attention. In a way, it was kind of humorous to see three grown men with egg on their faces cowering before the oldest member of our group. They knew they screwed up and would have to eat a little crow, before being forgiven for being late, at such a crucial time in the planning stages of an operation.

Despite their tardiness and late night debauchery, we were never once late for a pickup in Colombia. When it came time to fly a mission, our crews cut the festivities short and had me wake them up in time to attend a final briefing and pre-flight the undercover aircraft. Because of their overall outstanding performance, I looked the other way when they overdid it. After all, even though we paid these men a great deal of money to provide a service for Uncle Sam, the other special agents and I knew that our sources of information and contract personnel routinely performed above and beyond the call of duty. As I mentioned before, this included helping out on numerous occasions when they weren't being paid, or required to provide a service.

While Johnny Walker cracked a smile as he closed the cargo door and our crew took their positions in the cockpit, all I could do was write off their antics as boys letting off a little steam before the big game. A few minutes later, the four engines on the DC6 came to life. There was hope yet that this day would end on a positive note, or at least that's what I thought at the time.

WE DIDN'T DO SO WELL

The moment I saw our DC6 taxing our way, I had high hopes that the test flight went well. Whatever good feelings I had vanished, when I watched Johnny Walker open the cargo door and stand back as a stern faced Captain M quickly climbed down the ladder of the plane. I knew we were in big trouble, when the veteran DC6 pilot walked right past me and Pat without saying a word. Once Captain M left the building, he got in his car and drove away.

As soon as the rest of our crew climbed out of the plane and wandered over, I couldn't help but ask, "What the hell happened?"

While Johnny Walker snickered and the rest of our crew stood with the heads lowered, The Salesman looked at me and said, "We didn't so well."

That was it. I had to walk away and get some air. Pat R. and Eddie C. were not exactly jumping for joy either. After taking a few steps toward the door, I turned around and approached our contract aircrew and said, "Who's gonna fly this plane if Captain M quits?" Eventually, it all came out. It seems that despite his experience in a DC6, The Salesman did not do a very good job as a co pilot on the shakedown flight. To make matters worse, Captain Video wasn't much of a flight engineer on the DC6.

To know this particular type of aircraft is to understand that the job of the flight engineer is a crucial and must be performed to perfection. Despite his outstanding qualifications as our chief seaplane pilot, Captain Video had no experience as a flight engineer on a DC6. The fact that he had a late night didn't help. Fortunately, Johnny Walker knew enough about the flight engineer's duties to help Captain Video get through the test flight, even though he was no where near as proficient as he should be to satisfy a professional like Captain M.

Our crew had their work cut out for themselves, or this controlled delivery would never get off the ground. Fortunately, Captain M cooled off and returned to the undercover office. Once he had a private chat with Captain Video, The Salesman and Johnny Walker we were back in business. During this meeting they came together as a crew and things went fairly smoothly for the rest of the case, as far as the operation of the undercover aircraft was concerned. In fact, when it came time to fly this mission, Captain Video, with the help of both Johnny Walker and Captain M, became an accomplished flight engineer.

Even though Captain M didn't seem to get along with The Salesman as well as he did with the other members of his crew, I allowed them to fly together because this "chemistry problem" didn't seem to be serious enough to hamper the mission. One reason I kept The Salesman involved in this case, was because our contract personnel had to be more than pilots, crew chiefs and mechanics. We needed people who could operate aircraft under very demanding conditions, while also being able to effectively deal with bad guys.

To his credit, The Salesman was a former smuggler who made a full conversion to being one of the good guys. Hombre de la Calle was another experienced drug smuggler and undercover operative who knew how to deal with bad guys. Even though Chain Gang was a convicted felon, he also transformed himself into a Blade Runner when he joined our unit. Having Chain Gang involved in this case added an additional layer of credibility to this operation, because he served time in prison with Mr. Rogers.

Even though there were other aviators who knew more about the operation of a DC6, our crew consisted of people with different talents, because they were participating in a potentially dangerous undercover air operation, not a legitimate charter service. In other words, Captain M was recruited to be the Contract Pilot in Command and everyone else was assigned to go along to help him get to Colombia and back in one piece. Simply put, Captain M could not have done it with out them, any more than they could have flown this mission without him.

DON'T I KNOW YOU

After receiving the front money from Mr. Rogers the main target of our investigation was arrested and ended up in the Broward County Jail. Needless to say, the last thing we needed was to have Mr. Rogers incarcerated for driving with a suspended license (after a DUI arrest), when we were working hard to arrest him for his involvement in a more serious federal crime.

The night Mr. Rogers was released from jail, Eddie and I, along with Chain Gang and Hombre, were there to meet him. While driving Mr. Rogers home we were stopped by a uniformed police officer. Because Eddie and I were working in an undercover capacity we were armed but were not carrying our federal badges and credentials (ID). As far as identification was concerned, we did possess our undercover driver's licenses.

Even so, the last thing an undercover agent needs to have happen, is to get challenged by a police officer when you are armed and in the presence of a major violator. This is especially the case when you are smack in the middle of a 2000 kilo coke deal, that also involved thousands of pounds of marijuana.

The second this unformed police officer walked up to me and said, "Don't I know you," I had no idea where this encounter was going or how it would end. While I did my best to appear courteous, I responded in a very respectful tone of voice when I advised the officer that we never met before. When this police officer insisted that he knew me, I stood my ground and assured him that we never met.

During this encounter, I did my best to ignore the fact that I looked like a bad guy who had long hair, a beard and a $10,000 dollar gold Rolex watch on my left wrist. Being in the presence of Eddie C. (who also played his part well and looked like a bad guy) was further complicated by the fact that our two cracker jack Cuban American Sources of Information (Hombre and Chain Gang) also looked like bad guys. Last but not least, we had Mr. Roger with us. If this cop patted me down, I would have been taken into custody for being in possession of a concealed firearm. Once that happened, he would call for backup and everyone in the car as well as our vehicle would be searched.

Fortunately, this cop did not pat me down or pursue the matter further. Once we were free to go, we left the area as if all was well. Later on that night Pat R. went to police headquarters to ask this officer why he stopped me and he insisted that he knew me. According to this police officer, he was as sure as sure could be that I was someone that he arrested in the past. This encounter confirmed that I did in fact look like a bad guy and when you work undercover

it never hurts to look the part.

CHAPTER 11

INCHING CLOSER TO SUCCESS

O nce country clearance was approved, all we needed was to have the Colombians confirm that they were ready for our crew to pickup the load. According to our "clients" in Colombia, they had the fuel that we requested, as well as plenty of people to handle the loading of the DC6. To insure that everything would go according to plan, Fernando and Hombre met the week before the scheduled pickup, to work out the refueling and loading procedures. Immediately after this meeting, Fernando traveled to Colombia to personally supervise everything at the pickup point.

As far as their involvement in this case was concerned, Mr. Rogers and Fernando were partners who wore two hats in this deal. On one hand, they were the brokers who sold our transportation services to a group of Colombian suppliers for a fee. This fee included a kick back to them once we were paid. To be more specific, we agreed to charge a fee of $3000 per kilo to transport the cocaine shipment to the United States. We also agreed to pay Mr. Rogers and Fernando a $500 per kilogram commission for brokering the coke deal. In return for getting us the contract to transport the coke load, we agreed to smuggle the marijuana in for Mr. Rogers at no additional charge. This of course was predicated on the fact that we would be transporting 2000 kilos of cocaine.

Also be advised, that regardless of what we agreed during our negotiations, we knew that once it came time to execute the final phase of a controlled delivery, we would never get paid what we were promised. Our mission at that point was to squeeze every dollar we could from the stateside receivers, before we executed the "controlled delivery" and arrested every violator involved.

So far, everything was in the green as they say, when it came time to meet Mr. Rogers before our plane and crew left for Colombia. (Hombre was missing from this meeting because he was resting in a South Florida hotel with our crew.) After placing a phone call to Fernando's contacts in Colombia, we were reassured that the combination cocaine and marijuana shipment would be waiting for us to pick up in less than ten hours. Mr. Rogers was his usual cordial self and appeared to be very relaxed working with us. You could tell that he loved the intrigue as much as we did.

Despite the fact that he was the enemy, Mr. Rogers was a very brilliant man who was always meticulously dressed, even if his clothes were dated. I'm convinced that if he didn't allow himself to be consumed by the dark side, he could have made a valuable contribution to society. When he spoke of his travels to the jungle lab sites and marijuana fields, you thought that you were reading a Hemingway novel, or listening to the narrator on the Travel Channel.

Mr. Rogers was also just as committed to a life of crime, as my colleagues and

I were committed to being undercover operatives for the U.S. Customs Service. In a way, he was a blast from the past, a holdover from the 60's and 70's. His home was impeccably clean, his clothes always spotless and with the exception of his apparent love for cats (I'm allergic), Mr. Rogers was a "likable" guy as far as bad guys go. Clearly, the only reason we got along was because Mr. Rogers didn't know who we really were.

Once we placed our call to Colombia, Mr. Rogers wished us well and asked if we could call him as soon as we heard anything. Naturally, we agreed and shook his hand before we drove away and headed for our office.

GEARING UP TO FLY THE MISSION

Once we were clear of the area and we made sure that we weren't being followed, we raced down to the Group 7 office at Homestead Air Force Base. As soon as we drove through the main gate, we headed straight to the Customs ramp where we found Johnny Walker and Mr. Goodwrench busy working on the DC6.

Since our plan called for us to refuel in Colombia, we left enough room in the fuel tanks for our crew to take on the exact amount of aviation gas that we asked the Colombians to provide. Naturally, we included in our calculations the amount of fuel that our crew expected to use on the flight down south. Due to the capabilities of the DC6, our crew also had more than enough fuel on board to return to a safe location, whether they were refueled in Colombia or not.

Just when we thought that everything was going smoothly, we realized that we had to relocate several aircraft on the U.S. Customs ramp, in order to make enough room for the DC6 to taxi to the refueling station. The tension was broken when Customs Pilot Brooks B. showed up to help out while looking like a giant bug. Brooks looked this way, because he was wearing goggles and a goofy looking helmet that had a portable radio attached to his ears. When I told Brooks that Eddie C. was going to martial/guide the DC6 to the fuel pump, Brooks informed us in a dead serious tone of voice that only a pilot could handle this job.

While Eddie and I laughed so hard we had to hold our stomachs, I struggled to compose myself when I informed Brooks, that Eddie C. marshaled aircraft on the flight line under fire in Da Nang during the Vietnam War and he was only a corporal. (Eddie C. served as a member of a U.S. Marine Corps Crash Crew at Da Nang Airbase during the war. Brooks is also a former Marine but he did not serve in Vietnam.)

After ignoring my remarks, our favorite Customs Pilot held two large conned flashlights over his head and pranced backwards, while he directed Captain M when he taxied the DC6 to the gas pump. You had to know Brooks and be there to appreciate this moment for what it was worth. Brooks B. was a kind hearted soul who contributed more to our investigative efforts and ground operations than any other U.S. Customs Pilot. I should also add, that just like the rest of us, Brooks was an eccentric in his own right.

Brooks was also the kind of guy who would let his highly trained German

Shepard attack dog roam around the Group 7 office off the leash. Once I made the mistake of asking Brooks what would happen, if by some million to one chance, a stranger accidentally used the "magic" word in a conversation that signaled his dog Hondo to attack. Brooks looked right at me, while Hondo stood a few feet from my desk and said, "You mean, "Packard?" As I froze and waited to be eaten alive, a happy go lucky Brooks B. told me not to worry because anyone could say, "Packard, Packard, Packard," all day long and nothing would happen, because only he could signal Hondo to attack, when he used the right inflection in his voice. Brooks was right. The fact that I am still alive today, is living proof that his dog Hondo was very well trained.

As soon as we had a good laugh and the refueling process was completed, we had just enough time to conduct a briefing and cover the salient points of our operational plan. This was Captain M's first mission but you'd never know it. To his credit, Captain M fit right in and acted as if he had been with us for some time.

When Pat R. and I began the briefing, the Group 7 conference room was jammed packed with everyone who was involved in this operation, including the DC6 crew and the U.S. Customs air crews from Jacksonville, Florida and Corpus Cristi, Texas. As usual, we provided everyone with a copy of the operational plan and broke out the maps and air charts as we went over the flight plan to Colombia. We also assigned radio frequencies and separate call signs for our crew to use to communicate with the Colombians, as well as with the U.S. Customs surveillance and interdiction aircraft. In addition, we discussed the highlights of the case and briefed everyone on the major players and the undercover roles that Chain Gang, Hombre, Eddie C. and I played in this investigation.

Clearly, the scariest part of the entire trip would be the time spent on the ground in Colombia. Even though the Colombians had no shortage of warm bodies to serve as worker bees, we figured it could take thirty to forty five minutes to get the undercover aircraft refueled and loaded with 2000 kilos of cocaine and 14,000 pounds of marijuana. The refueling would take a lot longer to complete, if our crew had to used a hand pump and 55 gallon drums of av gas instead of a fuel truck. The Colombians were also famous for waiting until the plane was refueled, before they loaded the drug shipment into the aircraft. Barring any other issues that could arise, these factors determined the amount of time that the undercover DC6 would remain on the ground in Colombia.

As I looked around the room before we headed out to the flight line, I couldn't help but take a moment to examine each face closely. It was moments like this that made me feel proud to be a U.S. Customs Agent. Our mission was to take the fight to the enemy through unconventional means. The controlled delivery was one of our boldest tactics to employ, one that enabled us to seize large quantities of contraband and drug assets, while also arresting major violators. Knowing that what we did mattered, was enough to make us work a succession of cases with unbridled amounts of determination and enthusiasm. The fact that we were extremely successful, made our individual and collective sacrifices seem worth it. Regardless of the overall impact of our efforts, it was our way of doing something to contribute to the so called "Drug War" effort.

PILOTS MAN YOUR PLANE

I can't repeat this enough. Launching one of our crews was the hardest part of the job. After exchanging a few jokes and some kidding around, Captain M clapped his hands and said, "Let's go, if we're gonna do it!"

While Pat R., Eddie C., Chain Gang and I stood by the port side of the aircraft, we shook everyone's hand and watched Captain M, The Salesman, Captain Video, Hombre de la Calle aka Gordo and Johnny Walker climb up the aluminum ladder to board the plane. As Johnny Walker and Hombre stood inside the DC6 by the open cargo door, I smiled one last time as they sealed the hatch.

After walking up to the front of the plane, I could see the crew taking their positions inside the cockpit. As I strained my eyes to get a glimpse of our crew one last time, everyone was visible except Johnny Walker and Hombre. The moment Captain M yelled, "Clear," he leaned over towards The Salesman who was counting propeller turns. After The Salesman reached the number eleven, the first of four piston engines began to come to life when Captain M hit the starter switch. Once the right inboard engine rumbled to life, Captain M and his flight crew brought the remaining three engines to life until the plane was one thundering machine.

As soon as the Air Force Control Tower cleared them for take off, Captain M taxied the DC6 over to the active runway. The time was 0015 hours. While the undercover plane made its way to the runway, Eddie, Brooks, Chain Gang, Pat and I jumped into our cars and headed over to the control tower to watch the takeoff from center stage. By the time we made our way to the control tower, the DC6 was stopped at the end of the runway, while the crew conducted a "run up" of the engines and a check of all systems.

The moment Captain M applied full power to the throttles, the roar of the engines could be heard reverberating across the field as the DC6 began rolling down the center line. Initially, the DC6 moved slowly, but eventually her four engines began to pull the plane faster and faster down the 10,000 foot asphalt runway. After traveling less than 5500 feet, the undercover aircraft was wheels up and on her way to the pickup point. Immediately after the DC6 took off, the two U.S. Customs surveillance aircraft blasted off and followed the undercover plane into the night's sky.

Within a matter of seconds, the flashing strobe lights were invisible, as the DC6 and her two escort aircraft flew away from the South Florida coastline. Even though the undercover aircraft was out of sight, I continued to look up into the dark sky, while I asked Almighty God to protect our crew during their journey to an unholy land. After saying my prayer, I returned to my car with the others to wait out the night in the Group 7 office.

It was during moments like this that I aged quite a bit. Even though every morsel of information that we collected was evaluated from every possible perspective, the decision to send a crew in harms way was never an easy one to make

.

WAITING OUT THE NIGHT

From the moment he arrived in South Florida to work with us, Eddie C. fit right in to our undercover operation. Senior Special Agent Eddie C. also proved to be a fast learner, when he signed on to help us orchestrate an undercover air operation using a DC6 cargo plane. The fact that this was Eddie's first undercover air operation, meant that he was about to face a new kind of challenge, one that would complete his initiation into The Blade Runner Squadron.

Once the DC6 took off, Eddie C. joined a very select group of federal agents who knew what it was like to be responsible for sending a contract aircrew on a very dangerous mission. After we settled down in the Group 7 office, Eddie said that he didn't know how I managed to handle being responsible for our crews. Once again I felt normal, when another agent that I respected, reacted the way that I did to bearing such an obvious burden. It was also a lot easier for me to sit out the night with Pat, Eddie and Chain Gang by my side. I felt this way, because this was no time to be alone.

WE FLY AT NIGHT IF THE PRICE IS RIGHT

The flight from Homestead Air Force Base to the airstrip in Colombia where Fernando was waiting to meet our plane, took a little over five hours to complete. Throughout the entire trip our crew wondered what was in store for them once they landed. While it's true that before they left they had been thoroughly briefed, everyone knew that it was the stuff that wasn't included in the operational plan that could get you killed.

All the way to Colombia, the U.S. Customs Pilots in the P3 and the Jacksonville Air Branch Piper Cheyenne surveillance aircraft remained in constant communication with our crew. While doing so, the Customs aircrews provided our DC6 crew with navigational assistance and weather advisories. As usual, the air escort and surveillance support that we received from U.S. Customs Air Operations was a very important component of our undercover air operations. It was also comforting for our contract crews to know, that experienced U.S. Customs aviators were only a wing tip away, as they flew to one of the most dangerous destinations in the world.

Back in South Florida, I kept in touch with C3I, in order to check on the status of our undercover plane and crew. So far everything was going smoothly as our DC6 neared the Colombian coastline.

FIRST LIGHT

As our crew looked out of the cockpit windshield, they could see first light breaking through the cover of darkness at just past 5 AM local time. For the record, there's a difference between first light and daylight.

As I mentioned before, it was fairly common for us to be told when we planned a mission, that our plane and crew had to be feet wet (flying over the

ocean) and on their way back to United States territory, before a certain time,

or we couldn't go. This left no margin for error or problems. As a result, we had

to use every morsel of natural light, to get into and out of Colombia as soon as

possible.

This didn't mean that we couldn't operate during other times of day in

Colombia. Every approved country clearance request came with strict operat-

ing instructions. For example, during two other covert air operations that you

will read about, our undercover aircraft landed at an international airport in

Colombia in the late afternoon and early evening.

Once the DC6 was one hundred miles from the pick up point, they were

on their own. While the undercover aircraft headed toward the coast, the U.S.

Customs surveillance planes went into a holding pattern in off shore international

airspace. From now on, our crew had no escort and had to rely on their own

instincts and experience to get them through whatever they came up against.

As our DC6 neared the coast our crew had three concerns. Would the airstrip

be adequate to support a safe landing and take off, would they be found out once

on the ground and would they get shot down by a trigger happy Colombian Air

Force pilot, who didn't get paid off to look the other way.

While The Salesman started going through the checklist procedures in prepa-

ration for the landing, Captain Video looked like a kid playing Super Nintendo,

as he turned knobs and threw switches while Captain M blurted out commands like, "Watch the oil!" "Check the power settings!" Fortunately, Johnny Walker was close by and helped Captain Video stay on top of things while he performed the duties of a flight engineer. To prove that he had no favorites, Captain M also leaned into The Salesman when he relayed orders for his co pilot to follow.

The fact that our DC6 was nearing the coastline of Colombia on schedule, meant that our crew successfully completed the first phase of this covert air operation. Clearly, that achievement was worthy of some praise, because this particular undercover aircraft was being flown by the most eclectic DC6 crew that ever took off into the wild blue yonder.

GOOD MORNING SUNSHINE

By morning, I lost count on the number of cigarettes that I smoked, while I did some paper work as a way to take my mind off worrying about our crew. As I mentioned before, because I knew the op plan like the back of my hand, I could look at my watch and know where our plane and crew should be at any given time.

After checking my watch and doing some fast calculations in my head, I turned to Pat, Eddie and Chain Gang and said, "They're fifty miles from the Colombian coast descending to fifty feet." A few seconds later the phone rang. It was the U.S. Customs Duty Officer at C3I confirming what I just said. A few minutes later I checked my watch again and told my colleagues that our plane should be feet dry and over the strip. After contacting C3I to confirm that my calculations were correct, I turned to Pat, Eddie and Chain Gang and said something to the effect of, "A prayer now would be in order."

While Johnny Walker was getting the equipment ready to expedite the refueling and oiling procedures, Hombre de la Calle was curled up in a ball and sound asleep in the back of the plane. Hombre had the best job of all. Besides being the comedian on board, Hombre was the most streetwise member of the crew next to The Salesman.

As a former drug smuggler who never got caught, Hombre knew the game better than anyone. (I rated Hombre as a more successful former bad guy because he never got caught but The Salesman did.) After his ten year stint as a marijuana smuggler, Hombre developed a conscience of sorts and turned from the dark side in stages and eventually became an incredibly productive government informant/source of information. As the story goes, during his last days as a bad guy Hombre became incredibly paranoid. In an effort to protect himself from harm, he tried his best to buy loyalty. Whatever Hombre didn't spend on his associates, he gave away until he was broke. His transition began when he reportedly met some federal agents, who became suspicious of his activities and pulled telephone toll records on his home phone. Once this happened, Hombre began to trade information until he was no longer a target of any investigations.

As soon as he changed sides, Hombre became a free lance informant and sold information to the federal government, to prevent from being prosecuted and sent to prison. Almost five years to the day of my first meeting with Hombre de la Calle, my favorite Cuban CI was riding in the back of an undercover cargo plane, to pick up a record setting combination load of cocaine and marijuana in Colombia.

Just like our other documented sources of information and contract personnel, Hombre worked for us for several reasons, including for the money and the adrenaline rush. I also got the impression, that Hombre knew that it made more sense to be an informant than a defendant. The fact that we paid Hombre a lot of money for services rendered, made it easy for him to change sides. I say that, because when he made tons of money as a bad guy, he was always concerned about someone giving him up to the feds or the police. Working for us meant that he could make very good money, without having to become paranoid, providing of course that he played by our rules.

I should also mention that Chain Gang was instantly liked by everyone in our unit. In addition to being just as street wise as Hombre, Chain Gang possessed a certain class that his brother in law lacked. While they were both brilliant men in many respects, Hombre was more of a tragic and troubled figure. I also sensed that Chain Gang was a man who desperately wanted to clear his tarnished name. Even though Chain Gang knew that he would be well paid for his cooperation and services, I'm convinced that he would eagerly trade every penny that we would eventually pay him for a Presidential Pardon.

CHAPTER 12

FEET DRY

As soon as our DC6 went feet dry over the sovereign nation of Colombia, it was flying at 200 knots at an altitude of just under 1000 feet. Their destination was an unimproved landing area near Port Estrella, a small town on the northeast tip of the Guajira Peninsula. Once the DC6 reached Port Estrella, The Salesman pointed and yelled, "There's the field!" After hearing what his co pilot had to say, Captain M dipped the left wing a bit to get a better look. Sure enough, there was an open area that was large enough for a DC6 to safely land and take off.

The moment a sleepy eyed Hombre de la Calle entered the cockpit, Fernando contacted our crew via radio and said, "Carne, Carne, Wesso." While The Salesman passed Hombre a head set and the radio microphone, the Colombian on the ground repeated his message and said, "Carne, Carne, Wesso." The code for the plane was "MEAT" with the Colombians on the ground being the BONE or wesso.

Without wasting any time, Hombre responded with the proper code and said, "Wesso, wesso, carne!" While the DC6 approached the field, Fernando's excited voice could be heard over the radio when he responded and said, "Wesso,

Wesso we see you."

After receiving instructions from our contact on the ground, Captain M banked the huge cargo hauler to the east and flew toward the voice on the radio. Within a matter of seconds, the Blade Runners were flying over an LZ that was alive with people and crowded with different types of vehicles. "Carne, Carne, this is Wesso. Land, land, you're over us now," yelled our Colombian contact over the radio.

Because The Salesman and Captain Video were old hands at this, they were hoping to make at least one more pass before landing but Captain M said something to the effect of, "We're going in." Once again our crew worked as a team. While Johnny Walker helped Captain Video with his flight engineer duties and The Salesman assisted the Contract Pilot in Command, Captain M flew the DC6 as it descended from 800 feet to the ground.

GROUND ZERO

As soon as the DC6 landed, our crew made its way to the turn around point located at the very end of the runway. While Captain M turned the plane around, Hombre and Johnny Walker opened the door in the cargo bay. While our crew deployed the ladder, a group of machine gun toting gunman encircled the plane as a flatbed truck carrying fuel drums pulled up alongside of the DC6. The moment Fernando arrived on scene, he clapped his hands and ordered his helpers to refuel "his" plane. Without wasting any time, Johnny Walker and

Captain Video walked through the hatch in the cargo bay that led to the wings and passed a long hose to the Colombians to begin the refueling process.

By the time the rest of our crew assembled in the cargo bay, a very happy Fernando scurried up the ladder, followed quickly by Pacheco, the "manager" of this airfield. While an excited Fernando was happy to see Hombre and the crew, a more serious but friendly Pacheco asked the first stupid question of the day and said, "Why did you bring such a big plane?"

Since Hombre knew the nature of the business that we were supposed to be conducting, he looked somewhat baffled by such a statement and remarked, "What do you mean? What else would you use to pick up 14,000 pounds of merchandise?"

According to Hombre, Fernando interjected, "They only have the perico," meaning the cocaine. Typical, thought Hombre, as he continued standing in the cargo bay with our "clients," while another Colombian climbed up the ladder and asked our crew if they could come back in twenty four hours, to pick up the rest of the load. Fernando then handed Hombre a piece of paper that contained a radio frequency and asked him to call him later that night."

Once the refueling was complete, the head man motioned the load vehicle to move closer to the plane. Without wasting any time a small army of twenty Colombians started to load the cocaine into the cargo bay of the DC6.

While the loading continued, a medium size twin engine Cessna landed on the strip and taxied over to our plane. Again, without wasting any time, a few

Colombians ran over to the Cessna and removed more packages and delivered them to our crew in the back of the cargo plane. Moments later, a distinguished looking man dressed in a white suit appeared in the crowd. He seemed important because he rated a team of three bodyguards to escort him around.

Just when things seemed to be going according to plan, another Colombian drug trafficker arrived with a truck carrying the rest of the cocaine shipment that parked next to the DC6. When this pissed off Colombian approached the DC6, he went berserk and accused our crew of belonging to the DEA. He made this allegation because he previously lost a drug shipment that was put on a plane that looked just like ours.

No words can explain how our crew felt, when they were accused of being agents of the Drug Enforcement Administration while they stood on a runway in Colombia. Fortunately, Fernando immediately went to their defense. By the way Fernando reacted, you would think that we had done business with him many times in the past. In fact, while Fernando stood toe to toe with the irate Colombian, he said that he had no right to slander the good name of "his" people. Fernando reportedly then told the shit disturber to take his cocaine and leave. As the irate Colombian stormed off with his men and product (cocaine) in tow, the distinguished looking Colombian in the white suit congratulated Fernando for a job well done.

After taking on 400 gallons of 110 octane fuel and topping off the oil reserves, our crew took their positions in the cockpit, while Hombre de la Calle behaved like he was running for office. While Hombre shook everyone's hand and handed out cold drinks to the workers who serviced and loaded the plane, Johnny Walker finished securing the 1654 kilos of cocaine and a pathetically small bag of marijuana inside the cargo bay. It was also at this time that an anxious looking Pacheco whispered something into Fernando's ear.

After hearing what Pacheco had to say, Fernando told Hombre that they had to take off because a Colombian Air Force fighter plane was scheduled to patrol the area. At one point, a Colombian fighter pilot reportedly got on the radio and told everyone that he was delaying his patrol but couldn't wait forever. Fortunately for our crew, a Colombian Air Force pilot was reportedly paid a handsome sum not to shoot our plane down. After hearing this, Hombre de la Calle reportedly remarked, "It pays to have friends in high places."

Once Fernando and Pacheco said goodbye and climbed down the ladder, Johnny Walker secured the cargo door hatch, while Captain M and his cockpit crew cranked up the four R2800 engines. As soon as the undercover aircraft took off and went feet wet, the U.S. Customs P3 Orion (AWAC) aircraft intercepted the DC6 as it flew away from the coast of Colombia. Once the P3 crew made radio contact with the DC6 crew, I was notified by the C3I Duty Officer that all was well. The Blade Runner Squadron did it again! We tricked the bastards and it felt great.

At 11:30 A.M, the U.S. Air Force tower controller at Homestead AFB notified us that our plane was on final approach and about to land. After hearing the good news, we jumped into our cars and drove out to the Customs ramp to receive our crew. As soon as the undercover aircraft came to a stop and we climbed on board, it was easy to see that something was missing.

After hearing some details about what happened to the rest of the load, I couldn't resist teasing our crew. "I sent you guys all the way to Colombia in this big plane and all you came back with is 1654 kilos (3638 pounds) of cocaine?"

As soon as I finished, Eddie C. jumped in and teased Captain Video and said. "You piece of shit. I knew you'd let me down."

As usual, Captain Video gave it right back to Eddie and remarked something to the effect of, "I thought there was a height requirement to be a Customs Agent." After joking around handshakes and hugs were in order.

Even though the average law enforcement officer would be ecstatic over the amount of cocaine that we had in the cargo bay of our plane, we had become desensitized over the years and jokingly considered anything less than a few hundred kilos to be residue. While the average drug agent got excited over a few ounces, a few pounds, or a kilo of drug contraband, the "smallest" cases that we worked involved 300 to 350 kilos of cocaine.

After conducting a quick debriefing of our crew, we field tested the contraband and secured the cocaine shipment in the DC6. Even though we were operating on a very secure U.S. Air Force Base, we assigned an armed guard to watch the plane, until we knew what our next move would be.

We had to wait until at least 5 P.M. before we would be able to meet Mr.

Rogers. This was the case, because we had to "wait" until our plane made its

imaginary flight from Colombia to New Jersey, to find out if everything went

according to plan. It certainly didn't pay to call Mr. Rogers, to tell him that we

got stiffed for part of the load, before the plane would have landed up north.

MR. ROGERS WE HAVE GOOD NEWS AND BAD NEWS

At 6:30 PM Eddie C. pulled our undercover Cadillac into the driveway of

the modest house where Mr. Rogers lived in Pompano Beach, Florida. I had

already activated the recording equipment by giving the time and date to Pat

R., our one and only backup agent. Once again, we were working with little or

no help.

Either we were crazy for working under these conditions, or our superiors

were nuts for allowing us to operate in this fashion. Here we were, working a

major drug smuggling investigation and you could count the help that we had on

one finger (the middle finger). The fact that this happened at all was unforgivable,

especially on a case of this magnitude. (I explained why we lacked enough help

in other sections of this book series. Some of the reasons were legitimate and

involved the fact that we had a limited number of agents available to work in a

very active area of operation.)

Just like every other profession, the average investigative group of special

agents was made up of people who had different talents and capabilities.

While very few agents were cut out for undercover work, some were better at surveillance work than others. Some agents also lacked the "people skills" to be able to recruit and effectively direct reliable informants and sources of information.

While some agents were better investigators than others, many preferred to work certain types of cases. As an example, some agents were outstanding fraud agents and made all kinds of cases involving counterfeit goods that were smuggled into the country. Other agents loved to work drug smuggling cases. Within this group it wasn't uncommon for agents to specialize in investigating certain types of smuggling. This included air smuggling, marine smuggling, land based border smuggling and cargo smuggling cases. Other agents made a name for themselves investigating money laundering and technology/arms smuggling cases.

Some agents who never made a major case of their own, were really good at providing critical support on certain types of investigations and enforcement actions. Each office also seemed to have agents who had it in them to do more but failed to do so for various reasons. I always believed that one reason why this problem existed, was because some supervisors failed to counsel and if necessary discipline the agents who needed to improve their performance. It also wasn't uncommon for people who accomplished very little, if anything, to get promoted and become a supervisor, or a high ranking manager.

After several years of operating with very limited full time assistance, SAC Miami management did help us finagle getting Eddie C. assigned to Group 7 on a temporary basis. As I mentioned before, the main reason why this happened, was because we invited the SAC Newark to work this major case with us. By

agreeing to loan Eddie C. to SAC Miami Group 7, the SAC Office in Newark,

New Jersey was guaranteed a piece of the action; which in this case included

the publicity of making a major case and a 50/50 split of the trafficker funds

that were recovered. Naturally, this money would be used by the SAC Newark

to keep his undercover operation afloat. I can only assume that the prevailing

attitude was, why not cut Special Agent Eddie C. lose for a while, just in case

those crazy maniacs in SAC Miami Group 7 hit pay dirt again.

Despite some of my criticisms I'm not knocking this arrangement. The

Newark SAC Office under the command of SAC Robert V.E. was THE BEST

place that we ever worked, along with the Customs SAC Office in Boston. As I

said before, there was a secret economy of The Drug War that affected both sides.

From a law enforcement perspective, the life blood of covert operations was

trafficker funds and asset sharing. Every time a large amount of cash was depos-

ited into a local SAC office's certified undercover bank account, the local SAC

office became less dependent on headquarters and was capable of mounting oper-

ations at will. Renting cars, paying for cell phones, renting undercover aircraft and

boats, renting undercover apartments/hotel rooms and paying other legitimate

investigative expenses, were all things that could be done independently of head-

quarters, when you had plenty of Mr. Green in your undercover bank account.

While the state and local cops and other federal agencies provided assistance

because it was an integral part of the job and the right thing to do, it was also very important to be generous when it came time to share credit, proceeds and assets. Agreeing to share credit, trafficker funds and seized assets became the carrot on the stick, that motivated law enforcement agencies to provide support on a "joint" investigation.

Operation Excalibur was a perfect example of how the feds reimbursed a local law enforcement agency, for providing the manpower that was needed to make a major historical case. By allowing Detective Billy B. and Detective Danny De C. and a few other detectives to work full time and when needed on this case, we, meaning the feds, split $7 million dollars in seized drug assets with the Broward County Sheriff's Office.

While other law enforcement officers would always show up to help out in an emergency, most administrators wanted to know up front what was in it for their unit or their agency, when they agreed to assign sworn personnel to a major investigation. This was especially the case, when the commitment to assign sworn personnel to a federal investigation involved the paying of overtime to state and local cops. The fastest way to get plenty of help from another law enforcement agency, was to agree to share the publicity, the recovered "trafficker funds" (drug money) and the seized assets. Like it or not, we all creatively manipulated the system to serve the greater good and get the job done.

Every time we met Mr. Rogers or any other violator we had two main concerns. First and foremost was the issue of our personal safety. Even though there were times when we conducted undercover meetings with different amounts of back up, we always did the best we could with what we had. We also learned early on, that it was the quality of the back up protection that you received that mattered and not the quantity.

Personally, I felt very safe when an agent like Pat R. provided backup when I went undercover. In fact, I would rather have one OUTSTANDING agent like Pat R. covering my back, than a small army of agents who didn't want to be there, or were not as capable when it came time to perform this type of duty.

GETTING BACK TO THE CASE AT HAND

Mr. Rogers was all alone in his house when we arrived to give him the good news and the bad news. Mr. Rogers was alone because it would take Fernando two days to travel from the peninsula in Colombia to Miami. This meant that Fernando would be arriving on Sunday. He and Mr. Rogers had originally planned to head up to the New York City area on Monday to handle the exchange. Now things had changed and our plans would have to be reevaluated.

When Mr. Rogers welcomed us into his home he sounded very sincere, when he shook my hand and said, "You look beat, Mr. Nick, sit down." (In addition to being physically tired, my back injuries were also acting up. This made it was easy for me to look as if I was not running on all eight cylinders.) As usual, Mr. Rogers was a polite and courteous host. Despite his gentle outward appearance, Mr. Rogers had an utter contempt for authority. This guy literally looked at law enforcement officers as the enemy and actually used that term to describe us. As I mentioned before, just like other hardcore bad guys, Mr. Rogers acted like a nice guy because he had no idea who we really were. I truly believe that if he knew my true identity, Mr. Rogers would have loved to use my scull as an ashtray.

Without wasting any time, we informed Mr. Rogers that his precious 14,000 pounds of marijuana was not put on our plane when the DC6 landed in Colombia. Then we hit him with how we were promised 2000 kilos of cocaine but only received 1654. Naturally, we used this set of circumstances to remind Mr. Rogers, that this was exactly what we meant when we discussed how dis-trustful the Colombians could be. We also told the subject of our investigation that the Colombians wanted us to go back to pick up his marijuana.

After discussing the situation, especially the part about how the Colombians failed to provide us with the amount of cocaine that we were promised, Mr. Rogers said, "Can we get to a phone?"

"Sure, let's go," I answered as we headed for the door.

Since Mr. Rogers was recently arrested for driving with a suspended license he stopped driving. (The pay telephone that Mr. Rogers preferred to use was not far from his house.) Because we were just as interested as he was to find out what happened, we piled into our undercover car and headed over to a bank of pay phones in a nearby strip mall.

I had the transmitter on and as far as I knew, Pat R. was close by recording everything that was said. As soon as Mr. Rogers bailed out of our car, he pulled a non-filtered Camel cigarette from his shirt pocket and bent over slightly as I offered him a light.

After dialing the long distance country code and phone number, the voice on the other end seemed happy to hear from Mr. Rogers. After not making any progress, Mr. Rogers continued in very poor but passable Spanish and told the Colombian to hold on, while he put his associate Eddie C. on the phone to finish the conversation. (Eddie's undercover last name also happened to begin with the same letter as his real last name.)

After taking the pay phone in hand, Eddie C. wasted no time in talking to the Colombian about the apparent screw up. Then Eddie repeated, "7000 pounds are waiting for us." Then Rogers chimed in and said, "Ask them about the perico (cocaine)."

"They can have a thousand for us," responded my undercover partner.

"Make it two, tell `em," said Mr. Rogers.

As soon as Eddie finished relaying the message, he passed the phone back to Mr. Rogers, who continued speaking to the Colombian about the business at hand. After Mr. Rogers paused for a second, he looked over to me and asked, "When can we go back?"

I thought quickly. I had to agree to return, but how fast could we be granted clearance was the key. I also had to get the plane serviced and made ready to fly. With all of the confidence I could muster, I looked at Mr. Rogers and said, "Next Wednesday for breakfast."

To mount two major covert air operations within five days was a feat that very few agents if any have ever done. The preparation, logistics, coordination and overall effort required to put one of these operations together is very involved to say the least. The fact that we had mounted an impressive number of high risk undercover operations in the past, enabled us to work just as fast under pressure as a NASCAR pit crew. Still, as confident as we were, we had to deal with the fact, that using heavy equipment like a DC6 made things a bit more complicated. The average agent might think that all you had to do was put the crew in the plane, fill it with gas and adios amigo. Nothing could be further from the truth, but not many people knew that. Regardless, we had four full days to prepare for the return trip.

After we dropped Mr. Rogers off, he suggested that we all get some sleep and plan on meeting Fernando once he arrived in Miami. Mr. Rogers also agreed to cancel his trip to New York and hold a meeting between all of us on Monday. As he explained, Mr. Rogers wanted to hear the whole story from Fernando, to make sure that "our friends" down south didn't hose us again. We agreed to wait until Monday to firm things up.

As tired as we were and as much as we needed a break, we had plenty of work to do in order to get ready in time to launch on Wednesday. Saturday and Sunday were spent running back and forth from the undercover office to Homestead Air Force Base, to shuttle our mechanics and 200 gallons of oil to the DC6, so we could get the plane ready to fly the next mission.

Our next problem was believe it or not, due to the Environmental Protection Administration. In order to prepare an aircraft like a DC6 for another mission, you had to remove the cowlings (the metal covers over the engines) and inspect everything that makes the plane fly. While performing this critical maintenance procedure, our mechanics had to pull the screens to see if there were any metal shavings being thrown from the engine and as if that's not enough, filters had to be cleaned to keep the flow of air constant. Part of this pre-flight examination also involved cleaning the entire outside of the DC6, especially near the engines and where exhaust and oil can build up. (Once again, this wasn't something that the U.S. Customs Service taught any of us.) Fortunately, the U.S. Air Force was very cooperative and allowed Johnny Walker and Mr. Goodwrench, to taxi the undercover plane over to the C130 wash rack first thing Sunday morning.

As if I wasn't busy enough, I was still trying to help our Boston agents with the transportation cases that they were working on, including their joint investigation with the FBI. Once again, the Boston Agents asked me to come up and help out, but whenever they heard what I had to say, we had the usual disagreement over tactics. No matter how hard I tried, I could not get some of the Boston Agents to understand, that they had to negotiate the deal a certain way, in order to insure control, otherwise you had an OUT OF CONTROL CONTROLLED DELIVERY! My attitude was, we don't fly for free and we don't pay bad guys, they pay us to transport contraband.

At the risk of sounding like a broken record, I advised the Boston Agents that they needed to tell the Colombians who failed to deliver on their promises, that they needed to return the money that was given to them for expenses and we'll start all over. Naturally, for four months I was told, no, we can't do that. My attitude was, demand front money then hang up the phone and you'll get it. I knew I was wasting my breath, when I was told that the decision was made to give more money to the Colombians.

In order to be a good undercover agent you have to be an excellent negotiator. If you ever want to develop your negotiating skills, I suggest you go shopping for a car, even if you don't intend to buy one. Car salesman can be just as deceitful and treacherous as drug traffickers and smugglers. While you negotiate the possible sale of a new or used car, remember the Greed Factor then have some fun.

When you work undercover, you have to learn how to give things away that SEEM valuable to you, but are more valuable to your opponent, while at the same time not losing anything of real importance in the process. You also have to appear to be fair and very businesslike, yet have an air about you that makes your opponent respect you. You can't be too firm and you must appear confident in order to get people to trust you. When your opponent speaks, you must be able to remember everything that is said and be prepared to hold him or her accountable. This of course reinforces the standard piece of advice, which is never make a promise that you can't or don't intend to keep, unless you are prepared to see the case conclude.

I was also getting tired of telling the Boston based FBI and Customs Agents not to be afraid to hang up the phone and walk away from a deal, when things didn't seem right. Sometimes it paid to step back and remember the old adage about, "being too close to the forest to see the trees." However, I should mention, that even though we had a disagreement over the right tactics to use, I put one of our undercover planes in GITMO for over 2½ months, then got another undercover plane ready in order to accommodate the Boston Agents. I went this far, because the Boston agents were dealing with real bad guys. This is strictly my opinion, but months of not playing the game right, set Operation Snow Drifter back instead of driving it forward. While it's true that the Colombians occasionally made promises that sounded sincere, there was one ingredient missing, accountability!

GOOD THINGS COME TO THOSE WHO WAIT

On Friday, May 10th, 1991, Jimmy S. called to let me know that the Boston FBI Agents finally changed their tactics. Once they handled things the right way, the Colombian violators gave in and agreed to put up $35,000 in front money to pay our basic expenses, so we would provide the transportation services for their cocaine shipment. By using the right tactics, the Boston Agents secured the one ingredient that was necessary to make a deal, a real deal. It's called front money, dinero, lettuce, Mr. Green. After hearing the good news, I put Major Tom and Captain Dakota aka Johnny Churchill on standby and agreed to put the operational plan together once the Boston agents picked up the cash.

CHAPTER 13

ROUND TWO

As helpful as the Miami Air Branch was, the powers to be in U.S. Customs Air Operations did not want us to move their planes around again, or have us use any more of their aviation gas. This meant, that we weren't going anywhere on the Mr. Rogers case, unless we could refuel our undercover plane with our own supply of aviation gasoline. Needless to say, I needed this like I needed a hole in my head. My colleagues and I in Group 7 were smack in the middle of a major dope deal and I had to find a way to refuel the undercover aircraft for this mission, when there was an aviation gas pump a few hundred yards away from where the DC6 was parked.

Personally, I was a bit frustrated that the Miami Air Branch wasn't set up or equipped to assist us in this fashion. With all of the work that my colleagues and I had to do, the last thing that we needed to deal with, was the added burden of obtaining 9000 gallons of aviation gas for our undercover aircraft. After all, we were officially assigned to a U.S. Customs Air Smuggling Investigative Group that was co-located on a U.S. Air Force Base. Call me crazy, but you would think, that we could get all the aviation gasoline that we needed, in order to conduct a sanctioned covert air operation. (In addition to needing fuel to fly the mission, we needed aviation gas to fly to New Jersey, when we executed the final phase of the controlled delivery.) Despite my frustrations, I couldn't complain, because the personnel assigned to U.S. Customs Air Operations traditionally bent over backwards to support our undercover operations.

After going through intermediaries to conceal our true identity, arrangements were made to have an airport fuel supplier deliver 9000 gallons of aviation gas to Homestead Air Force Base on the night of our intended launch. To enable us to refuel our plane, The Gambler and Johnny Walker rigged up a refueling system using pumps, a long length of rubber hose and a generator. This is another example of the hoops that we had to jump through in order to launch one of our undercover air operations.

Renting an airline gasoline tanker truck to supply us with 9000 gallons of aviation gas would cost over $20,000. The good news was, money was no object and we had the cash on hand to pay for this fuel and everything else that we needed to orchestrate this mission.

After a flurry of phone calls, the fuel supplier confirmed that he would have our aviation gasoline delivered at 1800 hours (6PM) on Tuesday night. In the meantime, we had to meet Mr. Rogers and Fernando at Mr. Roger's house.

So far Eddie and I had gotten along just fine with Mr. Rogers, but we had no idea how well we would hit it off with Fernando until we met. The fact that Hombre and Chain Gang met Fernando and got along just fine with him meant that we should as well. After all, so far my colleagues and I lived up to the terms of our agreement, which is more than we could say about our Colombian "clients."

FERNANDO

The moment we entered Mr. Rogers' home, I spotted Fernando sitting in a chair near the entrance to the kitchen. As soon as we came into the house, he stood up and approached us first shaking hands with Chain Gang, a person he had already met once before. Much to my surprise, Fernando acted as if he knew me and Eddie for sometime as well. In fact, I could tell by his demeanor and the tone in his voice that he was glad to see us.

Even though the pot load and some of the coke load was never loaded on our plane, our business venture together was still partially successful. In fact, Fernando didn't seem all that upset about not having the marijuana shipment placed on board our plane. I could be wrong, but in my opinion, Fernando was more concerned about pleasing his Colombian associates than his gringo sidekick Mr. Rogers.

Our meeting went well and we talked for a fairly long time about future business and making money together. At the right time we interjected little comments to insure that our arrangement and agreement still stood. So far no one objected. Most of all, Mr. Rogers and Fernando knew, that at no time were we going to cut one gram of coke or one blade of grass loose, unless we got paid $900,000. When no one objected, we figured that our business associates accepted these terms.

As the discussion continued, Fernando explained why one of the sources of supply refused to allow his portion of the coke load to be transported on our plane. According to Fernando, the irate Colombian I mentioned earlier freaked out when he saw our plane, because one of his cocaine shipments was seized by DEA on a DC6. As a result, this particular supplier was concerned enough to remove his 400 kilos from the deal, while also making unpleasant accusations about our plane and crew.

I knew that Eddie and I were in good with Fernando, when he leaned closer to emphasize his next point and he told us how his contacts in Colombia banished the irate supplier from the area for insulting us. As Fernando put it, we were his people and above reproach.

While we sat and listened to Fernando, I imagined the events as they unfolded when our crew landed the DC6 and made the first pickup. As Fernando continued, he proudly told us that his people down south paid the Colombian Air Force $1 million dollars not to shoot our plane down. Deep down inside I wanted to scream, as I thought about how the irate supplier was the laughing stock of Colombia, but would soon be running the cartel, once we arrested Mr. Rogers, Fernando and their associates and we proved that his suspicions about our plane were correct. The only difference was, that our DC6 belonged to the U.S. Customs Service, not DEA.

The simple truth was, the fear of getting stung by various undercover operations was a valid concern. Even though the smugglers and drug traffickers knew that U.S. Agents were constantly running undercover operations, they also knew that plenty of contraband got through.

During the period that I call The Miami Vice Era of the Drug War, the success of U.S. interdiction forces and infiltration by undercover personnel posed the greatest threat to smuggling organizations. The third most effective group were the investigators who worked traditional and non traditional organized crime investigations, gang investigations and money laundering cases. These investigations dismantled criminal enterprises and resulted in the arrest of numerous violators, as well as the seizure of drug money and valuable assets.

To counter this threat, the smugglers were constantly trying to find ways to circumvent the system and avoid detection. As I mentioned earlier in this book, The Greed Factor made it possible for undercover personnel to infiltrate criminal organizations, cartels and gangs. In particular, greedy brokers aka middle men enabled undercover operatives to successfully infiltrate criminal organizations. Both Fernando and Mr. Rogers were excellent examples of major violators who served this purpose and made it possible for undercover operatives to successfully infiltrate a Colombian smuggling organization.

As we wrapped up that first meeting, we laughed and joked around a bit and agreed to be in touch soon. A telephone call to the suppliers guaranteed that the rest of the cocaine we were promised, along with 10,000 pounds of marijuana would be ready for pickup. Fernando also talked about other loads, including having us transport 10,000 kilograms of cocaine from Guatemala that was being arranged through the Cali cartel.

When Fernando noticed Eddie holding his stomach during the meeting, he sprang into action and pulled some weeds from Mr. Roger's lawn. These weeds were then used to brew up a green weed tea to help settle Eddie's stomach. After Eddie bravely drank the mixture, we shook hands with Mr. Rogers and Fernando and said goodbye as we left the house.

As soon as I got into our undercover car, I waited for Eddie to back out of the driveway, before I put the closing statement on the tape and included the license plate that was on the other car in the driveway. Once I was finished, I shut the transmitter off. With Pat R. backing us up, we left the area and made sure we were not followed, before we headed back to the undercover office. We met the main violator and his Colombian partner and raised no eyebrows. Our covers were intact and we were going to sting these bastards again. God, I loved this job.

IT WAS A DARK AND STORMY NIGHT

To use an expression made famous by the Peanut's Cartoon, "It was a dark and stormy night," when we prepared our DC6 for another mission under the illumination of the headlights of our undercover vehicles. While a light rain fell on South Florida, The Gambler and Johnny Walker assembled our makeshift pumping system in preparation of the arrival of the fuel truck. The time was 1830 hours (6:30 PM).

Once our crew finished doing everything necessary to inspect and service the plane, with the exception of filling her fuel tanks, a small reserve of oil was placed inside the DC6. The remaining 100 gallons of oil was stashed in our twin engine DC3; also known as a C47 by the U.S. Military and the Dakota by the British during World War II. Our DC3 was tied down on the tarmac next to the DC6 and was the aircraft that we intended to use in the joint Boston FBI/Boston Customs case. We also kept one of our seaplanes parked on the same ramp.

The moment my pager went off, I used my mobile phone to call the strange number. It was the fuel supplier informing me that the truck bringing us our Avgas (aviation gasoline) broke down with a flat tire on the way to Homestead AFB. The good news was that the repair was being made. The bad news was that the truck would be late getting to us. "Just great!" was all I said before I stuffed my portable phone in my pocket.

Because we had plenty of time on our hands and since everyone was tired, wet and hungry, we packed into three cars and left the base to get some diner in a local barbecue restaurant. Since all of us with the exception of The Gambler would be up all night, I figured we might as well take a break and have a good meal, before the fuel truck arrived and our crew departed for Colombia.

As I sat at the long dinner table and finished my food, I was confident that our crew would successfully complete their mission. I wasn't being cocky or delusional. I simply knew that we would be successful. Dinner went well and a good time was had by all. In fact, you would never know that our crew was planning to travel to Colombia on an undercover mission in a few hours. Even Chain Gang was in excellent spirits, for someone who would be flying his first mission with the rest of the DC6 crew.

By 8 PM we were on our way back to the base when my pager went off again. It was the fuel company representative, calling to tell me that his truck was waiting for me outside the west gate of Homestead Air Force Base. As soon as I finished my conversation with the fuel supplier, Special Agent Eddie C. blasted off in his undercover car to escort the fuel truck on base. Moments later my pager went off again. This time it was Eddie C. telling me that the fuel truck was no where in sight at the west gate. Right about now I was having a Malox moment, while I tried to figure out where the tanker truck was located. Sure enough, the fuel truck was located about two blocks from the west gate, at a 7-Eleven convenience store and not at the Circle K where it was supposed to be.

Once the fuel truck was escorted onto the base, I signed for the fuel shipment and paid the driver over $22,000 in cold hard cash. Since the driver had someone waiting for him outside the base to take him back to Ft. Lauderdale, I offered him a ride to the front gate.

"Hey, is that plane for jumpers, you know, paratroopers?" asked the fuel truck driver.

As I rolled my eyes and continued driving my undercover car, I was glad that this guy had no idea what the real purpose of our mission was. When he asked if we were getting ready to go on a mission, I looked back at the fuel truck driver and said with a straight face, "You were never here, you never saw any planes and as far as your boss is concerned, you dropped your tanker off on some deserted field on the base. OK?"

"Sure, Mister, I understand," responded the truck driver, who quickly added. "I got one brother in the Marines and one in the Navy."

To help the fuel truck driver get brain fade, I handed him a $20 bill and said, "Here's a few bucks to help you forget what you saw tonight." (Twenty bucks was a nice tip in 1991.) When he asked me if we were in some kind of secret Air Force unit, I ignored him at first, then said, "Sort of."

As soon as Pat R. and I drove the fuel truck driver to the main gate, we returned to the Customs ramp to get back to work. Within a few minutes of our return, The Gambler and Johnny Walker were busy pumping aviation fuel into the DC6 through 200 feet of brand new rubber hose. You had to be there to appreciate what we had done to get this plane ready to fly.

This was happening because The Blade Runner Squadron was a "can do" operation. As you know from reading this book, our capabilities as a sanctioned undercover operation did not happen overnight. It took me years of working long hours to develop the relationships that I had with my sources of information and contract personnel. The few special agents I worked with also had excellent people skills and helped to keep this band of eccentrics, patriots and social outcasts together and fully operational.

By 10:30 PM we had Captain Video, Captain M, The Salesman, Johnny Walker, Chain Gang and Hombre assembled in the Group 7 conference room, while we waited for our Jacksonville Air Branch crew to arrive for the briefing session. Rather than wait any longer, we kicked off the briefing by passing out copies of our operational plan. After Pat, Eddie and I passed out cups of coffee, we laid out a variety of maps and intelligence information that included a chart detailing the known clandestine airstrips in our area of operation.

When the Jacksonville Air Branch Cheyenne surveillance aircraft crew showed up, I saw some familiar faces from previous operations. The Customs surveillance aircraft crew was assigned to escort our undercover plane to a specific location off the coast of Colombia. Once the pickup was made, the JAX Air Branch crew would escort the DC6 back to Homestead Air Force Base in South Florida.

As usual, we purchased extra food, so when I heard that the Jacksonville crew hadn't eaten yet, we invited them to dig in and make some sandwiches while we finished the briefing. After I covered all of the bases, Pat R. read the crew the standard pitch regarding what to do if they were forced to remain in Colombia. With nothing else to do but fly the mission, we joked around a bit as we headed over to where the DC6 was parked.

In his time working with us, Senior Special Agent Eddie C. seemed to be just as affected by the stress and strain of our rather unusual duties as Pat. R. and I were. I knew that Eddie was just as concerned about the safe return of our crew and the successful completion of our mission, when he turned to me and said things like, "This is killing me" or "I'll never get used to this."

After hearing Eddie express his concerns, I turned to my undercover partner and said, "You never get used to it...you just get numb."

By 12:15 AM Captain M completed his pre-flight check and was satisfied that his plane was ready to fly. While Pat, Eddie and I stood by the cargo bay ladder, our crew lined up to say goodbye and board the plane. After saying goodbye to The Salesman, Captain Video teased Eddie as he scurried up the ladder. Hombre was next and did his best to brighten my spirits by telling me not to worry. Hearing Chain Gang joke around with his Cuban sidekick, as he followed him up the ladder and into the plane, was enough to put a smile to my face.

After shaking hands with Captain M and telling him to please be careful, the most senior member of our crew climbed up the ladder as if he was a man half his age. While Captain M walked up to the cockpit, Johnny Walker, Hombre and Chain Gang looked down and cracked a few more jokes, before our veteran crew chief smiled one last time and closed the double wide cargo doors.

After hearing Captain M yell, "Clear," we stood off to the side and waited while our crew started all four engines. The moment Captain M and The Salesman turned our way and smiled, I saluted our crew as they applied power and began to taxi the DC6 toward the active runway. As the DC6 taxied toward the runway, I couldn't help but think of the crazy chain of events that led us to have this night to remember. The last minute clearance approval, the flat tire and the very late fuel truck were only a few of the highlights of the evening.

Just when things seemed to be going smoothly, a U.S. Air Force Officer refused to let our undercover plane take off, because a maintenance crew was re-grooving the runway on base. When some enlisted personnel approached us on the side and said it wouldn't be a problem for our plane to take off, we decided to challenge the Officer who was being difficult.

This particular Air Force Major wanted to speak to the man in charge, as if I carried my boss around with me at midnight, to deal with a mid level government official who was making our lives miserable. When I tried to tell this pain in the ass that I was in charge, he didn't believe me. I guess my long hair and beard, as well as my rather relaxed attire, made me look more like a pirate than a supervisor, or a high ranking official of the U.S. Customs Service. Luckily, the problem was handled, but not before we had to sweat out a few phone calls.

While Pat, Eddie and I stood by the control tower, we heard the roar of all four engines coming to life as the DC6 began to take off. As the undercover aircraft picked up speed and raced down the runway, I said a silent prayer on their behalf. By the time I finished my prayer, the DC6 was wheels up and on its way to Colombia. A minute later the U.S. Customs chase plane from the Jacksonville Air Branch took off and joined up with the DC6. With nothing else to do but worry, I returned to the Customs trailer to wait out the night with Pat and Eddie.

ANOTHER LONG NIGHT

Throughout the night I had the usual contact with C31 while our plane headed to a familiar destination. Clearly, being with Pat and Eddie made it easier to survive the long wait until morning. Even though we knew that anything could happen during one of these missions, I was more concerned about what the Colombian Air Force would do if they interdicted our plane in Colombian airspace. All we could do was hope, that Fernando was right and that the Colombian Air Force was paid off to ignore the presence of our plane, when it flew into and out of their country.

WE'RE BACK

As the first rays of daylight began to shine on Colombia, the undercover DC6 went feet dry and headed straight for the same runway that our crew visited a few days before. Inside the undercover aircraft there wasn't much left to do except prepare the plane for a landing. Once again, Captain M steered the huge cargo plane lower and lower, while The Salesman read off the landing procedure checklist and Captain Video, aided by Johnny Walker, handled the flight engineer duties. As soon as the DC6 touched down and turned around, a smaller number of locals than last time met the undercover aircraft.

This time the crowd consisted of about twenty loaders, a ground crew to refuel the plane and some security people who were heavily armed. As soon as Johnny Walker opened the huge cargo door, Hombre de la Calle was leaning out of the plane looking for a familiar face. Then, Pacheco came through the small crowd again and smiled at the sight of Hombre, a man that he treated as if they were old friends.

After climbing up the ladder, Pacheco stood inside the cargo bay and prepared to direct the loading of the plane. With the rest of the crew except Captain M out on the wings to handle the refueling, Hombre was told that they had 7000 pounds of marijuana and 500 kilos of cocaine ready to be loaded. (The actual amount was 505 kilos or 1111 pounds.)

Just like last time, the numbers were off and the size of the load that was promised by the Colombians was inflated by the source of supply. Hombre had to appear despondent, especially since we were "allegedly" being paid by the kilo for the cocaine and were promised more than the amount delivered. Regardless, our crew worked quickly to refuel the plane in record time, while others loaded the 70 some odd burlap wrapped bales of marijuana and heavy white plastic sacks filled with 505 kilo size bricks of cocaine into the plane. As soon as Johnny Walker had the illicit cargo lashed down and secured, the flight crew took their positions up front. "Next week we want you to take 2000 kilos out of Cali for us," yelled Pacheco to Hombre, as the Colombian went down the ladder, while the engines on the other side of the aircraft came to life.

Once the hatch was secured, the crew prepared for takeoff. After hearing good news from his flight engineer, Captain M applied full power to the throttles. Not quite fully fueled and light on cargo, the DC6 was airborne in no time.

While cruising at treetop level, our undercover aircraft stayed low as she broke the coast and went "feet wet" (over water). After flying awhile just above the waves, the undercover plane climbed to a higher altitude and joined up with the U.S. Customs chase plane from the Jacksonville Air Branch. All was well and a brief coded message, that included the count on board and the amount of contraband that was picked up was relayed to me through C3I. The Blade Runner Squadron had done it again!

Rather than transfer the combination load of cocaine and marijuana to a U.S. military C130 cargo plane, our plan was to use the DC6 to transport Pat R., Eddie C., Hombre, Chain Gang and I, along with the entire shipment of contraband to New Jersey, so we could complete the final phase of the controlled delivery with the agents from the SAC Office in Newark.

As soon as the DC6 landed at Homestead Air Force Base we greeted the crew, joked around and field tested the cocaine. Once we were ready to depart, we loaded the DC6 with everything that we were taking with us to New Jersey and took off for Mc Guire Air Force Base. Since we had no seats in the back of the plane, we sat on lawn chairs and coolers and held on as best as possible whenever we hit any turbulence.

At one point during the trip we convinced Eddie to sit in the co pilot's seat and fly the plane. After he reluctantly agreed to do so, the rest of us walked back and forth in the long cargo bay. Doing so rocked the plane up and down and made it difficult for Eddie to hold the aircraft straight and level. Once we had a good laugh, we made some sandwiches and discussed the case, while we marveled at the sight of 11,449 pounds of marijuana and cocaine in the cargo bay of the aircraft. It was truly a sight to behold.

CHAPTER 14

CAPTAIN DAKOTA AKA JOHNNY CHURCHILL

When an infantry unit transmitted the need for assistance over the radio, the contract pilot known as Captain Johnny Churchill aka Captain Dakota fire walled the throttles of his FAC (Forward Air Controller) aircraft and flew toward the encircled troops. The Cessna 337 was called a "push pull" because it had one engine up front pulling and one right behind the cockpit "pushing" in between a twin tail section. (This is the same plane that was used in the movie BAT 21.)

As Captain Dakota raced closer to the contact area, he used his radio to alert the ambushed squad of grunts (infantry) that help was on the way. Two helicopter gunships and a medivac helicopter were also en route. Luckily for the troops on the ground, Captain Dakota arrived on station in his Cessna 337 ready to lend a helping hand in the nic of time. Armed only with some small rockets, Captain Dakota planned to mix it up with the opposing force, until other combat aircraft with more substantial offensive weapons arrived.

From his front row seat in the cockpit of his plane, Captain Dakota could see the battle brewing in the distance. The combination of tracer rounds emanating from a nearby tree line, followed by the billowing smoke from a red smoke grenade, indicated that things were getting a bit dicey on the ground. The moment the friendly ground troops spotted Captain Dakota, the radio came alive with chatter as the Cessna 337 went into the attack mode.

The first two rockets that he fired hit the mark, in the patch of trees where the enemy troops were firing a heavy machine gun. As Captain Dakota flew his aircraft over the embattled area, he pulled back on the controls to put some badly needed airspace between his plane and the enemy forces below. Unfortunately, the sound of bullets hitting the undercarriage of his plane, meant that the enemy gunners were violating the integrity of his aircraft with small arms fire.

Captain Dakota knew from experience, that his presence over this battle was a definite thorn in the enemies side and helped to protect the beleaguered friendly forces on the ground. With little or no concern for his own safety, Captain Dakota turned his shot up aircraft back toward the battleground below. While timing it perfectly, Captain Dakota put his plane in a much steeper dive and fired two more rockets at the cluster of enemy troops who were determined to shoot him down.

The second the rockets were fired, Captain Dakota pulled back on the controls and climbed to a safer altitude. It's important to note, that the enemy gunners were more interested in shooting down a plane, than finishing off an ambushed infantry unit. This was the case, because the ambushed soldiers in Captain Dakota's army weren't going anywhere, or at least that's what the bad guys wanted to believe.

To his credit, Captain Dakota was buying time, valuable time, until the choppers arrived, even if it meant that he had to expose himself to an immense amount of ground fire. While the ambushed friendly troops on the ground did all that they could to prevent from being overrun, Captain Dakota made another pass over the contested battlefield. Just as the two rockets left the launchers that were under each wing, several rounds of machine gun fire hit the cockpit. Wounded but still alive, Captain Dakota broke right and flew away from the ground fire, just as more rounds could be heard and felt hitting his plane.

With leaking fuel dripping all over his wounded body, Captain Dakota had difficulty controlling his plane, because his ailerons were shot up and badly damaged. While struggling with the controls, a wounded Captain Dakota circled the area and directed the helicopter gunships in their attack on the enemy positions.

Despite the fact that the ground element was still in serious trouble, they were heard over the radio asking the FAC pilot (Forward Air Controller) if he was OK; a concern that made Captain Dakota feel that no matter what happened, he did the right thing. Fortunately, in a matter of seconds, the area was covered with machine gun fire from helicopter gunships that softened up the LZ enough to allow a medivac helicopter to extract the wounded.

While all alone in his cockpit and bleeding from several wounds, Captain Dakota flew his shot up FAC plane back to his base. Fortunately, the man I call Captain Dakota survived his war in a far off land and emigrated to the United

States.

It's been quite a few years since this incident took place. I also hope that I accurately documented this combat action after it was relayed to me. In fact, it was his wartime experiences, in particular his flying abilities, that eventually led me to meet and recruit Captain Dakota aka Johnny Churchill into The Blade Runner Squadron. You see, this particular contract pilot did not fight in one of America's wars. His military service was in a foreign air force, one that was strongly influenced by the British Royal Air Force. The way we met is an interesting story, one that involves me being contacted by a veteran CIA Officer, who got to know Johnny Churchill when he was stationed overseas.

As I mentioned earlier in this story, two CIA employees would occasionally visit the Group 7 trailer complex at Homestead Air Force Base. After several of these visits, I received a hand written message that a certain CIA Officer wanted to speak to me. As soon as we finally got in touch with each other, this particular CIA Officer explained that he heard about our operation and he knew an experienced pilot who I might like to recruit. Since I liked what this CIA Officer had to say, I asked to be put in touch with the man I ended up calling Captain Johnny Churchill aka Captain Dakota.

The day we met, it took all of about two seconds for me to welcome Johnny Churchill aka Captain Dakota into our undercover operation. I decided not to use the nickname that Johnny Churchill aka Captain Dakota wanted me to use in this book, because it would easily identify him to his friends. Even though I would prefer to use his real nickname, I have no choice but to protect his true identity. This is the case, because only the Commissioner of Customs is authorized to reveal the true identity of a documented source of information or a contract employee.

The day I met Johnny Churchill I immediately knew that he was a Blade Runner. In addition to the fact that he had the right disposition for our kind of work, Captain Dakota aka Johnny Churchill was one of our most qualified contract pilots. While Captain Video was our most qualified mutli-engine sea-plane pilot, Captain Dakota/Captain Johnny Churchill was type rated to fly everything from large four engine cargo jets to corporate jets and bush planes. Johnny Churchill was also very sociable and had the kind of class you would expect from a military combat aviator, who served in a foreign air force that was largely influenced by the British Royal Air Force.

Since I was eager to put Captain Dakota into a deal, I assigned him to fly with Major Tom on the Boston FBI/Customs mission when and if it ever materialized. The plane that we originally selected for this mission was one of The Gambler's old war birds. Due to a change in plans, we rented a DC3/World War II C47 cargo plane from Airport Sam. (I also called Johnny Churchill Captain Dakota because the British RAF in World War II called the twin engine American C47 cargo plane a Dakota.)

Because it was impossible for me to be in two places at once, Pat R. and I agreed to send Major Tom and Johnny Churchill to GITMO, so they could be positioned closer to Colombia, as soon as the Boston Agents were ready to have us make the pickup. I had no problem doing business this way, because I knew the Boston Agents could be trusted directing my contract pilots. Not every special agent felt the same way. In fact, some agents would never allow anyone to work with their sources of information or contract personnel, unless they were present at all times. Agents behaved this way to prevent a CI or a contract employee from being stolen or recruited by another criminal investigator/law enforcement officer.

I also agreed to send our crew to GITMO without us being present, because I knew Major Tom could help the Boston Agents, if they needed to make a last minute call to the Colombians before leaving to make the pickup. After all, the last thing I wanted, was to have a well intentioned special agent from Boston agree to something that our pilots and plane could not, or should not do.

Not only did Major Tom know how to run a covert air operation according to our guidelines, but he also spoke passable Spanish and knew how to deal with Colombian drug smugglers. Even though Johnny Churchill had no experience working drug cases, he knew enough about guerrilla warfare to learn the ropes from Major Tom. Since Johnny Churchill was the Contract Pilot in Command for this mission, he also had to be present during all planning stages to insure success. I also felt good about having Johnny Churchill fly with Major Tom, because both of these incredibly brave men were highly decorated former military combat aviators. The fact that they survived flying numerous combat missions, meant that they were well prepared to fly a covert air operation.

Even though it bothered me a little, that I couldn't be with our DC3 crew when they launched, I had complete faith that they would be well cared for by the Boston Agents during their stay in GITMO. I also believed that Major Tom and Johnny Churchill would be protected by a higher authority once they went operational. I say this, because I could pray for Major Tom and Johnny Churchill just as easy from a hotel room in Newark, New Jersey, as I could while standing on the side of the runway in Cuba.

This photo shows the cargo bay of the undercover DC 6 aircraft loaded with 2159 kilos of cocaine (4749 pounds) and 7,000 pounds of marijuana that was delivered to the U.S. Customs SAC Office in New Jersey.

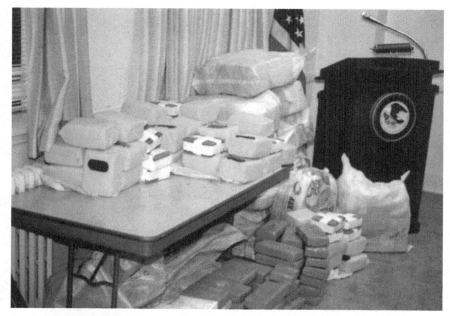

2132 kilos or 4690 pounds of cocaine being displayed at a press conference at the U.S. Customs SAC Office in Boston.

Using former military seaplanes enabled us to conduct certain controlled delivery air operations that would have never been conducted if we lacked access to these types of aircraft.

This photo shows the box containing $900,000 dollars that was partial payment for the 2,159 kilos and the 7,000 pounds of cocaine that was delivered to the U.S. Customs SAC Office in Newark, New Jersey on our undercover DC 6 aircraft.

The author behind the controls of a rented undercover aircraft.

Night Take Off From GITMO

Long before the U.S. Navy Base at Guantanamo Bay, Cuba was used to house prisoners during The Global War on Terrorism, GITMO was used as a forward operating base to launch undercover air and marine operations during The Drug War

The remains of the Group 7 Office after Hurricane Andrew.

500 plus kilos of cocaine for the 2ⁿᵈ New Mexico CD

The undercover DC6 arrives at Mc Guire Air Force Base with 2000 kilos of cocaine and 7,000 pounds of marijuna and our undercover team

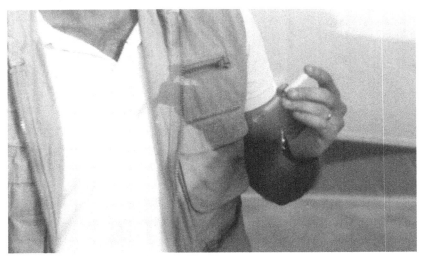

Customs Agent Kip H. holds a test kit that shows positive (blue) for cocaine

A SAC Miami Group 7 undercover Grumman Albatross Seaplane flies in formation with a U.S. Customs Air Operations C12 aircraft in route to launch a covert operation from the U.S. Navy Base at GITMO, Cuba.

Cocaine and Cash. Another view of a successful Controlled Delivery executed between U.S. Customs SAC Miami Group 7 and the U.S. Customs SAC Boston Office.

U.S. Customs Black Hawk Helicopters lined up to provide assistance during Hurricane Andrew

Undercover Grumman Albatross Seaplanes were effectively used by the author and other U.S. Customs SAC Miami Group 7 Special Agents to execute a number of high risk covert air and marine controlled delivery operations. Shown is one of The Blade Runner Squadron seaplanes taking off after a water landing on the open ocean.

The author (standing on right) with Undercover Agent Eddie C. with the trafficker funds that were recovered during the Controlled Delivery in New Jersey involving 2159 kilos of cocaine and 7,000 pounds of marijuana.

A Miami based U.S. Customs Citation Jet provided critical support during the first and the fourth CD that we executed for the U.S. Customs SAC Office in Boston.

This photo shows how the U.S. Navy conducted an Underway Replenishing (UNREP) at sea to provide fuel, fresh water and other supplies and assistance as needed to U.S. Customs undercover vessels from SAC Miami.

This photo shows how the marijuana shipment was packaged in the controlled delivery involving 2159 kilos of cocaine and 7,000 pounds of marijuana that were picked up in Colombia in the undercover DC6.

CHAPTER 15

MAKING HISTORY IN NEW JERSEY

After arriving at Mc Guire Air Force Base in New Jersey, our DC6 was escorted by Air Force security personnel to a remote part of the field. Waiting for us was a contingent of U.S. Customs Agents from the SAC Office in Newark, one Special Agent from Air Force OSI (Office of Special Investigations) and the duty agent from the U.S. Customs SAC Office in Philadelphia.

Once we unloaded our luggage and equipment from the DC6, we waited on the tarmac next to the plane and joked around with some of the SAC Newark agents, while a fork lift was used to load the 11,449 pounds of cocaine and marijuana into a tractor-trailer. After waiting a lot longer than we expected, we decided that it was time for us to make the long drive to our hotel in Newark, New Jersey.

The reason we needed to get on the road, was so we could place a very important undercover phone call to Mr. Rogers at a certain time. This was necessary, so we could keep things as realistic as possible and call Mr. Rogers shortly after our plane "safely" landed in New Jersey and was off loaded by "our people." In order to do so, we needed to secure ground transportation. After Pat R. had a brief run in with a Group Supervisor from the Newark SAC Office, we rented cars and took off for Newark, so we could make our undercover phone call to Mr. Rogers on time.

TAKING CARE OF BUSINESS ON ALL FRONTS

My recorded telephone call to Mr. Rogers was short and sweet. Basically, all I wanted to do was touch base with the main subject of our investigation and let him know that our plane and crew, along with "his merchandise," made it safely to New Jersey. Since Mr. Rogers was having a difficult time getting everyone on his side lined up, we made arrangements to meet him in the morning. Once we took care of this phone call, we were free to unwind and go on R&R in New Jersey.

After a sumptuous dinner at the Hearth Restaurant in Rosell Park, New Jersey, we grabbed a few hours of sleep and met at the SAC Office in the morning for coffee and bagels. Just when I thought that we might actually have a good day, Eddie C. went off like a grenade with the pin pulled, when his group supervisor (the one who gave us a hard time when we landed at Mc Guire AFB) didn't want our sources of information and contract pilots in the office. Even though this guy was still Eddie's immediate supervisor, Eddie wasn't going to let anyone throw our hired hands out in the street, especially since these men were responsible for helping to make the largest drug smuggling case in the history of the State of New Jersey.

In an effort to nip this reoccurring problem in the bud, Eddie and I went to visit Marty F., the Assistant Special Agent in Charge. When Marty F. heard that we were moving the deal to the SAC Office in Boston, he interceded on our behalf and got Eddie's group supervisor to back off and leave us alone.

Now that we were free to work without any more interruptions, we held a briefing session to plan our next move. After the briefing, I placed the recorded call to Mr. Rogers and made arrangement to meet at the Hilton Hotel near Meadowland stadium. Then, just as we were getting ready to leave, my pager went off with a 911 page from Jimmy S., our favorite Group Supervisor from the U.S. Customs SAC Office in Boston.

As I sank in a chair in the conference room and picked up a phone, Rob and the others could tell by the look on my face that something was wrong. Once I punched in Jimmy's phone number, I looked at everyone and said, "It's a 911 page from Jimmy S. This can't be good news."

When Jimmy answered his phone, I imagined him pacing back and forth behind his desk, while he told me that Captain Dakota and Major Tom had engine trouble going into the strip in Colombia. To complicate matters even more, Major Tom and Captain Dakota were in police custody in Aruba. As I shook my head in disbelief, I felt years peeling off the tail end of my life, while I quickly filled Rob K. and the others in on the situation at hand.

When Jimmy S. continued, he told me that even if the FBI was able to get our pilots released, we still had to get the undercover plane fixed in order to complete the mission. Since time was of the essence, I spoke fast as I looked up and briefed Rob and Pat while the back teams were assembling by the elevators.

My plan was to get Johnny Walker with his tools to Aruba ASAP, so he could repair our DC3, while the FBI worked on getting Major Tom and Captain Dakota out of the slammer. When Rob told me that he would handle everything, I felt the weight of the world lifted from my shoulders. After telling Jimmy S. that I had to run, or I would be late for a very important UC meeting, he wished me luck before I handed the phone to Rob.

As I left the SAC Office, I filled Pat and the others in on what had happened to our DC3 crew. Needless to say, our pilots were lucky they diverted to Aruba, when they experienced engine trouble during their aborted their landing in Colombia. From what Jimmy said, our crew buzzed the airstrip with the bad engine sputtering, to let the Colombians on the ground know they had a legitimate reason for not landing to pick up the load. This reassured the Colombians that they were dealing with professionals and arrangements were made to have our crew return to the LZ in Colombia, to make the pickup as soon as their engine was repaired.

This also meant that we were still in the game. Instead of trying to fly 400 miles to GITMO or our base in Puerto Rico with a bad engine, Captain Dakota and Major Tom decided to fly to Aruba and see if they could get the plane repaired. Since they were working for Uncle Sam, our contract pilots knew that we would run interference for them when they encountered the local authorities.

Even though this was a set back of sorts, I was grateful that our crew was all right. Certainly, things could have been a lot worse, had Major Tom and Captain

Dakota thrown caution to the wind and landed in Colombia but were unable

to take off due to engine problems. Unfortunately, the police in Aruba had no

choice but to take the suspicious DC3 and crew into custody, especially when

our contract pilots landed in a plane with fictitious tail numbers and without

the proper identification.

NEXT STOP THE MEADOWLANDS HILTON

With our surveillance teams in tow, Eddie C., Chain Gang, Hombre and I

drove north and parked our rented undercover car in the Hilton Hotel parking

lot. After I tested the transmitter, I waited until Special Agent John G. flashed

his headlights, to let me know that he and Pat R. were receiving us loud and

clear. Without wasting any time, I exited the vehicle with my undercover team

and walked to the lobby of the hotel to meet Mr. Rogers.

It was a short walk from the parking garage to the entrance of the Hilton. All

the way to the front door of the hotel, I wondered how things were going to go

once we met the bad guys. After all, there was always the unexpected.

Whenever I went undercover I was prepared for anything. Facetiously

speaking, even if my badge fell out of my pocket in the middle of a deal, I had a

perfectly logical explanation why I was carrying a U.S. Customs badge and ID.

(I never carried my badge unless we intended to shut a deal down and arrest

violators.) I was so confident in my role as a drug smuggling pilot/transportation specialist, that I could probably wear my U.S. Customs raid jacket to an under-cover meeting and explain to bad guys, that all my men wore these jackets in case we got stopped by the police, whenever we transported a drug shipment. I even instructed my two sons how to react and what to say, if we ever ran into a bad guy while I was off duty with my children. I did that to leave nothing to chance and because we lived in a small world.

For various reasons, I felt like my favorite Hollywood actors, even though no one considered me to be a celebrity. The fact that we didn't have a screenplay to memorize, that directed us what to say when we went operational, was a minor detail that made the experience of working undercover a lot more exciting. Simply put, it was a pure adrenaline rush to pretend to be someone else, when the price for a bad performance could be your life. The fact that we used real bullets instead of blanks and we did all of our own stunts, made being an actor with a real badge and gun more of an adventure than a career.

So far, we had successfully infiltrated a smuggling organization and after convincing the main players that we were real smugglers, they gave us $30,000 in expense money to travel to Colombia by plane to pick up 2159 kilos or 4749 pounds of cocaine and 7000 pounds of marijuana. All we needed to do to make this case a complete success, was collect $900,000 dollars and arrest every violator involved. That sounded simple enough.

As soon as I spotted Mr. Rogers, he looked tired and a little frayed around the edges. When we approached Mr. Rogers he was standing in the lobby and pacing around a sand filled ashtray. I could tell the instant we made eye contact, that things were not going well. The moment we shook hands and I asked where Fernando was, I was surprised to hear Mr. Rogers say that Fernando was being held captive by some real nasty Colombians.

According to Mr. Rogers, he and Fernando were being harassed by a very angry and tyrannical Colombian, who had a female partner who was just as ugly as she was scary. From what Mr. Rogers told us, all he and Fernando did since they met the local Colombian receivers, was drive around in their BMW listening to them scream and yell orders. When Mr. Rogers finished filling us in, he explained that the Colombian boss from Queens, New York and his nasty female sidekick would not honor the terms of our agreement.

As usual, the promises made to the transportation people were being reneged on. My associates and I had a deal with Mr. Rogers and Fernando and they knew exactly what that deal was. The fact that we had to make two trips to accomplish what we were originally promised, made our position even stronger.

Even though we originally negotiated a fee of $3000 dollars per kilo, we knew that we would never be paid anything even remotely close to that amount. As a result, we focused on taking the Colombians for as much cash as possible, before we announced who we really were and we made our arrests. Since we knew this was the case, we came up with the $900,000 dollar figure, as a reasonable percentage of what we were owed. It should also be noted, that when we negotiated this deal, we expected to experience problems, but could not predict the level of problems that we would run into.

Mr. Rogers knew all too well how we viewed a deal. We did our job and now we expected to be paid. We also advised him that we expected some hanky panky, but in the end, we would hold him to our arrangement because business was business.

According to Mr. Rogers, the Colombians were willing to pay us a $100 grand ($100,000 dollars) for 300 kilos. Since that wasn't the deal that we made, we refused to do business with them. After we asked Mr. Rogers where we go from here, he asked if we could help him place a call to Colombia. His plan was to see if Mr. Big down south would be willing to intercede on our behalf and direct the receivers in New York to pay us the exact amount that we were owed.

As we walked over to a nearby payphone, Mr. Rogers knew he had a problem. While some really scary Colombians kept his partner Fernando on a tight leash, Mr. Rogers was allowed to try and convince his gringo transportation people to start delivering hundreds of kilos on the lick and promise that we would be paid. On the other hand, Mr. Rogers had me and my undercover team refusing to deliver any cocaine unless we received $900,000.

As I say elsewhere in this book, we played it this way for several reasons. One reason was to lure out the money people so we could arrest more significant violators. Reason number two was to recover a significant amount of drug money known as trafficker funds. We demanded a suitable payment for services rendered, because money was the lifeblood of all criminal enterprises, including drug cartels, domestic drug trafficking organizations, gangs, warlords and terrorist organizations. It was also good tactics to play it this way, because who in his right mind would voluntarily agree to change a prearranged business deal and postpone getting paid cash on delivery, for a job that was already completed. After all, we weren't delivering groceries. This was a dope deal involving a massive amount of cocaine and 7,000 pounds of marijuana.

If we were real smugglers, we also wouldn't want to be involved in making a number of smaller deliveries in order to get paid. As far as my colleagues and I were concerned, this nickle and dime way of doing business was bad business. By proposing this, the Colombians were asking us to assume additional risks, when we already "risked enough" by making two successful pickups in Colombia and flying all the way to New Jersey. Remember, every time you transport a drug shipment and make any type of exchange of contraband, you risk being interdicted by the police and or the feds. This was especially the case when you were dealing with complete strangers. We also had to act legitimately concerned about sitting on 2159 kilos of cocaine and a warehouse full of marijuana.

Unless the Colombians met our previously agreed upon terms, the 7000 pounds of marijuana would rot in our warehouse. This was a real problem for Mr. Rogers, who was also banking on making a substantial profit from distributing the marijuana load, in addition to receiving a commission for setting up the coke deal.

Once Mr. Rogers finished dialing the long distance telephone number, he removed a Camel cigarette from his half empty pack and slipped the unfiltered cigarette in between his lips. No sooner did I offer him a light, was his party on the line.

"Buenos diaz," said Mr. Rogers in a cheerful tone of voice as he began to converse to his Colombian associate from Bogota. Since Mr. Rogers was not capable of carrying on a serious negotiation while speaking Spanish, he asked if Hombre de la Calle aka Gordo could take over. Naturally, I had no objections, so I instructed my Cuban CI to explain our dilemma to the voice on the other end of the phone.

While I sat on the curb, I listened to Hombre tell the Colombian down south, that the Colombian receivers (in the U.S.) were being difficult and refused to meet the original agreement regarding the transportation fee. As Hombre carried on this conversation, Chain Gang translated and told me and the others what was being said. Hombre then excused himself for a moment, before he turned to me and said that the only Colombian who could help us was killed in a car accident. According to Hombre, the Colombians wanted us to front them merchandise a little at a time, so they could earn enough money to pay us piecemeal, until they distributed the entire load.

Despite the fact that Mr. Rogers and Fernando assured us that the people we were dealing with were honorable, the Colombians were doing exactly as I predicted they would do, once we arrived up north with the "coke" load. By now I was standing up and projecting a different kind of body language to Mr. Rogers.

After pacing back and forth, I stopped and took the telephone from Hombre's hand and said, "You're out of the translating business, Gordo," before I handed the phone to Mr. Rogers, so he could conclude the phone call to Colombia without our help. As soon as Mr. Rogers hung up, I gave him the bad news and said, "Bob you're a gentleman but this is bullshit."

While Eddie left to get our undercover car, I gave Mr. Rogers some more bad news. "You can tell the Colombian Napoleon that he just met his Waterloo and that this call just cost him a hundred grand. Now you owe us one a million dollars."

Needless to say, Mr. Rogers was not a happy camper. We were in control now and he knew it. The more the adversaries tried to change the deal, the more control we exerted. While I waited for Eddie to show up with our getaway car, I ignored Mr. Rogers pleas and said, "I'm not waiting around here for a week until your friends raise my million."

Naturally, Mr. Rogers desperately wanted us to hang in there. He even tried to give us a bullshit version of a pep talk. As soon I heard the sound of screeching tires of our rented Lincoln Continental Town Car, I concluded my remarks by saying, "I'm heading back to Florida to take care of some other business. Call me when you've got the cash." Personally, I could care less that Mr. Rogers did not want us to go anywhere. After all, we played by our rules, not his.

Even though Mr. Rogers believed that the cocaine and marijuana load was stashed somewhere in New Jersey and was under guard by my brother and

Eddie's people, the fact that he didn't have access to the shipment, meant that it might as well be on the moon.

According to Mr. Rogers, he had one more call to make at diner time. He also pleaded with us to return to the Hilton and help him to negotiate with the Colombians down south. As polite as we were to Mr. Rogers, we had no choice but to be firm and businesslike. After all, we warned him and Fernando that this might happen.

Instead of playing it his way, we left the area to meet with Pat R., John G. and the other agents who were covering us. Once we were far enough away from the Meadowlands Hilton, we rendezvoused with our backup teams and were surprised to find Johnny Walker and Captain Video tagging along to help out on the surveillance. (Shortly after this undercover meeting Johnny Walker caught a flight to Aruba with his tools to repair the undercover DC6.)

While we grabbed a quick lunch in a nearby Jersey City neighborhood bar restaurant, we planned our next move. We had mixed emotions and were undecided about returning to help Mr. Rogers make another call to Colombia. After discussing the matter, we decided to call him from a nearby payphone.

In a very short conversation that got a little heated, Mr. Rogers slipped and told me that I was being unreasonable. The second Mr. Rogers pushed the wrong button, I became Nick Franco the scumbag drug smuggler. As far as I was concerned, nothing else mattered except playing my part to the hilt. Once again, I was an actor with no Q Cards, or script to rehearse from. I was an undercover federal agent, smack in the middle of a world class dope deal, that was as big as they can possibly get. Worse yet, there was no chance for a second take, if any of my colleagues or I screwed up.

Under the circumstances I did what I had to do and told Mr. Rogers, "Page me when you have my million dollars. If it goes past a week you can add $25,000 for my warehouse people! Goodbye," was all I had to say, before I slammed the phone down. Keep in mind that outside of a cell phone number, or a pager, Mr. Rogers, Fernando and their Colombian associates didn't have a clue where or how to reach us. That meant, that if we were real smugglers, the bad guys risked having us sell the combination cocaine and marijuana load if our terms weren't met. Even though I suspected that some people thought I was crazy, my colleagues and I walked away from that payphone having stood our ground. Now it was up to Mr. Rogers and his Colombian associates to do right by us.

The reception that we received in the SAC Office in Newark was beyond belief. If Marty F. the ASAC, or Bob V.E., the SAC, shook my hand one more time to congratulate me, I would have had to be fitted with a wrist brace. Even though these moments were few and far between, it felt great to be so well received by such well liked and distinguished Customs managers.

Once again, Eddie C. was a cordial host. Just like we had done our best to take care of Eddie during his thirty day detail in Miami, he was doing his best to take care of us during our stay in New Jersey. Eddie was also an incredibly brave and hard working special agent, who fit in right in with our group of eccentrics and social outcasts. After a well deserved night on the town, my colleagues and I from SAC Miami Group 7 headed home to wait for the call from Mr. Rogers.

WAITING FOR THE CALL

Portraying a smuggler was easy for me to do, because I had worked enough smuggling cases to know how my adversaries behaved. Participating in a number of high risk controlled deliveries also made it possible for me and the other members of our undercover operation to know exactly what we had to say and how we had to act, when we met with major violators. The fact that I had an overactive imagination also helped a great deal.

LET THE GAMES BEGIN

By late May of 1991 I was about as undercover as an undercover agent could get. I carried two mobile phones, a small micro recorder, spare batteries, spare tapes and two handguns. In addition, I also kept a short barreled 12 gauge Remington 870 pump shotgun and a 9mm Walther MPK submachine gun with three spare 30 round magazines in my undercover car.

On Tuesday, May 28, 1991 Chain Gang got the call that broke the silence. When Chain Gang contacted me to report that Mr. Rogers wanted to talk to me, I said, "Great, let the games begin." Unfortunately, this call couldn't have come a worse time, because I was literally on my way out the door to watch my oldest son's little league baseball game. This meant that when Mr. Rogers contacted me on my pager, I would have to leave the game to return his call.

Since there was no way that I could hook up my tape recorder to a pay phone in the park and I would have to leave anyway to record the conversation in my undercover car, I set up my recorder on a table in the backyard of my home and waited for my pager to go off. While I smoked a cigarette and paced back and forth, I prepared to go into role as a drug smuggler. Looking back, I must admit that my nerves were shot. I had been through some hairy moments without being overly concerned, but for some reason when it came time to make this call, I felt as if I would shake apart.

As soon as Mr. Rogers contacted me on my pager, I checked my recording equipment one more time to make sure that everything was in fine working order. Just about the time that I was ready to place the call, the front door to my house opened and my two sons burst into the living room followed by their mother.

The moment my family spotted the recording equipment attached to my mobile phone, they knew that my job followed me home again. Worse yet, was the look of disappointment on my oldest son's face, as he walked by and headed to his room. I knew I messed up big time by missing his little league baseball game, but there was nothing that I could do about it now. All I could do was hope that my wife and sons would understand, that there was no way I could walk away from a controlled delivery involving two thousand plus kilos of cocaine and thousands of pounds of marijuana.

After putting my index finger up to my lips to alert my family to be quiet, I finished placing the header on the tape to log the date, time, case number and purpose of the call, before I dialed the number. While I stood all alone in my backyard, I felt unbelievably guilty that I spent so much time away from my family. Even when I managed to make it home at a so called reasonable hour, my time with my family was constantly interrupted by my pager going off and a flurry of phone calls.

At the time, I was so immersed in my work, I never stopped to think how my sons viewed my life and our relationship from their perspective. Once I put myself in their shoes, I realized that it must be pretty scary at times for my sons to have me for a father. When I was home, our time together was constantly being interrupted. On other occasions, I was loading magazines, strapping on two guns and leaving the house in a hurry with my bags packed. I'm also sure, that witnessing some of the arguments that I had with their mother didn't make them happy either. Still, there were times when our life was as normal as everyone else, or so it seemed.

One reason I had little or no balance in my life was because business was booming. The good news bad news was, that we were being inundated with a steady stream of major cases; cases that were a dream come true for a U.S. Customs Agent. Any one of these transportation cases were a once in a lifetime opportunity. To have one major case right after another come our way, was like being a kid with the keys to his very own toy store and having someone tell you that you had to go home once in a while. Even though we were on a roll, I knew that this roll would not last forever. My plan was to ride this wave as long as possible, then transfer to another duty station, or medically retire as a result of my worsening line of duty injuries. In the meantime, I had work to do.

As soon as I heard Mr. Roger's voice, I focused on the matter at hand as I recorded our conversation. After making some small talk Mr. Rogers got down to business. From a professional standpoint, I respected the challenge of dealing with such a brilliant and cunning smuggler as Mr. Rogers. After all, it's not fun to win when your opponent is the village idiot. I also knew that because Mr. Rogers and his associates were blinded by greed, they would be unable to see who we really were. This fact alone empowered me and my colleagues and made us feel confident, that the bad guys were no match for us, as long as we played the game the right way.

"How are things on your end?" I asked. "Hectic but coming together," he responded. "I should have it all in a day," he said.

"Fine, call me tomorrow once you have it all," I responded, referring to my million dollar payment. After some small talk we hung up. I quickly shut off the tape and put a closing on it with the time and date.

Later that night I was contacted by Mr. Rogers after he and Fernando met with the Colombian receivers of the coke shipment. When Mr. Rogers asked me with a sense of urgency if I could come up to New Jersey tomorrow I said, "Will you have my one for me?"

"Yes, I'll have it all," he said, before he added, "I don't have to tell you that I'm in the hot seat."

Even though his tone was polite and friendly, I could tell Mr. Rogers was going through some difficult times. I could also tell that things were improving, but only after he had gone a few rounds with the Colombians.

In order to drive the point home that I wanted my money, I told Mr. Rogers that I would call him in the morning, to make sure that he had all my money before I headed north. After discussing some details about how we would make the transaction, I said goodbye and hung up.

As soon as I finished this recorded conversation, I called Eddie, Pat R. and Rob K. We had our first disagreement over tactics that night, when I wanted to blast off at first light to meet Mr. Rogers. Pat R. and Rob K. disagreed and wanted to wait until Mr. Rogers confirmed in more certain terms, that he had all of our money. After an hour of trying to convince Pat to see it my way, I called it a night and went to bed feeling miserable.

As far as I was concerned, Mr. Rogers had no reason to invite me to return to New Jersey unless he had the money he owed us, or the Colombians intended to lure us into a trap. My attitude was why put off the inevitable. If the bad guys had the money we would get paid and shut the case down, once we executed the final phase of the controlled delivery. If the bad guys had other plans, they would be the ones with the problem, not us. Either way, we would never know unless we met them face to face on neutral turf.

After a concoction of weird dreams and a miserable night's sleep, I woke up feeling eerie and in danger. By this time in my career I had become a bit paranoid.

Clearly, enough people knew what we were doing to create a leak big enough to get someone killed. The job stress and the intrigue was generally very intense. Constantly taking calculated risks and playing non stop mind games with bad guys played heavily on your sanity.

As a coping mechanism, undercover agents often made light of the things that most people would be concerned about. I was also obsessed with considering EVERY possible detail, because people's lives, including my own, were at stake whenever we went operational. Clearly, operating this way for several years took its toll. A bad situation was made worse by the fact, that I rarely if ever took a day off, let alone a real vacation. My attitude was, why bother, because whenever I tried to take off, I was usually contacted by various people.

The fact that all we did was create one fictitious scenario after another, also left little room for reality. One minute you're a federal agent, the next you're a smuggler, or at least acting like one. One minute you're creating a cover story, to convince a drug smuggler that you or your CIs and contract personnel were genuine bad guys and the next minute you were shopping for groceries, or playing with your kids at the beach. What little time you have with your family and friends helps to some extent, but the only cure seems to be retirement, or a different job. When you're involved in a succession of major cases, you also have to worry about running into bad guys when you're off duty. After all, like I said before, it's a small world.

When you're 38 years old and twelve years away from being able to collect a regular pension, you begin to wonder if there is anything else you can do for a living that will be rewarding and fulfilling. I was also getting more and more concerned about the physical injuries that I sustained in the line of duty, because they were getting progressively worse. The reason I felt this way, was because I was experiencing more episodes when the discs in my neck and lower back were so badly compressed, I was finding it painful and difficult to walk.

Regardless of the various risks involved, I was still very devoted to my work and wasn't ready to ask for another assignment. As I said before, despite what some people thought, I had a plan that did not include me working undercover until I dropped. While I was being cheered on by some and criticized by others, I knew exactly what I was doing, even though I wasn't quite sure when or how I was going to get off this merry go round.

WAITING FOR THE HOOK TO SET

When my pager went off at 1:30 PM Pat and I were sitting outside our undercover office looking at some planes taxi by. After I jumped into the front seat of Pat's Lincoln Town Car, I punched in the 1-800-SKY PAGE then Mr. Rogers' pin number and waited in silence for Mr. Rogers to call back. In a way, I felt as if I was deep fishing and waiting for a giant marlin to take the bait.

As I stared at my mobile phone, I thought about what I would say when Mr. Rogers returned the call. The sight of the light screen being illuminated was a dead giveaway that the call was coming through the line. After exchanging some small talk with Mr. Rogers, he informed me that he had the money and was ready to make the exchange. When I pressed him to clarify the part about the money, Mr. Rogers admitted that he didn't personally have possession of the cash at that time, but he confirmed that he did see the money in the trunk of a car.

After making a few comments about the exchange, Mr. Rogers remarked, "Sounds great, Mr. Nick, see you later."

"OK, see ya," was my response, before I ended the call. To make sure the phone connection was severed, I pulled the battery from the hand held mobile phone, before I put a closing remark on the tape.

When Pat asked for my opinion, I said that Mr. Rogers told me what I needed to hear. Between his tone of voice and the words that he used, my instincts told me that Mr. Rogers had the money. Based on my recommendation Rob and Pat agreed that it was time to wrap this case up. At 3 PM we boarded a flight to Newark, New Jersey.

CHAPTER 16

THE PLOT THICKENS

After arriving in Newark, New Jersey, I placed a recorded call to the subject of our investigation to firm up our plans for the exchange. As much as I didn't want to do it, I agreed to meet Mr. Rogers very early in the morning in the lobby of the Meadowlands Hilton.

I knew the minute that Mr. Rogers and Fernando asked us to be ready at 6 AM to make the exchange, that it would never happen at that hour in the morning. First of all, the Colombians were notorious for either being late, or not beginning their day until well after sun up. Nevertheless, I played the game as requested and agreed to meet Mr. Rogers at the ungodly hour of O dark 6:30 AM. I figured I broke his balls enough, so why not give in to his request. Besides, I knew it might come in handy, to have something to throw up in his face when and if things didn't work out.

Once the undercover phone call was completed, I joined Pat, Eddie, Hombre, Chain Gang and some of the Newark agents for dinner at one of our favorite restaurants. When it was time to call it a night I felt uneasy and anxious about the next day. For various reasons I was unable to sleep the night before the exchange. After tossing and turning all night, I finally dozed off around 3:30 AM.

With a solid hour and a half of restless sleep under my belt, I dragged myself out of my hotel room at 5 AM. We met in the lobby and after grabbing coffee and juice, Pat, Hombre de la Calle, Chain Gang and I drove over to the nearby SAC Office in Newark, New Jersey. As usual, we had a contingent of agents, that included three agents from the local DEA office providing backup. After holding a quick briefing session to go over the operational plan, we were on our way. With plenty of heavily armed agents trailing behind, Eddie, Chain Gang, Hombre and I drove to the Hilton Hotel where Mr. Rogers was staying.

All the way up to the hotel I wondered what was in store for us. In the event that things got a little dicey I carried a five shot .38 caliber Smith & Wesson Model 49 Bodyguard Model revolver concealed under my shirt and a decent supply of spare ammunition. Just in case things got really ugly, I also secured my fourteen shot 9mm SIG 228 pistol with two spare 13 round magazines in the glove box of our undercover car. My undercover partner Eddie C. carried a Walter PPK.380 caliber pistol tucked in his waistband under his shirt.

Even though we had plenty of backup, Eddie and I knew from experience, that even with the best intentions in the world, the agents covering us might not be able to come to our rescue in time to prevent a disaster. In addition to technical equipment failing at the most inopportune time, shit happened in plain English. As a result, we were armed with concealable handguns, so we could take care of business if any of the bad guys made a move against us.

At 6 AM my pager went off while we were en route to the Hilton Hotel.

Apparently, Mr. Rogers was up bright and early and decided to page me when we didn't arrive exactly on time. After calling Mr. Rogers, I informed him that we were on the way and would be there in a few minutes. At 6:15 AM we were in position.

As I exited the undercover car, I activated the transmitter and said, "OK, guys, here we go." After making the short walk from the parking lot, I walked though the revolving front door of the Hilton Hotel with Eddie, Chain Gang and Hombre. As soon as we entered the lobby, we found a smiling Mr. Rogers standing in almost the same spot he was in, when we met him at the Hilton Hotel the day after we flew the load to New Jersey.

After being told that the Colombians had not arrived but were en route, we resigned ourselves to hang out in the lobby and pass the time by talking to Mr. Rogers about the deal. While we drank coffee and smoked God knows how many cigarettes, I noticed Mr. Rogers signaling me with his eyes to look over to my right. I was hoping that the eagle-eyed smuggler hadn't noticed, but we were surrounded by a group of very young cops. Inside I was screaming, "I don't fucking believe it," as I realized that the hotel lobby area was filled with police officers attending some kind of seminar or conference. What else could I say to Mr. Rogers but, "You picked a great place to do the deal, Bob."

The presence of so many cops actually eased the tension that was brewing. Before long we quietly slipped out the back door and waited on the veranda. By noon we started to wear out our welcome at the hotel. Even Mr. Rogers was getting anxious to move things along, so he began to place call after call to the Colombian receivers.

Miraculously, the Colombians finally showed up and asked us to meet them out front. In an effort to move things along, Mr. Rogers charged down the block to find Fernando, while we stayed in front of the hotel to wait for further instructions. How they missed each other I'll never know, but the sight of Fernando walking quickly up to us was a sight for sore eyes. Unfortunately, I could tell by the look on his face that something was wrong. "The police are everywhere," remarked Fernando, while he frantically looked around as if he was paranoid about being under surveillance.

When I responded, I made sure to sound both friendly and a bit sarcastic. "No shit, Fernando, there's a fucking police convention going on here. We've been freaking out all morning waiting here for you."

While Fernando nervously looked around, he sounded like he was having a melt down when he continued and said, "The truck is here but the people are getting nervous. They see cops everywhere."

As far as we knew, inside the Ryder truck was our million dollars. We were literally a half a block away from our money and we needed this to happen. Then I wondered if our surveillance teams had been made. (I had no idea of knowing it at the time, but members of our backup team were doing one hell of a job and had the Ryder truck under surveillance.)

In an effort to play down the fact that the area was packed with law enforcement officers, I tried to sound as reassuring as possible when I looked at Fernando and said, "They're probably eating lunch. Tell your friends to relax."

"They're gonna be moving. We have to pick another spot," snapped Fernando as began to jog back to the Colombians, who were waiting by the yellow Ryder rental truck. Meanwhile, Mr. Rogers was still missing. I assume they missed each other when Mr. Rogers went to get his van, so he could drive around to find his Colombian partner.

Now that we were alone, I decided to relay a message to our back up team. "I hope you guys are getting all this." Rather than take any chances, I acted like I was talking to Eddie and the others when I quickly added, "If you guys can hear me call me on my mobile phone."

Just about this time, Mr. Rogers returned to the front of the Hilton and exited his van. His dope dealer for a driver looked like a biker type and remained in the vehicle that was parked nearby. Then my pager went off. It was Pat. As soon as Mr. Rogers approached, I told him that I had to call my people at the warehouse, because they were probably wondering what happened to us.

"Hey, we've got a delay here," I said as I spoke to Pat on my mobile phone. While I continued to act as if I was talking to our warehouse, I went on to say, "Our clients are getting hinky so we're moving to another location."

As soon as Pat asked me some fast questions, I continued to sound as if I was talking to one of our associates at our warehouse, when I responded and said, "Yea, they say they've got our green, so hang in there. OK, Bye." A second later I hung up with Pat.

When Mr. Roger's pager went off, it was the Colombians calling him to set up a new place for the exchange. As usual, Eddie C. was thinking ahead and pulled our undercover car out onto the street where I was standing with Chain Gang, Hombre and Mr. Rogers. While we waited to move, Mr. Rogers placed a quick call to the car phone number that was displayed on his pager. Then Fernando returned, huffing and puffing as he ran over to our car. "Let's go, Nick. They're waiting for us at a spot close by."

All I could think of when I got into our undercover car, was what a circus this exchange was turning into and how was Hollywood going to portray this scene, if this book was ever made into a movie. Before I knew it, we piled into our Lincoln Continental and raced off toward Tonnelle Avenue in Secaucus, New Jersey.

While we drove to the new location, I spotted one of our backup units close by and felt more confident knowing that we weren't alone. I also knew that a U.S. Customs helicopter was flying overhead to relay our position to the back up units on the ground. This enabled the majority of backup units to hang back and stay out of sight. Fortunately, none of the bad guys spotted the helicopter, or any of the agents who were providing cover for me, Eddie, Chain Gang and Hombre.

As luck would have it, the road that we were on passed right by the Holiday Inn, where Mr. Rogers's marijuana smugglers were staying. Even though Mr. Rogers was eager to officiate the transaction of the cocaine shipment, he was just as eager to see that his pot people got on the road, with their portion of the marijuana load. While we knew this was asking a lot, we hoped to be able to pull off a double play and arrest both groups of bad guys, before we completed this controlled delivery. As s result, Mr. Rogers made our day, when he pointed to the Holiday Inn and told us that his pot people were staying in that hotel.

Once we arrived at the new location to pick up our money and the truck to put the cocaine shipment in, we spotted a Colombian kid behind the wheel of a two door Chevy Lumina. Unfortunately, there was no truck in sight. We also spotted a second Colombian exit a white Ford van that was parked nearby.

When Mr. Rogers and Fernando left the car and went over to use the pay-phone, I looked at Eddie and he looked at me. Chain Gang was also streetwise enough to begin to feel real uneasy about the scene that was unfolding before our very eyes. After all, if these bastards were this kinky over just giving us their truck and $1 million in cash, how would they react when it came time for us to give them their cocaine and arrest them.

Instinctively, I removed my 9mm SIG Model 228 Pistol from the glove box and put it under my jacket that I kept on the front seat. There was still a chance that these characters would try to persuade one of us to wait with them, until the transaction was completed. Should that happen, my colleagues and I would stand our ground and refuse to comply with any plan that they proposed.

It took almost two more hours for the Colombians to finally settle down and show up.

Even Napoleon and his ugly female sidekick (a women called Lucy) were present and waited in their car, as they barked orders to a very nervous Fernando. The tension was relieved when we spotted the Ryder truck pull into the rear parking lot of the doughnut shop.

As soon as the driver parked the truck, he jumped out and entered the doughnut shop to hand the keys to Fernando. Once this happened, Mr. Rogers walked over and instructed me to meet Fernando inside the doughnut shop.

Without wasting any time, I got out of the UC car and walked across the parking lot to the entrance of the shop. As soon as I met Fernando, he slapped the Ryder truck keys in my hand and asked me to hurry back with the cocaine, because his people didn't want to do business after dark. After being asked to meet at 0600 hours and putting up with all of their delays, I was in no mood to be told that we had to jump through hoops, to satisfy a timetable that was set by the Colombians.

Instead of playing it their way, I reminded Fernando that his Colombian pals were no where to be seen, when my colleagues and I were ready to do business at 6 AM in the morning and as a result, I had no intention of rushing just to make them happy. I thought for sure that Fernando was going to have a heart attack after he heard my response.

After Fernando turned and looked in the direction where Napoleon was standing, he faced me again and started to plead with me. (I could see the Colombian Napoleon standing outside the coffee shop through the large glass windows) When I heard Fernando repeat that his people didn't want to business at night and that I should get back as soon as possible, I got a little sarcastic and asked him if Napoleon was afraid of the dark, before I walked out of the doughnut shop and headed straight for our undercover car. (By the way, if the Colombian I called Napoleon was such a tough guy, he would have met me himself, but he chose not to.)

As soon as I handed the Ryder truck keys to Eddie, I got in behind the wheel of the Lincoln and told Hombre and Chain Gang to hang on. Once Eddie was ready, we left the parking lot at flank speed and headed south, with our back up teams covering us all the way. While I drove behind the Ryder truck, I spotted some of our backup teams moving into position all around us.

After taking us on a tour of Newark, New Jersey, Eddie pulled into a New York Port Authority facility. As soon as I joined him by the side of the truck, Eddie was all smiles as he pointed to the large cardboard box, that was on the floor of the cab on the passenger side of the compartment. Without saying a word, I slipped the heavy box out of the truck and walked over to Special Agent John G.'s surveillance van.

Call us paranoid or very careful, but we initially remained quiet in the event that the bad guys placed a transmitter in the box to see if we were bad guys or cops. After Pat slid the door open, he used a sharp knife to slice a long opening in the top of the box and expose a layer of paper that the package was wrapped in.

With a small crowd of agents standing by, I helped Pat R. carefully open the box and inspect the contents that included stacks of hundred and fifty dollar bills. Handshakes and hugs were in order, especially between the members of The Blade Runner Squadron who made this case happen. Our mood quickly changed when a quick bundle count revealed that the box contained $900,000 instead of the million dollars that we were owed because of the delay. Normally, you might think that being paid an outrageous sum money in an undercover operation would have satisfied us, but it didn't.

As far as the Colombians were concerned, we were real smugglers. I say this because no self respecting bad guy knowingly hands the police or the feds $900,000 dollars in cash. Still, as far as I was concerned, a deal was a deal. Because the Colombians screwed with us, I decided to screw with them.

After racing back over to the SAC office, we met in the conference room to go over our game plan and our intentions. As far as I was concerned, the large number of agents who were out there all day deserved to be in on our discussion. My position was simple. We should refuse to deliver the cocaine shipment, unless we got paid the full one million dollars that the Colombians owed us. After all, they caused the delay after they reneged on our original deal. As soon I finished explaining my position, to Rob K, Pat R. and everyone else, Rob responded and said, "Go for it."

Once we had the green light to proceed, Eddie and I decided to double team the bad guys. In order to execute our plan, I kicked things off by calling Mr. Rogers. As soon as Mr. Rogers answered my page, I went on the offensive and in a very firm tone of voice told him that we had a deal for one million dollars not $900,000. Without wasting any time, I told Mr. Rogers that the delivery was on hold until I got the rest of my money. Mr. Rogers and Fernando were definitely behind the eight ball now. The flurry of phone calls that followed were one right after the other, with each call becoming more and more intense.

When Fernando told me that we had to deliver the coke shipment no later than 5 P.M. I laughed and repeated my earlier remark and said, "Why, are your people afraid of the dark?"

The moment Fernando began to whine, I sounded as determined as ever when I responded and said, "You gave me $900,000 dollars. You owe me one million dollars. Where's my money?" When Fernando responded he told me that the Colombian female had it.

"Where is she keeping it?" I asked. His answer was a painful one as he whined, moaned and pleaded with me to let the load go by accepting the $900,000 for now. When I wasn't moved by any of his remarks, Fernando reluctantly said, "The money's in her house in Queens."

After hearing Fernando's response, I did my best to sound like a first class prick when I responded and said, "Good, you tell that Colombian bitch that this is the United States of America, not Bogota. $900,000 from $1 million is $100,000...I want my money! You tell her to drive home and get it, then call me when you got my money." The second I finished, I hung up and ended the call.

As soon as I did so, the conference room at the SAC Office in Newark erupted, as every special agent present, as well as Hombre and Chain Gang, started clapping and cheering after witnessing my performance. This was one of the greatest moments of my life as an undercover agent. If I ever gave an Academy Award Performance, that unleashed all of the frustrations that my colleagues and I experienced after years of dealing with drug smugglers this was it.

The die was now cast and things were bound to get ugly before the night ended. We had the cocaine shipment and $900,000 in drug money, so no matter how pissed they were, the Colombians and their associates would do business our way, because they had no other choice. Even though some of our critics might say that we were provoking the bad guys, we decided to look at another way. For starters, the bastards made us get up very early in the morning and dance to their tune all day long. Now it was our turn to call the shots and that's exactly what we did.

I also believed, that the loved ones and friends of a drug addict would truly enjoy seeing how we operated, when we put the screws to a group of drug smugglers and drug traffickers. These bastards have been killing people and destroying lives for decades with no end in sight. I don't mean to sound pious, but it was moments like this that really made being one of the good guys worth it.

CHAPTER 17

A NIGHT TO REMEMBER

While we waited for Fernando and Lucy to drive back to Queens in rush hour traffic, we decided to use the free time to chow down and eat some dinner. Once again, we decided to call on our favorite Portuguese restaurant, The Golden Eagle, to provide us with something to eat. The fact that The Golden Eagle was a short drive from the SAC Office in Newark, meant that we didn't have to go far to pick up our order. This particular establishment had a very friendly atmosphere and good food for a bar restaurant that was located in a dingy neighborhood.

To keep things simple, we ordered the same dish and had Armando the owner of The Golden Eagle, whip up a huge batch of picadillo and loaves of fresh Italian bread for twenty five agents. As soon as our dinner arrived, we formed a line in the huge conference room and ate buffet style.

We needed the break and I for one used this time to recharge my batteries and prepare for the rest of the night. When my mobile phone rang the room around me went dead silent. As I quickly stuffed the earpiece into my right ear, Eddie hit the record button on the tape recorder as the word "Hello" came out of my mouth. As I heard Fernando relay the good news that he had our money,

I gave everyone the thumbs up.

According to Fernando, the Colombians wanted us to meet them in the parking lot of the doughnut shop, where we picked up the truck earlier that day. In return, they wanted me and my people to turn their truck back over to them loaded with the entire shipment of cocaine. After I hung up with Fernando, we went over the game plan and left the SAC Office for the field.

While Eddie and I were en route to the Tonnelle Avenue doughnut shop to pick up the balance of our million dollars, Hombre and Chain Gang were positioned at a nearby hotel in Newark, so they could hand over the keys to the truck to some of Napoleon's assistants. This meant, that we would have one team covering me and Eddie and one team covering the load truck and our two Cuban Sources of Information.

Just when I thought we were moments away from culminating this deal, my pager went off. This time it was Mr. Rogers telling me that Fernando and the Colombians were going back home to Queens. As soon as I said, "What," and repeated what I was told, Eddie listened in total disbelief. According to Mr. Rogers, when Fernando and his contingent showed up at a doughnut shop, some cops came in for coffee. Apparently, the Colombians freaked out and ran for the safety of the New York border.

I couldn't believe these people. It wasn't as if one of our surveillance teams got burnt. These were regular street cops who stopped to take a break in a local doughnut shop. My only recourse was to tell Mr. Rogers to let the Colombians know, that if we didn't do the deal tonight, we would put off the delivery for several days and want more money for our additional grief.

Once again, we were off and running getting paged and called on our mobile phones. At one point, Fernando wanted to meet Eddie alone in bar in New Jersey that was frequented by a large Colombian clientele. That suggestion went over like a lead balloon. After more discussions, we finally wore them down and got our way. We would meet on neutral turf.

Meanwhile, Hombre and Chain Gang were standing by to turn the truck keys over to the three Colombians, who pulled up to the rear entrance of a large hotel that was located near an exit off the New Jersey Turnpike. Hombre was acting under strict orders not to release the load until he heard from me personally. As you can expect, these were some very tense moments. Things got even more tense, when I called Hombre on his mobile phone to tell him to hold off on making the exchange and he calmly reported that the Colombians were armed with a machine gun. As I repeated the word "machine gun" Pat, Eddie and Agent Jack G. listened closely, while I told Hombre that we would let his back up team know that the Colombians were heavily armed.

As Hombre stepped away from the small sedan, that the Colombians used to transport the driver to the hotel parking lot, I asked him if he and Chain Gang were all right. "Yes," he answered with confidence. While he stood a few feet away from the three Colombians, Hombre continued to tell me in a low voice, that he told the bad guys to get rid of the gun or we wouldn't do the deal.

Then, after he paused briefly, he added, "I don't want to see any agents get shot!"

Regardless of the reasons why they worked for us, guys like Hombre and Chain Gang made such a valuable contribution to The Drug War, that without them, we would never be able to be as effective as we were. This is the reason why reliable sources of information and contract personnel deserved to be paid well for services rendered.

By midnight, Eddie and I, as well as everyone else who was involved in this case, were physically and emotionally drained. While Hombre had gotten rid of the machine gun toting three amigos, Eddie and I were en route to meet Mr. Rogers and his driver, a guy called Angel. Fernando had also agreed to meet us, but as luck would have it, the Colombians were being difficult again.

As soon as Eddie and I walked into the lounge at the Holiday Inn on Route 1&9 in Newark, we spotted Mr. Roger's biker type associate sitting on a stool near the end of the long bar. Angel was a Vietnam veteran who looked like he had experienced a few flashbacks in his day. As soon as we joined him and Mr. Rogers at the bar, Angel paid me a compliment and told me how much he liked the way I handled the Colombians.

Even though he was primarily involved in the pot deal, Angel was obviously well aware of the coke load and knew that the Colombians were responsible for holding up the delivery of Mr. Roger's marijuana. I can only assume that he also knew, that Mr. Rogers and Fernando were brokers for the entire shipment, including the cocaine load.

After ordering a round of drinks and mixing serious business with some jokes about our rough day, Angel asked me if I served in Vietnam. Even though I didn't serve in Vietnam, I acted as natural and friendly as I could when I responded and said, "Yea, I was in the Battle of Moo Goo Gy Pan in the Tae Kwuando Delta." (This was a line that I first heard from my older partner Bob S. I should add, that when a law abiding person asked me if I served in Vietnam, I usually responded by saying, "No, they were holding me in reserve for The Drug War.)

While Angel laughed and began filling me and Eddie in on some of his exploits, Mr. Rogers got paged and headed for the bank of pay phones that were located just outside the hotel bar. When he returned, a tired but nevertheless excited Mr. Rogers told us that the Colombians were ready to do business and were waiting for us on 1 & 9 South at the Queen Elizabeth Diner. Mr. Rogers finished making our day when he told me and Eddie that he had our hundred grand in his van.

This is great, I thought. Our transmitter is dead and we were all alone except for Pat R. and John G., because everyone else was either back at the SAC Office, or covering the load vehicle and our two Cuban CIs. The question was, how do I let Pat R. know where we're going and why, without raising any suspicions?

As Eddie and I followed Mr. Rogers and Angel out of the bar, I got the bright idea to tell the bad guys, that I was going to call Hombre on a pay phone, to let him and Chain Gang know that we were getting ready to finish the deal. While Eddie followed Mr. Rogers and Angel to their van in the parking lot, I stopped at the bank of pay phones by the rear exit to the hotel and faked placing a call to Hombre.

The moment I broke free, I noticed Pat R. and John G. leaving the lounge and heading my way. Once again Pat R. proved that he was without a doubt the best back up team agent in the U.S. Customs Service, when he read my mind and had Special Agent John G. fake placing a call near where I was standing, while he headed for his car in the parking lot to cover Eddie.

Once I saw that John G. and I were on the same sheet of music, I said, "Queen Elizabeth Diner, right now, OK?" As soon as I saw John nod once, I continued and said, "The hundred gees are in Mr. Rogers' van, OK?" Again I saw John nod his head and finished my remarks by saying. "Gotta go, OK." For a third time John G. shook his head and smiled as he stood two pay phones away from me and faked placing a call. (Agent John G. was another outstanding agent, who did an amazing job of backing us up during this controlled delivery.)

As I walked away from the bank of pay phones, I couldn't help but think that they didn't teach special agents this shit at FLETC. We learned these "tricks of the trade" from having an overactive imagination and a tremendous desire to survive. At the risk of repeating myself, I also feel compelled to say that I'm sure that Divine Intervention had something to do with our survival as well.

As soon as I met Eddie and company by Mr. Roger's van, Mr. Rogers handed me a Manila envelope containing $100,000 dollars. After getting into our undercover car, we led Mr. Rogers and Angel down 1 & 9 South to North

Avenue, where we pulled into the parking lot for the Queen Elizabeth Diner. The moment we drove into the crowded parking lot, I spotted at least two car loads of Colombians parked on either side of the side street entrance.

As I rolled my eyes, I slipped my fourteen shot 9mm SIG P228 pistol into the waistband of my jeans and said something like, "Oh shit." Eddie spotted the bad guys as well and remarked, "Nick, this could get ugly." With nothing else left to do except complete the final phase of the controlled delivery, we got out of our undercover car and proceeded with the exchange as if we didn't have a care in the world.

The really bad news as far as we could tell, was that we had absolutely no backup in the immediate area. If we did, I had no idea where these agents were hiding. Worse yet, Pat R. and John G. were no where to be seen. The fact that we were surrounded made the situation at hand seem worse. Since I felt very much in danger, I decided to go on the offensive rather than show any fear or concern.

While we walked toward the front of the diner where Fernando was pacing like an expectant father, I stopped short and turned around and said, "Eddie, I'm going over to talk to those guys," referring to the three Colombians that Hombre had seen earlier with the machine gun. With Eddie by my side, I made sure to wave and present a friendly face, as I approached the three Colombians who were parked by the side exit to the diner.

As I approached the car, I could see by the expressions on their faces that they didn't believe that I could be so bold. Personally, I liked being unpredictable.

For one thing, being unpredictable was an important tool of the trade, not to be misused, but kept in reserve for emergencies and moments like this.

As soon as I approached their car, I did my best to sound as friendly as possible when I said, "Hi, I'm Nick," and extended my hand to shake with the shocked driver. All this time I quickly scanned the inside of the passenger compartment looking for any signs of weapons.

"My name's Nick too," said the driver. Then he added, "Oh, yea, you're the crazy pilot."

Under the circumstances I took his remark as a big compliment. As I laughed, I stepped back a bit then said, "Do you guys want a drink, maybe some coffee?" Now all three of them were off guard and seemingly more relaxed as they thanked me and said they were fine.

From our brief conversation, Eddie and I learned that they blamed Lucy for screwing up the deal and causing the delay by holding back my $100,000. That proved, that even the bad guys had to deal with people who were a royal pain in the ass.

Before I walked away, I asked the three amigos to stay put and wait to go to the hotel parking lot to pick up the load, until I gave them the word that the truck was in position. My explanation for giving them these instructions, was to prevent them from having to wait around unnecessarily. After telling the three bad guys that I had to meet with Fernando, I walked toward the front entrance of the diner with Eddie C.

As soon as we approached Fernando, he looked sick and scared as he blurted out, "The police are inside, the fucking cops are everywhere!" In an effort to reassure Fernando that everything seemed OK, I told the nervous older man that he had nothing to worry about, because the two most favorite places for cops to hang out were doughnut shops and diners. "Besides," I said, "You picked the spot."

While Fernando looked around as if he was being followed, he continued and said, "Look, Nick, I am being held hostage."

"By who" I said, "You're here alone with us."

After rolling his eyes, Fernando looked toward the second carload of very unfriendly looking Colombians and described to us that Lucy had him on a very short leash.

For some reason Lucy and her two associates didn't like us talking about them and left the parking lot like a bat out of hell. As they stared at us while they raced away from the diner, I smiled and waved as I called out and said, "Hey, wait up." Off they went into the night leaving us with Fernando and the three amigos still parked in the small Japanese sedan.

Pat R. and John G. were a sight for sore eyes, when I spotted their four door Oldsmobile pull up to the green light on the corner of North Avenue by the diner. As far as I was concerned, they couldn't have showed up at a better time, because I didn't know how much longer I could keep everyone contained in the relatively small parking lot. Mr. Rogers and his biker-type chauffeur Angel were getting ready to drive away, while the three Colombians in the small sedan were anxiously awaiting my order to leave. Once I spotted Pat and John in the corner of my eye, I knew I could start cutting bad guys loose.

As the traffic light changed and Pat R. and Jack G. began to slowly roll through the intersection, I leaned on the passenger's side door of Mr. Rogers van and said, "OK, we'll talk tomorrow." Mr. Rogers looked beat and was anxious to get on his way. Just like in the movies, Angel pulled Mr. Roger's van away from the diner and headed south of Route 1&9, just as Senior Special Agent Pat R. and Agent Jack G. pulled up behind their vehicle.

Knowing that Pat R. and John G. had Mr. Rogers and Angel covered, I turned my attentions to the three Colombians in the sedan. As I approached their car, they seemed comfortable and ready to hear from me. While I spoke to the Colombian driver, I pointed north and told him that the Ryder truck containing the entire shipment of cocaine was on the way to a local hotel parking lot that was on Route 1&9 North. As I smiled and stepped back from the car, the Colombian driver backed the sedan up and proceeded to pull out into the flow of traffic.

Once I returned to Eddie and Fernando, I said something about the need to call Hombre to make sure that everything was going as planned. As I placed a quick call to the command post, to tell the duty agent to alert all units to move in, I was shocked when Hombre de la Calle answered the phone and said, "U.S. Customs, can I help you."

"Why are you answering the phone, Hombre? Where's the duty agent?" I whispered. When he responded, a happy go lucky Hombre proceeded to tell me that he answered the phone because all of the agents were in another room. Under the circumstances, I shook my head as if I didn't believe what I was hearing. With no time to waste, I told Hombre to tell the agents that we needed help out here and to move in and take the bad guys down ASAP.

Moments later, two teams of U.S. Customs and DEA agents, followed by a contingent of New Jersey State Troopers, pulled into the parking lot of the diner and exited their vehicles with guns drawn. While Fernando was placed face down across the hood of a car, I removed my gold badge that was secured to a chain around my neck and let it hang outside my shirt. As soon as I leaned over and made eye contact with a very surprised Fernando, I looked at the main Colombian subject of our investigation and said, "U.S. Customs, you're under arrest." It's hard to describe the look of complete disbelief on Fernando's face, when he realized that Eddie and I were federal agents. My colleagues and I had waited a long time for this moment and it felt great.

As Fernando was taken away, Eddie and I jumped in with a New Jersey State Trooper and headed over to the hotel where the final phase of the controlled delivery was being executed. By the time we pulled into the parking lot, there were over a dozen agents wearing raid jackets, some carrying shotguns and automatic weapons, converging on the three Colombians. (In the so called fog of war, our agents mistakenly challenged a young couple on their honeymoon, who just happened to be in the parking lot when the stateside receivers were taken down. Once our agents explained the reason for the mistaken identity, the couple thanked them for the excitement and went on their merry way.)

As soon as our agents moved in, the truck driver was immediately pinned by the Ryder truck, while his two associates were ripped through the open windows of the Japanese sedan and arrested by a team of U.S. Customs Agents. Meanwhile, down the road by the entrance to the Outerbridge Crossing to Staten Island, Pat R. and Jack G. executed a felony car stop on Mr. Rogers and Angel. (Lucy and Napoleon were no where to be found when we executed the final phase of this controlled delivery. If I remember correctly, they were eventually arrested by DEA Agents.)

It took exactly 21 days for us to put this deal together and complete one of the most interesting, complex and dangerous controlled deliveries we ever worked. As soon as we wrapped everything up in the field, we headed back to Newark SAC office to process our prisoners and see if anyone wanted to cooperate.

The moment I presented my credentials to Mr. Rogers and I identified myself as a U.S. Customs Agent, he acted as if he was captured by the enemy and had nothing to say. Fernando was no different and had nothing to say.

CLEANING UP LOOSE ENDS

By 5 AM, the crowd fizzled out, leaving only three of us along with Hombre de la Calle and Chain Gang to handle the less glamorous part of the job. Once we had Mr. Rogers, Fernando, Angel and the three young Dominican mobsters from central Jersey in the Union County Jail, we headed back into the field to put the finishing touches to this case. (We didn't know they were Dominican until after we had them in custody.)

As I mentioned before, earlier during the day, Mr. Rogers identified the Holiday Inn where his marijuana contacts were staying. The fact that the Winebago that Mr. Rogers pointed out to us, was still parked at this Holiday Inn, was a clear indications that the marijuana receivers were still checked into this hotel. A stop at the front desk led us to a room on the third floor, where two subjects I call Smoking Joe and Walter, were waiting for Mr. Rogers to drop off their camper loaded with marijuana. Since Mr. Rogers was in custody, Eddy C. and I along with John G. decided to stop by and finish things off.

As if they hadn't done enough already, we had Hombre and Chain Gang hanging out with us when everyone else was in bed. After all these guys had done for the government, they asked us to honor one request and let them come with us when we made an arrest. Hombre went a step further and asked us if he could put the handcuffs on someone. Maybe it was the late hour, or the fact that none of us were thinking clearly due to exhaustion, but we agreed and allowed them to come along, providing they did everything that we told them to do.

Because it was almost 6 AM when we got off the elevator, the sound of a door opening to one of the rooms on the floor didn't strike us as being suspicious. As we walked down the narrow hallway of this Holiday Inn, we passed a young man on his way to the elevator. As we turned around, it must have hit all of us at the same time, because we looked at each other and wondered if he was one of the guys we were looking for. Before any of us could react, the subject known as Walter walked into the elevator and vanished from sight.

Regardless, we had a room to hit, so once we reached the end of the hallway, we set up on both sides of the door. As soon as Eddie knocked on the door, a marijuana smuggler I call Smoking Joe answered the door. In no time, Eddie had this subject acknowledging that he was expecting to receive a thousand pounds of marijuana. As Eddie stepped aside, we charged the room and took Smoking Joe into custody. Once the prisoner was face down on the floor, we signaled Hombre to move in. While Agent John G. rolled his eyes, as if he didn't believe what was happening, Hombre initially fumbled a bit, but eventually got the hang of it and was able to get the prisoner secured. (If the agents in the SAC Office could leave Hombre alone in the command post, I figured there was no harm in having him place handcuffs on a prisoner who was pinned to the floor of a hotel room.)

After leaving the prisoner with Agent John G. and his two deputies (Hombre and Chain Gang), Eddie and I went downstairs to catch the marijuana trafficker that we passed in the hallway earlier. According to Smoking Joe, his sidekick went out for some coffee and a newspaper and was expected back soon. Eddie and I were beyond beat by 6:30 AM but we kept our vigil in the parking lot while we waited for Walter to return.

When Walter pulled into the hotel parking lot driving his rented car, Eddie and I pulled in behind him. Just when we thought Walter was going to park he kept going. Rather than lose him, I pulled our undercover vehicle around his car and cut him off. After executing a felony car stop, Eddie and I had Walter in custody without incident.

By 7 AM we were transporting our two prisoners to the Union County jail. After working with little or no time off for the last twenty one days, we were all wiped out and in need of a shower and a good night's sleep. By 8 AM we were all in bed.

When I woke up I felt like I could roll over and go back to sleep for another eight hours or more. After dragging myself out of bed, I took a shower then dressed and packed my bags, before I made my way to the Newark SAC Office with the others. Once we arrived, we set up camp with the agents in Eddie's group, while we wrapped up some lose ends on the Mr. Rogers case.

While we feasted on huge hero sandwiches from a local Italian deli, my pager went off. It was Jimmy S. When I returned the call, Jimmy answered on the first ring. Our favorite Group Supervisor from the SAC Office in Boston was in very good spirits and almost screamed into his mobile phone when he said, "Those crazy bastards of yours did it again!"

Now that Major Tom and Johnny Churchill were successful, the Boston agents had over 600 kilos of cocaine to use as bait, to lure out a group of major violators operating a drug ring in New York City. As Jimmy continued, he gave me a quick run down of events, while he waited for a U.S. Coast Guard C130 to land in Weymouth, Massachusetts. On board that C130 was the cocaine shipment that our contract pilots picked up that morning in Colombia.

The moment I heard the sound of the C130 in the background, I knew Jimmy had to go. After Jimmy told me that my pilots were safe and on their way back to Miami, we agreed to keep in touch. As I hung up the phone, I stood up and smiled as I faced the others and repeated the good news. The most important phase of Boston CD # 1 for 1991 (our second CD with our Boston Office) aka Operation Snow Drifter was complete. It would now be up to the Boston based FBI and Customs Agents to complete the delivery and arrest the stateside receiver.

OUR SUCCESS WAS MEASURED IN KILOS, TRAFFICKER FUNDS AND ARRESTS

After an enjoyable but hectic week in Newark, New Jersey it was time to return home. According to the press coverage and our unit statistics, the 7000 pounds of marijuana and the 2159 kilos (4749 pounds) of cocaine represented the largest single drug seizure in the history of the State of New Jersey. As far as breaking existing records were concerned, to the best of my knowledge, no other undercover agents were ever paid $1,030,000 dollars to provide transportation services in any other controlled delivery in the history of The Drug War. In fact, as far as I know, this record still stands.

In addition to seizing an estimated $69 million dollars in drug contraband, we also managed to arrest several major violators. As a result of the cocaine shipment that Captain Dakota and Major Tom delivered to the Boston Agents in Operation Snow Drifter, we beat our previous record and shared the credit with our fellow agents up north, for seizing the largest shipment of cocaine in the history of New England.

As far as the controlled delivery we just completed in Newark was concerned, my colleagues and I would go on to help Chief Assistant U.S. Attorney Stuart R. put Mr. Rogers and Fernando behind bars for life and secure long prison sentences for the other violators. Even Chain Gang would testify and help in the prosecution. In the process, The Blade Runner Squadron had the chance to do some fancy flying and log in more frequent flier miles while executing another high risk covert air operation. In addition, some new friendships were made and a good time was had by all of the good guys who worked on this case. Best yet, we managed to accomplish all this without sustaining any casualties.

GOING BACK TO MIAMI

After saying goodbye to Eddie C. and the other agents in Newark, Pat R. and I along with Chain Gang and Hombre de la Calle boarded a flight to South Florida. Once we landed, we decided to meet Major Tom, Johnny Churchill aka Captain Dakota, The Gambler aka Mr. Lucky, Johnny Walker, Airport Sam and the rest of the boys at one of our favorite restaurants to celebrate our recent victories.

Even though I probably should have gone straight home, I couldn't pass up the chance to spend some time with the men who made our operation the

success that it was. As soon as we met, we sat down at a long table and ordered

dinner and drinks, while we exchanged war stories in a very relaxed atmosphere.

Another reason Pat and I didn't go right home was because we had to debrief

Major Tom and Johnny Churchill, so we could write the closing case report and

complete the request for POI/POE (Payment for Information/Payment for

Evidence). Once these POI/POE payments, along with the payments for the

DC6 crew were processed and signed off by headquarters, Pat and I would be

able to pay our contract pilots and sources of information for services rendered.

This included paying Airport Sam for the use of his DC3/C47.

As usual, we always debriefed our crews after every mission. My colleagues

and I amassed the intelligence for our own use and shared whatever knowl-

edge we accrued with the agents we worked with and any agents who needed

assistance. With the exception of a few visits from two CIA employees, no one

from the U.S. Customs Service ever "officially" seemed interested in what we

learned in our dealings with drug smugglers, major violators and their underlings.

Personally, it always amazed me that we were never "formally" debriefed. (For

the record, the two representatives from CIA were only interested in what was

taking place on foreign soil in a "source" country like Colombia.)

As I mentioned before, Major Tom and Johnny Churchill were combat

veterans of two different bloody wars, where all of the technology available

never replaced the fact, that raw courage was all it took to make the difference between victory and defeat. In our conflict, no drug cartel was able to defeat us once we latched onto their representatives. No drug smuggler could pit their greed against our determination and hope to win.

Once our debriefing session was over, I made a few notes and sat back with the others while we had dinner and some refreshments. While we sat together, Johnny Churchill turned to me and spoke with his classy British style accent and said, "Nick, you've been gone for weeks, set this deal up, left and did another big one, then came back the day we returned and instead of going home to be with your family, you had to come and see us." "That's right," I said.

As Johnny Churchill smiled, he looked at me and said, "You've got a good operation here and I'm proud to be a part of it."

The feeling was mutual. Maybe the system didn't always care, but my colleagues and I who ran this operation did and that's all that mattered. If the government only had one, two or three agents at any one time running this operation, then we made sure that we did the work of twenty. When our crews risked their lives to pick up a load, we risked ours when it came time to make the delivery in the states.

The sources of information and contract pilots who worked for us were 110% committed to our mission and purpose in life. On numerous occasions, these men left their normal jobs and families to help us prepare and execute every operation with the skill of true professionals. As I repeat elsewhere in this true story, when two or three of our contract crewmen were gearing up to go operational, we could always count on other members of our group to help out. When another federal agent we were assisting noticed that our entire contingent of contract pilots, mechanics and confidential sources of information responded to help two of our contract pilots prepare for a mission, he seemed surprised when he looked at me and said, "You mean these guys show up to help out even when they're not getting paid?" Personally, I was one proud agent when I responded and said, "That's correct."

When our contract personnel, sources of information and CIs did get paid, they usually waited several months to collect their money. Some of our contract crews flew other missions, or helped us make other cases while they waited to get paid for previous operations. In fact, it wasn't uncommon for some of our contract personnel and sources of information to have multiple payments waiting to be approved. Best yet, as crazy as we acted at times, you couldn't find a more dependable group of pilots, crew chiefs, sources of information and undercover personnel to work with, when it came time to put the tequila aside and go operational.

While I sat at the table surrounded by our wacky band of contract pilots, sources of information and confidential informants, I knew without a shred of doubt that everything that we did together was meant to be. As I watched the men who made up The Blade Runner Squadron tease each other and tell war stories, I sat back and enjoyed the moment because I knew it would not last forever.

CHAPTER 18

AND THE BEAT GOES ON

While the final phase of the joint FBI/Customs controlled delivery was being executed, I was contacted by Jimmy S. and told that he and his agents needed my help on another deal. According to Jimmy, Special Agent Gary S. and Special Agent Russ P. picked up $60 grand in front money with the help of Codfish, a CI with a rather extensive criminal history.

To his credit, Special Agent Russ P. pursued Codfish for a long time and never gave up until he was able to arrest him on federal charges. The informant I decided to call Codfish for this book was a hardcore veteran of revolving door justice, who spent a good portion of his life behind bars. Despite the crimes that he committed, Codfish had a personality that made it easy for the Boston Agents to cut him some slack.

The moment of truth came, when Jimmy S. walked into a small holding cell where Codfish was being detained and he made their prisoner an offer he couldn't refuse. Jimmy reportedly told Codfish that he had gotten away cheap, by getting nailed on a dry conspiracy and not on a much bigger case. Regardless, they had him dead to rights and as a previously convicted felon, it didn't look good for the man I call Codfish.

Codfish listened to what the Boston agents had to say, because he was facing at least a solid decade in jail if he was convicted. Jimmy and Russ both knew that their prisoner could deliver some major cases if he flipped (cooperated), but the question was, would he?

Codfish was a hardcore career criminal, one who had handed a few bad guys their heads for getting in his way. During his reign as a bad guy, Codfish did some traveling and had contacts in various sources countries, including in Colombia.

As I was told, after hearing Jimmy's proposal, Codfish sat back and appeared to be considering his options. While Jimmy and Russ waited patiently to hear his answer, Codfish thought long and hard about what he should do next. As I documented at the time, his response was something to the effect of, "You know, once I come over to your side, there's no going back."

Throughout his adult life, Codfish lived under a code of honor that made it disgraceful to turn cooperating witness or informant. He also knew that his life would be worthless, if anyone learned that he was working for the feds. After wrestling with his decision, Codfish shook the agents' hands and agreed to change sides.

Wanting to cooperate and being able to cooperate are too different things. Fortunately for Codfish, he had enough connections in the underworld to make himself useful. For our purposes as U.S. Customs Agents, Codfish proved to be an invaluable "defendant informant," because he was able to help us infiltrate two different Colombian based smuggling organizations. Once Codfish learned how to do things our way, he was able to act like a smuggler, while gathering evidence that could be used to prosecute good quality cases in federal court.

So far, Codfish had successfully infiltrated two Colombian smuggling organizations in the span of four months and was given a sizable amount of front money to provide transportation services for two large shipments of cocaine. The trick was to orchestrate the first controlled delivery in such a fashion, as to insure the success of the second. Needless to say, this would not be easy to pull off. In fact, this particular "double header" had all of the trappings of an impossible mission.

This was the case, because both controlled deliveries were being orchestrated in New England by Codfish and "his people." This meant that we had to be very resourceful, when it came time to explain to the Colombians, that we had nothing to do with the misfortune of others. Naturally, if the Colombians involved in the second load became suspicious of Codfish, or anyone he did business with, there would be no new business and someone might get hurt. Even if the Colombians trusted everyone involved, they might not trust our route and would be justified to have someone else provide the transportation service for their shipment.

After making fourteen arrests on the joint FBI/Customs controlled delivery, our Boston Agents were able to concentrate on their next transportation case. By the time I was asked to help plan the third undercover air operation that we worked with our Boston agents, I had been working three weeks straight with no time off. Two days after being handed this assignment, I completed the first draft of the operational plan and had a plane and crew lined up to fly the mission.

By this time in 1991, the level of activity was at an all time high. It was also interesting, that the size of the coke loads that we were being asked to transport, were doubling and tripling in size from the old days. This meant that there was a need for new planes and fresh crews. Fortunately, I had taken the steps necessary to recruit new pilots and acquire access to different types of aircraft that could be used in our up coming operations.

Even though there was a sizable rift between SAC Miami Group 6 & 7, special circumstances existed that enabled me to work with Special Agent Kip H. again. Originally, I had The Colonel aka Captain Mona slated to fly this mission with another pilot, but since I wanted to work with Kip again, I decided to put one of his contract pilots into the deal.

The contract pilot that Kip and I documented for this mission was called Captain Band Aid. Captain Band Aid flew jets for the rich and famous and had the personality of a gentleman from the south. After flying corporate jets, he tried his hand as an airline pilot, but eventually went into business for himself. In time, Captain Band Aid managed to build a top shelf executive class private jet service. Unfortunately, Captain Band Aid had a prior brush with the law that eventually caught up to him.

In Captain Band Aid's case, his crime against society was relatively minor, especially when you compare his actions to the activities of the people that we were used to dealing with. Unfortunately, he got arrested in a rural part of the country, where even the most minor drug infractions were taken very seriously and resulted in the harshest penalties imaginable. Fortunately, a federal judge and the local U.S. Attorney gave Captain Band Aid a chance to repay a portion of his debt to society by flying a mission for us. In order to give Captain Band Aid time to complete his substantial assistance to the federal government, his sentencing was postponed. Fortunately, we always had room for one more social outcast in The Blade Runner Squadron.

As soon as DEA Miami Group 6 processed our request for country clearance, we received the green light launch in less than three days. It was also very good news that we would be working very closely with the DEA Agents from Boston on this deal.

So far, things were going quite well in Operation Pale Dry, a case involving 2000 kilos of cocaine that we were scheduled to transport from Cali International Airport in Colombia to Boston, via our base in GITMO. This meant, that our undercover plane and crew would not be landing along a remote stretch of beach, on the open ocean, on a runway carved out of the jungle, or on a relatively secluded airport along the coast. This time, our crew would be landing at a major international airport, where the control tower would direct them to a secluded part of the field, without having to go through Colombian Customs. Once our plane was loaded with over 4000 pounds of cocaine, the tower would clear our crew for take off.

ON TO GITMO

With nothing else left to do except fly the mission, I departed South Florida with Kip, The Colonel and Captain Band Aid in a private business class jet. Gary S. (Customs SAC Boston) and Ed M. (DEA SAC Boston) flew to GITMO on another aircraft. The flight down to the U.S. Navy Base at Guantanamo Bay, Cuba didn't take long, given the capabilities of the executive class jet that we were using to fly this mission. Compared to our slower and older fleet of oil leaking cargo planes, the undercover jet that we were using for this mission outclassed them all.

This time our stay in GITMO would hopefully be a short one. Our plan was to prepare for a 1600 hour (4 PM) departure from the U.S. Naval Air Station at Guantanamo Bay. By launching at this hour, our undercover plane was expected to arrive at Cali (Colombia) International Airport at 7 PM. Due to the time difference, our scheduled departure had to be moved up to 5 PM instead of 4 PM.

Even though there were times when The Colonel had the personality of a fast talking used car salesman, he was one of the most experienced undercover contract pilots in our unit. Despite that fact that The Colonel aka Captain Mona could be a royal pain in my ass, I kept him on board, because he had a great sense of humor, that came in handy when the going got rough. Whether I called him The Colonel or Captain Mona, there always came a time when he would stop being a handful and become part of the team.

Even though Captain Band Aid was a likable guy, I was a little concerned that I might have to scrub the mission, when I saw him show signs of being scared beyond the limits of a bad case of pre game jitters. Fortunately, The Colonel saw it too and immediately went to work calming his new partner down, while I conducted the pre-flight briefing and reviewed the operational plan again.

Even though he had a bad case of sweaty palms, Captain Band Aid sucked it up and seemed ready to go when it came time to launch. After saying goodbye to our crew, Kip and I, along with U.S. Customs Agent Gary S. and DEA Agent Ed M. (one of the nicest DEA Agents I ever worked with) stood off to the side as our crew fired up their engines. The time was 4:15 PM.

After saying a brief prayer, I smiled and gave The Colonel and Captain Band Aid a casual salute, as our undercover plane received clearance to take off from the U.S. Navy control tower. As our crew applied some power to the engines and began to taxi the UC aircraft to the runway, the other agents and I were forced to turn away, when we were pelted with a burst of jet blast that sent bits of sand and small pebbles flying our way.

While I watched our plane taxi toward the active runway, I felt good about bringing a veteran like The Colonel in on this deal. If anyone could get a rookie pilot through a dangerous mission, it was a veteran Blade Runner like The Colonel.

The moment our crew applied full power to the engines, the undercover aircraft raced down the long runway as if it was being scrambled to protect

America from attack. In a matter seconds, the undercover plane was out of sight and on its way to Colombia.

As I sat in the old gray U.S. Navy World War II era Jeep, I cracked a smile when I noticed that the words Blade Runner Squadron were still secured to the top edge of the windshield in quarter inch high black letters. Somehow, the U.S. Military personnel on GITMO left our year old artwork alone. Even though the black plastic letters were somewhat faded and not government issue, seeing our unofficial name displayed on the old Jeep, reminded me of where we had been and what we had accomplished.

After watching our plane take off, Kip H., Gary S., DEA Special Agent Ed M. and I headed back to the Customs trailer to wait for the safe return of our crew. After picking up some diner at Danny's Hideaway Restaurant, we settled into the Customs trailer to wait out the night.

To provide support for this mission, the U.S. Navy positioned an E2C Hawkeye surveillance aircraft and a U.S. Navy surface warfare vessel off the coast of Colombia, to track and monitor the undercover aircraft as it went feet dry on its way to the pick up point. The same military assets would also track the UC aircraft when it went feet wet on the return trip back to GITMO.

The Navy's job was to report their observations through channels to C3I, who would then relay messages to me and the other agents on GITMO. For obvious reasons, this was a Drug War mission that U.S. Department of Defense assets conducted that was never made public at the time. One reason I included this information in this book, is remind anyone who says The Drug War is not a real war, that you don't receive assistance from U.S. military surveillance aircraft and combat naval vessels to conduct "police work."

After finishing my steak, potato and salad, I called C3I in Miami and got the news that our crew called once on the HF radio to say that all was well. As soon as I hung up the phone, I looked at my watch and realized that if the undercover plane was on schedule, they should be very close to the heartland of the Cali cartel's headquarters.

CALI INTERNATIONAL AIRPORT HERE WE COME

After making radio contact with the Colombians our crew prepared to land at Cali International Airport. Just as we expected, the control tower proved to be very helpful to our crew. As soon as our undercover aircraft touched down, the crew was instructed to follow a small truck. Once the undercover plane taxied to a rather secluded part of the field, an Esso fuel truck parked in front of our plane. (A row of tall grass provide an additional modicum of privacy for the refueling process and the loading of the contraband.)

As usual, the Colombians preferred to fuel the plane first, before they loaded the aircraft with the cocaine shipment. Once the refueling was completed, a large canvass covered stake bed truck appeared out of no where with about twenty Colombians. While some of the local Colombians stood by and watched, the rest loaded the plane.

While our crew did what they could to direct the loading, the Colombians packed the jet to the gills with cloth sacks that were filled with kilos of cocaine. Our plane was so jammed packed with cocaine, there was almost no room for our crew to get into the cockpit. Unfortunately, the Colombians put the square kilos into square sacks that looked like over stuffed pillow cases. Had the bad guys packaged the shipment to conform to the cigar like shape of the plane, they would have been able to put a larger load on board. If we thought this was going to be a problem, we could have removed some of the seats in this jet, to make room for more cocaine.

When The Colonel and Captain Band Aid became concerned that the load would affect the weight and balance of the aircraft, The Colonel told the Colombians to stop loading the plane. This resulted in a rather odd number of 1673 kilograms of cocaine being placed on board the undercover aircraft, instead of the expected 2000 kilos.

After saying goodbye to our Colombian clients, The Colonel and Captain Band Aid climbed back into the plane, secured the cabin door and took their seats in the cockpit. In no time, the undercover aircraft was rolling down the long runway. As soon as our jet blasted off into the night's sky and the crew retracted the landing gear, my colleagues and I were on our way to breaking our own record in New England for the third time.

At 2200 hours Kip H., Gary S., DEA Special Agent Ed M. and I waited on the tarmac, while the orange and white U.S. Coast Guard C130 taxied over to the

U.S.C.G. Air Station on GITMO. We intended to use this C130 to transport the coke load and three of us to Massachusetts, while Kip H. returned to Miami with our contract pilots in the UC aircraft. Moments later the undercover aircraft landed at GITMO and was directed to taxi over to our position.

Once we opened the door to the undercover plane, handshakes were in order when we greeted our crew. As the other agents and I looked inside the executive class jet, we marveled over the fact that the UC aircraft was jammed packed with square sacks of cocaine. After taking some photographs, we transferred the cocaine from the UC aircraft to the Coast Guard C130.

As the ramp in the back of the C130 closed, I waved goodbye to Kip, The Colonel and Captain Band Aid. Since this was a Coast Guard plane and not a Blade Runner flight, I had to refrain from sitting up front with the crew. Once I found a long row of unoccupied seats, I stored my travel bag and buckled in. As soon as the C130 was wheels up, I stretched out across a row of empty seats and fell into a deep sleep under a constant blast of ice cold air-conditioning. (The AC unit on this monster of a cargo plane turned this aircraft into a flying ice box in a matter of minutes.)

At 5:30 A.M. we arrived at Weymouth Naval Air Station where we were met by Jimmy S., Bob C., Boston Customs SAC Bob C., Assistant U.S. Attorney Jeff L. and a contingent of U.S. Customs and DEA Agents. After being warmly greeted by the Boston Agents and the AUSA, we headed into Boston with the contraband to start working on the final phase of the controlled delivery.

I LOVE IT WHEN A PLAN COMES TOGETHER

Despite the success of Phase One of this controlled delivery, Codfish lacked confidence in my belief that we would be able to recover hundreds of thousand dollars from the Colombians for our "transportation fee." In fact, for some reason, the figure $500,000 dollars popped into my head, as far as the amount of drug money aka trafficker funds, that we would recover from the bad guys in this case. While I am not sure how many people believed me, I was convinced that $500,000 was the magic number for this particular Controlled Delivery.

Whenever the opportunity presented itself, we used the time in between recorded undercover phone calls and face to face UC meetings to learn a lot more about our adversaries. In this case, even though we knew the identity of the middle man in this deal, we had no idea who the main violator in the states was. (I called the middle man Fred Flintstone.)

Once a drug shipment arrived safely in the United States, all parties involved were in good spirits until the bad guys reneged on their end of the deal. At the risk of repeating myself, I ask you to remember, that when we held back and demanded payment things started to unravel for the broker, who made certain representations to the source of supply and the transportation people. What can the broker say, when he was asked to explain the reason why the deal is stalled and not going forward; that he's really not asshole buddies with the pilots who provided the transportation service and that he doesn't really know how to get in touch with the transportation people, except by cell phone or pager?

In a typical deal involving substantial quantities of drug contraband, the transportation people traditionally get promised very large sums of money to handle moving a drug shipment from point a to b. The transportation people take a huge risk for minimal expenses or front money, then they're asked to start delivering contraband on the lick and the promise that they'll get paid. Most people involved are virtual strangers, but they want you to trust them as if you're an old friend. No one wants to front any cash, but they expect the transportation people to provide a plane and their flying services for peanuts, then deliver a portion of the drug shipment for free.

As I mentioned before, the owner of the load, or the primary representative of the source of supply, were the best violators to deal with when the terms of our agreement were reneged on. One reason for this, was because the owner of the load had the power to get large sums of money released. In contrast, the drug traffickers and smugglers that operated in the U.S. moved with more caution, because they were the ones who were at risk of being taken into custody by U.S. law enforcement officers.

DRIVING A HARD BARGAIN

When the opportunity presented itself, Gary S. and I had Codfish apply the right pressure on the middle man (Fred Flintstone) by saying NO to everything he said. As soon as the deal stalled, we asked to speak to someone who could discuss the money issue, because the middle man we were dealing with, was unable to raise the kind of cash that was needed to satisfy our demands. Five minutes didn't go by before we received a page. That pager going off led our agents on a manhunt and eventually sealed the fate of the main stateside violator. Not only were we now in direct contact with a more important violator, but we had a phone number to run and cross reference.

The main violator in this case did his best to sound like a real tough guy. During the negotiations that followed with the man in charge of the stateside receivers, we were threatened with the wrath of 40 to 50 Colombians. "OK, send them up. We'd love to talk to them. Besides, we're not getting anywhere with you," was our response to the big man from New Jersey, who was directing this deal for the dark side.

When the main violator remarked, "If the Colombians come up to you they won't want'a talk," we had the last laugh, because we knew where the coke load was stashed and he didn't.

The violators in this case were tracked and later fully identified by tracing the phone numbers from pager and cell phone calls and conducting surveillance operations. Once the combined U.S. Customs and DEA surveillance teams latched onto a violator in this case, they were followed day and night. When the two bad guys we identified as drivers were followed to a hotel in Boston, our agents obtained copies of the telephone charges to their room. Once we had these phone numbers, agents were able to link the two drivers to their associates. By this time in the investigation, we had three of the four violators fully identified and under constant surveillance.

One of the biggest breaks of all came, when agents supporting this controlled delivery traced the main violator to a first class hotel in New York City. Another break came when Jimmy S. had an idea who the main violator was. When more telephone analysis gave us an address on the Jersey Shore, I wasted no time in calling Eddie C.. Eddie was back in Miami wrapping up the search warrants on the Mr. Rogers case. Once I briefed Eddie about the on going Boston deal, he told me not to worry and that the assistance we required from SAC Newark would be provided. After Eddie made one phone call, Special Agent Don M. from our SAC Newark, New Jersey office, was following leads in the Garden State for our Boston Agents.

As soon as Special Agent Don M. located the house on the Jersey Shore that was listed on the telephone tolls, we were able to fully identify the main violator. (Actually, the name we were initially using to identity the main violator was an alias, but either way, Jimmy S. was right.)

As hectic as things were, we always had time for a good laugh. While coordinating a massive surveillance effort, Jimmy S. had approximately seventeen U.S. Customs Agents working out on the street, with a contingent of DEA Agents at any one time. As a result, Jimmy looked more like a stockbroker sitting with several telephones on his desk, with at least one ringing off the hook every few minutes.

At any one time, you could find Jimmy answering one phone, while he was already talking to someone on another line. Jimmy would then jump up and grab a portable radio and yell into it with his loud Boston Irish brogue and say, "Alpha 143, this is Alpha 140. Call me on the mobile ASAP." Seconds later a mobile phone would ring, while it rested in a charger on the floor. As soon as Jimmy answered his mobile phone, he relayed instructions to the agent with the call sign Alpha 143, while he tossed one of his hard lines (desk phones) down.

During this flurry of activity, I did what I could to help field calls and when necessary I directed traffic, when Jimmy entered the outer office to grab another phone off an agent's desk. While Gary S. was talking on the only telephone that was left in the Group 4 squad room, Jimmy S. ran back into his office and called out, "Garry, get Dick on the phone." (Jimmy needed to relay an important message to Senior Special Agent Dick O'C. who was directing one of the surveillance operations on the south side of town.)

When Jimmy ran out of his office into the open squad room, he once again called out to Gary S. "Come on, Gary, I need to talk to Dick." Then, without saying a word, Jimmy disconnected the phone line that Gary was on and dragged it into his office. There was mild mannered Special Agent Gary S., sitting behind his desk, holding the telephone that was now disconnected next to his ear. While Gary S. held the phone that was no longer attached to a telephone line, he called out to his group supervisor and said, "Jimmy, that was Dick I was speaking too."

While Jimmy smiled from ear to ear, he entered his office and plugged Gary

Stephan's line into a desk phone that had no extension cord. Gary and I looked at each other, shook our heads and began to laugh hysterically. We had a lot riding on this deal and if anyone handled the pressure well it was Jimmy S.. Despite his office antics, U.S. Customs Group Supervisor Jimmy S. coordinated this surveillance operation with the grace of a big band leader, even if he acted like the Phantom of the Opera when he did so.

U.S. CUSTOMS YOU'RE UNDER ARREST

The day we decided to execute the take down, turned out to be so hot and sticky that Boston felt just like Miami. With all of our agents in position at the North Peabody Mall and a South Shore Mall in Braintree. the only thing that was missing was the signal to move in. After weeks of working this case, the Boston Agents were tired and in need of a break. While other Americans were enjoying the summer months in New England, two full groups of U.S. Customs and DEA Special Agents missed their days off and scheduled vacations, to do a job that received very little public recognition, primarily because The Drug War is generally fought in secret.

Once the signal was given, the North Shore teams moved in. Even though the two drivers were nothing more than errand boys and messengers, every kilo of cocaine that ever hit the streets in the United States did so, because these worker bees were the delivery men for the stateside drug trafficking organizations.

The second the two drivers took control of the load vehicle, a horde of special agents moved in to make their arrests. While one of the drivers reacted in a more docile fashion, the other driver made a run for it, when he spotted a small army of federal agents wearing raid jackets coming his way. Fortunately, Special Agent Don L., Agent Bob C. and a team of DEA Agents were able to capture the driver after a brief foot chase through a shopping mall.

When we moved in to arrest the middle man (Fred Flintsone) at the South Shore Mall, I was surprised to see the U.S. Customs Special Agent in Charge in Boston (Bob C.), out there with the rest of us. The Boston based Customs SAC seemed especially happy, when he saw that we recovered over $500,000 in drug money in the trunk of the prisoner's car.

For the record, the ONLY time I ever saw a Special Agent in Charge of a major field office participate in enforcement actions, was when I worked with my fellow U.S. Customs Agents in Boston. Even though I teased the Boston SAC and called him Windex Bob, because his glass covered desk was always spotlessly clean, I had the utmost respect for him, because SAC Robert "Bob" C. went in harm's way with the rest if us, even though he didn't have to do so.

While the main violator waited for the middle man and his drivers to pick up the load, we entered the hotel where he was staying and had the manager seal off the hallway on the floor where his room was located. Once a small squad of agents lined up in the corridor on either side of the room, I called the main violator from a phone in another room and suggested that he surrender. Moments later, we took the main violator into custody.

During the press conference the U.S. Attorney for Boston, along with AUSA

Jeff L., U.S. Customs SAC Bob C., Jimmy S. and other dignitaries were on

hand to discuss the case and take questions from the media. During the press

conference, an inquisitive media probed for a bigger story. Rumors were afoot

about a top secret undercover air unit that made cases like this possible. One

particular reporter wanted to know if this case was made by such a unit. Instead

of spilling the beans and divulging the existence of The Blade Runner Squadron,

the Special Agent in Charge for the U.S. Customs Office in Boston addressed

the reporters and said, "No comment."

I also need to mention, that the excellent working relationship between the

DEA Agents and U.S. Customs Agents in Boston was made possible, because

DEA Group Supervisor Joe G. and Customs Group Supervisor Jimmy S. worked

very hard to conduct this investigation in a professional fashion.

GOING BACK TO MIAMI

At 2:30 PM on June 19, 1991, it was time for me to catch a Delta Airline

flight at Boston Logan Airport and return to the Sunshine State. Dick O'C of

Operation White Christmas fame was the first to shake my hand, then Agent

Bob C., Steve D., Gary S. and Don L. Before I knew it I was facing my friend

and colleague Jimmy S.. It wasn't easy saying goodbye, but my base of operations

was in Florida not Boston. Even though Jimmy and I said goodbye to each other

in the office, he walked me to my car in the garage where we shook hands and hugged each others like brothers. Before I left I promised Jimmy that we would do it again soon.

CHAPTER 19

MORE NIGHTMARES

After retuning home, I had a series of nightmares of megaton proportions. In one of the scariest nightmares I ever had, two of my contract
pilots were dragged from their plane after being identified as undercover operatives for the U.S. Customs Service. This nightmare ended when a Colombian
drug smuggler walked up behind my pilots and shot them in the back of the
head with a pistol.

No matter how hard I tried, I could not erase this nightmare from my memory banks. The sight of my contract pilots kneeling on a runway in Colombia,
with their hands tied behind their backs as they were executed, was enough to
make me afraid to fall back to sleep. This nightmare stayed with me for weeks
on end and was an ugly reminder of what could happen to one of our crews, if
the Colombian smugglers we were dealing with found out who they really were.
I can only assume, that this particular nightmare was a result of the incident
that took place, when a pissed off Colombian accused our DC6 crew of being
with the DEA.

Another nightmare that I had, that was just as scary, took place on the U.S.
Navy Base at Guantanamo Bay, Cuba. During this incredibly eerie dream, the

base was bristling with activity as I walked to the flight line. As soon as I arrived, I observed a World War II era B25 bomber preparing to takeoff. I knew the crew had an exciting mission to fly and I desperately wanted to go along. I remember feeling terribly disappointed, when the base commander told me that there was no room on the plane for anymore passengers.

As I continued watching the B25, I saw a crew of four, including one man that I met earlier in my dream. Then, almost as if the side of the plane was cut away, I saw a handful of bloody men lying on stretchers in the rear of the aircraft. As unusual as all of this was, I also noticed that the wheels of the plane were strapped down to the runway. As I stepped back, the engines roared to life, until finally the straps broke and the aircraft lifted off the ground in vertical take off like a helicopter. As the plane banked to the left and looked as if it would fly away, it flipped over on its back and crashed right in front of me killing all on board. The moment I saw what happened, I was consumed with incredible grief and a feeling of complete helplessness. As I knelt down on the runway, I cried hysterically while I viewed the carnage. Once again, I woke up from a nightmare of megaton proportions that rattled me to my core.

As if this wasn't bad enough, another nightmare woke me up at 5:18 AM feeling completely overcome with sadness. In this nightmare, a U.S. Customs Black Hawk helicopter crashed in front of a place that I had never seen before, but I knew was my home. These three nightmares were in living color and very vivid.

After waking up and walking around my house, I went back to bed and said something to my wife, about how they sent twenty one out, but I sent one at a time and one had to come back, before I dozed off. I knew exactly what I meant by my babbling. Whether the U.S. military sent two combat aircraft in harm's way, or a thousand, generals and admirals considered the loss of life, as tragic as it was, as an "acceptable loss." In The Drug War, there was no such thing as an acceptable loss, because we sent one plane on every mission and one had to come back.

I didn't have to be a student of Sigmund Freud to know, that the fear of losing one of our crews was continuing to eat away at me like cancer. During my last trip to Boston, I confided in Jimmy S. and told him that I was having terrible nightmares and problems coping with being responsible for the lives of others. As I sat in the Fours Restaurant by South Street Station in Boston, Jimmy looked across the table from me and said, "You're gonna lose one someday. It's only a question of time. Are your prepared for it, Nick?" My answer was, "No," I wasn't prepared for that for to happen.

The thought of having any of our crew members killed during our very carefully executed controlled deliveries had been bothering me ever since the first mission we flew. At times, the responsibility I shouldered was unbearable, but somehow I managed to repress my concerns and act as if I was as confident as ever. As I considered Jimmy's comment, I thought of all the close calls that we had. Were these close calls signs of impending doom, or were my concerns just a case of an over active imagination?

The men who worked for us were not expendable because they were contract pilots, sources of information or confidential informants. Regardless of whether some of us had badges, carried guns and received a civil service salary, or others served as highly paid contract personnel or confidential sources of information, we were all in this together.

Every time we planned an operation, my colleagues and I focused our attentions on every detail. We did so, to prevent from overlooking anything that could result in the loss of life or the compromising of a case. Clearly, I was not alone in this regard. Every Special Agent I worked with on controlled delivery operations also worried about the hired hands who worked for us.

My problem was twofold: First, I worried the longest, because I started this operation and ran it until it ended. Even when I was on sick leave or annual leave (which wasn't very often) I was usually the agent who was called at home and disturbed on my days off. One reason for this, was because I was the primary day to day point of contact with our core group of sources of information and contract personnel. This was the case, because I recruited the bulk of these individuals to work for us. In other instances, whoever I was working with at the time was involved in the recruitment process.

I was also the agent who generally had the most day to day contact with the special agents and supervisors from other offices that we assisted in various ways. When the one or two agents I worked with were on leave, I covered the operation on my own. In fact, I was such a workaholic, that I hardly took time off and routinely carried my accrued vacation time over from one year to another.

I should also mention, that the decision to launch was mine to make. Even though I shared this burden with others, I got the distinct impression that the so called "system" viewed me as being ultimately responsible for the outcome of our activities. In fact, I was told in no uncertain terms by a high ranking Customs manager, that it was my call to make whether we launched or canceled a mission. That sounded plain enough to me. Despite this comment, I knew that the other agents I worked with felt exactly like I did and worried a great deal about the safety of our contract personnel/undercover operatives.

In order to insure that we covered every possible detail, my colleagues and I worked excessive hours on every controlled delivery, often with little or no time off. Unfortunately, after a large wave tore open the bow hatch on our undercover vessel and we crash landed one of our undercover aircraft in New Mexico, I wasn't all that reassured that our attention to detail could prevent every disaster from occurring. This was the case, because certain events were beyond our control. In other words, shit happened.

My cure, if you can call it that, was to stop orchestrating high risk undercover operations and move on to other duties or retire. When I considered leaving the U.S. Customs Service to transfer to another agency, I was concerned that my line of duty injuries would force me to medically retire, so why bother going to another organization. Unfortunately, I was just as addicted to my job, as the people who used the drugs that managed to get smuggled into this country. In a way, this made me very sympathetic to the folks who were tormented by their addictions.

It was also difficult to move on, because The Blade Runner Squadron had grown in size and was now in big demand. Even though I knew I was closer to the end than the beginning, I decided to hold on a little longer, because I believed that we still had a mission or two left to fly.

CHAPTER 20

TO LAUNCH OR NOT TO LAUNCH - THAT IS THE QUESTION

D espite the publicity from the last two controlled deliveries that we executed in New England, the Colombians were willing to have us back again. Fortunately, Codfish was able to convince the Colombians, that the loss of merchandise and the arrests that were made in Boston had nothing to do with him or his people.

After being properly coached, Codfish reassured his contacts in Colombia that it was safe to use his smuggling route. To prove our point, we developed a flight plan for this smuggling venture that the Colombians loved. (Once again, we used our knowledge of smuggling to develop a plan that impressed our clients.)

Even though we were excited about the prospects of picking up another 2000 kilos, we also wondered if we were being lured into a trap. To make matters worse, our plane and crew would have to make the pickup at Cali International Airport, the same location were we picked up the last load. Once the Colombians provided Codfish with an ample amount of front money, I began to draft the operational plan and assemble a crew and a suitable plane. However, I did so with reservation.

In August of 1991, I made one of the hardest decisions of my career since we executed our first covert air operation in December of 1988. The question was, could we sting the Colombians again (in Boston) and get away with it? On the positive side, we had a sizable amount of front money and a few other factors in our favor that I cannot divulge. Unfortunately, as a result of the losses they were sustaining, the Colombians were beginning to strongly suspect, that American Agents were running some type of undercover operation, that was seizing large shipments of drug contraband.

When Jimmy S. called to let me know that they had another 2000 kilo deal to work, I wanted to be convinced that it was safe to fly this mission, before I volunteered our services to pick up this load. As a result of everything that was taking place, we agreed to proceed very slowly and thoroughly evaluate everything the Colombians said and did.

The first turning point of a positive nature came when the Colombians authorized the release of an additional $50,000 in front money. It took one face to face meeting in Miami to solidify the deal and finalize the arrangements. We secured the clearance to go and were counting on two of our contract pilots to pull this mission off, in the most expensive plane that we used to date.

As I stated throughout this book, my colleagues and I in Miami were constantly looking for new planes that we could use in future operations. In addition, we needed to periodically screen new crews. Our hiring techniques usually involved "the old boy network," where one Blade Runner recommended another. Simply put, we never recruited anyone who wasn't highly recommended by one or more people that we trusted with our own lives.

Due to the aircraft that we selected for this mission, this deal was tailor made for our newest pilot, a gentleman I decided to call Top Gun. Top Gun was a crackerjack corporate test pilot, who flew for Uncle Sam during the Vietnam War. Like many of our pilots, Top Gun had seen action years ago and until he met us, his flying days were peaceful and boring. Once again, The Gambler aka Mr. Lucky came to the rescue when he introduced us to our newest member.

The Gambler also surprised me and Pat when he volunteered to fly this mission as Top Gun's co pilot. Since I also called The Gambler Mr. Lucky, I decided to let him go along, because everything he touched turned to gold. In addition to him being one of my best confidential sources of information, The Gambler aka Mr. Lucky was a very experienced aviator and successful businessman, who could wheel and deal with the best of them and always come out on top.

COUNTRY CLEARANCE CANCELED

There we were, preparing to get airborne and for a very good reason our request for country clearance was canceled. For the next two weeks that we were shut down, we had no choice but to stall the deal. I cannot reveal the specifics for this delay, but the intelligence information that we received warranted us to move cautiously. Even when we were finally cleared to go, we still weren't sure if we should allow our crew to take off. If we ever split hairs in our lives to make a judgment call, this was it. During this delay, my colleagues and I in Miami and Boston evaluated some very sensitive intelligence information that was provided by DEA. After a number of face to face meetings and telephone discussions, Rob K., Jimmy S., Pat R. and I agreed to allow our crew to fly the mission.

In order to be fair to our crew, Pat and I went over every morsel of case information so our crew would know who the players were and why we had some initial reservations about executing this mission. We conducted these types if in depth briefing sessions, so our crews would have the right answers, if and when they were ever questioned by any of the Colombian violators, when they landed to make a pickup. Our crews also had to have this information so they could act like legitimate members of a smuggling organization.

PREPARING FOR ANOTHER MISSION TO CALI INTERNATIONAL AIRPORT

As soon as we received the necessary clearance to fly the latest Boston mission, Pat R. and I worked for the next three days to prepare to launch our crew. When it came time to select a suitable plane for this mission, we decided to rent a Gulfstream G2 executive class jet.

The day that Pat R. and I traveled out of state to pick up the Gulfstream G2, I thought I died and went to airplane heaven. After we paid the broker $20,000 in cash and signed the lease agreement, Pat and I sat in luxury accommodations, while Top Gun and The Gambler aka Mr. Lucky flew us back to our base of operations in South Florida. Simply put, this was the way to travel by plane. The Gulfstream G2 was a luxurious aircraft that had eleven super comfortable high back leather chairs positioned in a spacious cabin. This amazing aircraft, that cost over $1 million bucks, was also equipped with a bar, a television, an amazing sound system and all sorts of munchies to feast on.

INCHING CLOSER TO LIFT OFF

Monday morning, August 6, 1991 was a typical hectic day before a scheduled launch. While I handled some last minute details in our office, Pat was off repositioning the undercover plane to another airport. When Pat returned, I was dealing with changes to the op plan. After making a total of five revisions, the operational plan was approved and distributed. (In order to accommodate the frequent changes, we amended each version by the time of day and the date.)

Just about the time that we finished the op plan, U.S. Customs Pilot Robbie V. from the U.S. Customs Air Branch in Miami notified me, that a U.S. Air Force E3 AWAC from the North American Air Defense Command (NORAD), just touched down to provide support for our scheduled operation. Once again, the purpose of this high tech eye in the sky was to provide surveillance coverage for our undercover crew and any other assistance they required during the duration of their flight. This included, tracking the undercover aircraft on his flight from South Florida to Cali, Colombia to a small suburban airport in Norwood,

Massachusetts. Clearly, assigning such an expensive U.S. military surveillance asset to provide support for this mission, proved that the Department of Defense took their involvement in The Drug War very seriously.

As soon as the U.S. Air Force E3 AWAC flight crew was picked up on the flight line, they were immediately escorted to the Group 7 trailer complex. During the detailed briefing session that we conducted, I sensed that some of the U.S. Air Force E3 crewmen were very surprised to hear that we were conducting these types of undercover operations. My suspicions were confirmed, when a U.S. Air Force Captain approached me and said that he couldn't believe that the U.S. was conducting these types of operations. Clearly, this Air Force Officer was surprised to learn that our government had the balls to allow us to operate in this fashion. I had heard this type of comment before. Naturally, my response was to smile and say, "That's why they call what we do a secret."

Our briefing went well, but not without problems. Based on what we were told at the time, the U.S. Air Force E3 AWAC aircraft would not be able to operate close enough to Colombian airspace to adequately support this under-cover mission. The reason for this operational constraint had nothing to do with the technical capabilities of this particular surveillance aircraft. Unfortunately, I feel I should avoid addressing the specific reason why we had this problem, because if I tell you what I was told, you will shake your head in disbelief that this issue even came up. This meant, that in order to get complete coverage, we had to go to Plan B.

The reason we needed complete coverage on this operation, was because the Colombians planned on putting an observer on board the undercover aircraft on the return trip to Massachusetts. According to the Colombians, their "observer" was a licensed pilot and would be wearing an airline pilot's uniform. In order to provide protection to our undercover crew and insure that we remained in complete control of the 2000 kilos of cocaine, we had to covertly escort our undercover plane from Colombia to Massachusetts.

If the U.S. Air Force E3 AWAC aircraft was unable to fly close enough to Colombia to perform this part of the surveillance mission, we had to find another asset that could get the job done. This meant that we needed to add another "asset" to our surveillance package, that could intercept the Gulfstream G2 as soon as it departed Colombia. Once this was done, the UC aircraft had to remain under escort, until the U.S. Air Force E3 AWAC aircraft could assume responsibility to perform the rest of the air surveillance mission.

In addition to tracking the Gulfstream G2 on its return flight to Massachusetts, the U.S. Air Force E3 AWAC surveillance aircraft was also responsible to alert U.S. Customs Air Operations, if the UC plane diverted off its intended flight plan. Should this happen, a U.S. Customs aircraft would covertly interdict the undercover aircraft and follow it wherever it went. In order to provide this type of coverage, we needed to use every radar and surveillance asset that we had at our disposal, to blanket an entire corridor from Colombia to Boston with an armada of interdiction aircraft.

One problem we encountered involved the endurance and speed of the under-cover aircraft. This was a concern, because the Gulfstream G2 could fly at 540 miles an hour at an altitude in excess of 40,000 feet for some 3000 miles without refueling. (The G2 had a fuel capacity of 2100 gallons or 23,300 pounds.) Since U.S. Customs Service Citation Jets were not as capable as the Gulfstream G2, the primary U.S. Customs chase plane would make its way north along the coast and run parallel to our undercover aircraft as it flew further off shore. The chase plane's job was to deliver my partner Pat R. to any airstrip that our undercover plane was forced or compelled to divert to, before arriving at Norwood Airport in Massachusetts. Other U.S. Customs air units and ground units stationed along the east coast, could also be called upon at a moments notice to provide assistance if required.

We made these rather elaborate plans because the words "controlled delivery" meant just that. Our mission in life was to transport the drug contraband/evidence to Boston, so we could use the cocaine as bait, to lure out the money people before we arrested every violator involved. At no time would the cartel representative on board the undercover aircraft (G2), have the ability to remove any amount of cocaine from the undercover aircraft without our intervention. If the undercover aircraft had to divert from its predetermined flight plan, one or more U.S. Customs aircraft would follow the Gulfstream G2 to any destination, to protect our crew and the drug contraband that they were transporting on our behalf.

Our operational plan also allowed our undercover crew to use coded language to alert us, if they had a mechanical problem that caused them to land at a location other than at the Norwood, Massachusetts airport. Should that occur, the UC aircraft would be secured by our crew and I would be immediately contacted on my undercover pager. If our crew was forced at gunpoint to land somewhere else, we had a plan for that contingency as well. Even though we prepared for every possible contingency, the odds were in our favor that the cartel representative on board would behave and go along for the ride.

If everything went according to plan, I would be in a position in Norwood, Massachusetts along with other undercover agents and our backup team, to receive the plane and off load the contraband. While the off load was taking place, Codfish would escort the Colombian observer/pilot to his hotel. Naturally, while the Colombian observer was under complete surveillance, he would report back to his superiors, that Codfish and I ran a first class smuggling operation, that successfully delivered their cocaine shipment to Massachusetts as promised.

To solve our air surveillance problem, Lori C., Robbie V. and Roger G. from U.S. Customs Air Operations arranged for a U.S. Navy Northrop Grumman E2 Hawkeye surveillance aircraft and a U.S. Navy surface warfare vessel to provide additional surveillance coverage during this mission. Once again, the United States Navy was coming to our rescue.

In this instance, the U.S. Navy's mission would be to use their surface warfare vessel and their E2 Hawkeye aircraft to track the undercover aircraft from the time it departed Colombian airspace, until it reached the vicinity of Haiti. Once the UC aircraft was escorted to airspace near Haiti, the U.S. Navy E2 aircraft would turn the surveillance mission over to the U.S. Air Force E3 AWAC plane. (Again, don't ask why the U.S. Navy was able to operate closer to Colombia, but the U.S. Air Force AWAC was prohibited from doing so during this particular mission.)

When the final operational plan was completed, we had one U.S. Air Force E3 AWAC aircraft, one U.S. Navy E2 surveillance aircraft, two U.S. Customs Citation Jets and a U.S. Navy surface warfare vessel providing support for this mission. In addition, as I mentioned before, we also had other U.S. Customs aircraft available to provide assistance in an emergency.

At the risk of being factious, you could almost hear Kate Smith singing, "God Bless America," as this armada of U.S. government military and federal law enforcement aircraft and one U.S. Navy surface warfare vessel prepared to engage the enemy in another secret campaign of The Drug War. It was moments like this when I truly loved being a U.S. Customs Agent assigned to the Miami Air Smuggling Investigations Group 7.

Being the ad hoc commanding officer of such a successful covert air operation made me feel like a four star general, as I jockeyed everything into position in time to launch our incursion into Colombia. One thing was certain. Orchestrating these operations and working undercover on cases of this magnitude was an exciting way to earn a living. Just being in a position to request and be given access to all kinds of military and federal law enforcement aircraft and vessels, was something that the average federal agent rarely if ever got to do. Clearly, moments like this were to be savored and remembered because they didn't happen every day.

Flying drug interdiction missions and directing such complex undercover air operations also reminded me of the days of my youth, when I envisioned myself serving in some type of government aviation unit. I guess you can say, that as a result of my adventurous career, I became a firm believer in the fact that dreams do come true.

BRIEFING THE GAMBLER AND TOP GUN

After a long day of finalizing the plan to launch our crew, Pat R., Customs Pilot Brooks B., The Gambler, Top Gun and I were scheduled to rendezvous at one of our undercover airport offices for an 8 PM briefing. Once we arrived, we put on a pot of coffee and were joined by Ricky Ricardo and The Gambler's wife. Even though I was surprised to find her present, none of us objected to The Gambler's wife attending the briefing. Besides, how could I ask her to leave?

Even though The Gambler and Top Gun were about to go on a very dangerous mission, they were amazingly calm, cool and collected as they listened to our briefing. Before we discussed the flying part of the mission, Pat and I provided our contract crew with their cover stories. During this part of the briefing we went over the most important details of this case. This was done to familiarize our contract pilots with every aspect of this investigation, to include the rolls that Codfish and I were portraying in this deal.

We then provided our contract pilots with the primary and the alternate radio frequencies, that would be used to communicate with the U.S. DOD (military) and U.S. Customs assets that were providing support during this mission. After telling our crew that their undercover call sign was Mohawk, we informed them that the call sign of the U.S. Air Force AWAC was Eagle and the call sign for U.S. Customs aircraft was Renegade. We also let our contract pilots know that U.S. Customs Pilot Brooks B. would be their point of contact in the U.S. Air Force AWAC surveillance aircraft and Pat. R. would be flying in the lead U.S. Customs Citation Jet chase plane.

In addition, we advised our crew that when they communicated with the Colombians in Cali, the UC plane would use the call sign Panther and the smugglers on the ground would use Tiger. We also provided our contract pilots with a different set of primary and alternate radio frequencies, that they needed to use to communicate with the Colombian smugglers.

Our crew was also given a flight plan and a set of way points for the rendezvous with the U.S. Air Force E3 AWAC aircraft. This rendezvous would take place after they departed Colombia and they were escorted by the U.S. Navy E2 Hawkeye aircraft to a location near Haiti. Even though a percentage of what we discussed would never have to be used, we provided this information to our crew to cover every possible contingency.

We also gave our crew a list of preferred alternate airports to use in case of an emergency. In addition, we had our crew memorize the recognition signals they were expected to use when they met our "clients" in Colombia. Last but not least, we discussed how our crew should handle certain situations that forced them to remain in Colombia. The briefing was concluded at midnight.

After I promised to call The Gambler's wife when I knew her husband was safe, I shook hands with our crew and wished them well. As I walked Top Gun to his car, I went over a few of the more important details again and wished him good luck. I then turned to The Gambler aka Mr. Lucky and told him to be careful for the umpteenth time.

As a special agent who had a love for flying, I was new to aviation when I first met The Gambler. One of the reasons we hit it off, was because The Gambler and I both had a can do mentality. In fact, everyone we worked with had the same disposition, which is why we worked so well together. Over the years The Gambler and I spent many days and nights together making one case after another. During our time together, we became professionally close and enjoyed each others company. Even though it was difficult at times not to get too close, somehow we managed to find a way to maintain a very friendly professional relationship.

After all that we had been through, it was especially difficult for me to send The Gambler AKA Mr. Lucky on such a potentially dangerous mission. I felt this way, because he was personally responsible for helping me get this undercover operation established and off the ground. Even though he was a wheeler dealer, who loved receiving big payments from Uncle Sam, I am convinced that The Gambler truly enjoyed being a Blade Runner. I feel feel this way, because no man who was as intelligent and successful as he was, would risk his life and his business ventures just for money.

CHAPTER 21

THE BALL WAS NOW IN PLAY

On August 6, 1991, I traveled to Boston to get into position to meet the undercover aircraft, when it returned to Massachusetts carrying 2000 kilos of cocaine and the Colombian observer. While I was in Boston, our crew departed South Florida in the Gulfstream G2 bound for Colombia. The ball was now in play.

While the undercover aircraft traveled to its destination and the armada of surveillance aircraft and one U.S. Navy surface warfare vessel moved into position, I waited in the Boston SAC Office for a progress report from C3I. Even though Jimmy S. and I were old hands at running high risk undercover operations, we knew this was an exceptionally dangerous mission. In fact, I'd say that this mission pegged the danger meter, as far as the amount of "calculated risks" that I was personally willing to take, to authorize the launch of a crew that I was responsible for. Based on the discussions that my colleagues and I had during the planning stages of this operation, Jimmy S., Rob K and Pat R. felt the same way that I did. In other words, we were all in this together.

As I looked at my watch, I made a few calculations in my head. Since I drafted the operational plan, I knew the time-table like the back of my hand. As usual, I knew every phase of the flight plan, including the time the G2 was expected to go feet dry and land in Colombia. According to my calculations, the undercover plane should be touching down at Cali International Airport in the next few minutes. (The undercover G2 aircraft was scheduled to land at Cali International Airport at 1800 hours local time or 1900 hours in Miami.) Until our crew was wheels up and on their way back to the CONUS (Continental U.S.), there was nothing else to do but pray and wait.

FLAPS DOWN, GEAR DOWN

The time in Boston was 1900 hours. Top Gun had his watch set for daylight savings time, even though the Latin American country that he was about to land in was an hour behind the U.S. So far, so good. Both The Gambler and Top Gun had successfully flown to the pickup point without incident. As they streaked across the night's sky, they placed the required call to the Colombian tower controller and asked for permission to land.

With clearance to land approved, the undercover plane settled down on the runway and was directed by the tower to turn off a taxiway and proceed to a part of the field, where a group of fifteen Colombians were waiting to meet the aircraft. The first person spotted by our contract pilots was a man I have decided to call Captain Cocaine.

While serving as a drug smuggling pilot, Captain Cocaine boasted of flying over 40 cocaine flights for a Colombian drug cartel. After nearly five months of negotiations, followed by over $150,000 in front money being delivered to Codfish, Captain Cocaine appeared very happy to see the Gulftream G2 taxing over to where he was standing.

Codfish deserves the accolades for our success, because he made a Colombian violator I call Fast Freddie a true believer in our smuggling capabilities. Based on their relationship, Fast Freddie sold our transportation services to his associates, even though he had no real reason to believe that we were legit bad guys. Just like the chain reaction that takes place when you knock over the first Domino, Captain Cocaine followed suit and believed that any friend of Codfish was a friend of his. Once again, I also believe that The Greed Factor had a great deal to do with our success.

The moment the undercover aircraft came to a complete stop, Captain Cocaine moved closer to the Gulfstream G2 as The Gambler opened the door and extended the stairs. Once he made his way up the gangway, Captain Cocaine hugged our crew and called the Colombian called Fast Freddie over to examine the million dollar luxury jet. As he climbed on board, Fast Freddie greeted the crew and exchanged a few words with them, while the plane was refueled for the long trip to Massachusetts.

Just as we expected, Fast Freddie was no fool. Thanks to Codfish, we knew enough about Fast Freddie to expect that he would be the one bad guy, who would test our crew one last time, before the plane was loaded with cocaine. On two occasions after Fast Freddie met our contract pilots, he tried to trip up our crew, but they were ready for him and fired back the appropriate responses to his remarks. Our incredibly brave crew met the enemy face to face on their turf and passed muster. So far so good.

The presence of a machine gun toting Colombian had little effect on our crew, other than to remind them that these people were hardcore bad guys. Fortunately, The Gambler and Top Gun were able to put on a good show. In fact, whatever our contract pilots did when they were on the ground in Colombia worked, because once the undercover plane was refueled, the signal was given to load the aircraft with the cocaine shipment.

Once the 4690 pounds or 2132 kilos of cocaine that was packed in flower boxes was put on board the Gulfstream G2, our crew handed the local ground crew a customary case of American beer as a gesture of friendship and appreciation. In return, our plane was filled with fruit, sandwiches, soda and bottled water. After saying goodbye to Fast Freddie, Captain Cocaine and our crew boarded the G2. Once the stairs and the cabin door were secured, everyone took their seats.

While Captain Cocaine sat in a comfortable leather seat and buckled his seat belt, our undercover crew prepared for takeoff. Outside on the tarmac, Fast Freddie and his band of merry men stood by and waited for the plane to taxi to the active runway. Once the word came from the control tower to proceed, the undercover aircraft taxied past the watchful eyes of an airport security vehicle and headed for the active taxiway. In less than three minutes our undercover plane was airborne. With the sound of the landing gear retracting, both Top Gun and The Gambler could rest a little easier, knowing that they had completed the first phase of a very dangerous mission.

OFF WE GO INTO THE WILD BLUE YONDER

The first indication that our crew was safe and proceeding as planned, came when the U.S. Navy surface warfare vessel and a U.S. Navy E2 aircraft began tracking our undercover plane as it left Colombian airspace. As soon as the U.S. Navy relayed the information to C3I, I was contacted at 9:15 PM local time in Boston and advised that the undercover aircraft was feet wet and heading north on the projected flight plan. Now that we knew that our crew and plane were safe, we were anxious to hear the results of their mission.

As instructed during our briefing, our undercover crew maintained radio silence until it was well away from Colombian airspace. The moment our crew made the covert rendezvous with the U.S. Air Force E3 AWAC surveillance aircraft, they contacted U.S. Customs Pilot Brooks B. while Captain Cocaine dozed off in the back.

Even though our sources of information, confidential informants and contract pilots were a wacky bunch of characters, they took their work very seriously. When it came time to go undercover or fly a mission, our contract crews, sources of information and informants became as professional as a space shuttle crew and proved it when they executed their duties with precision. This mission was no different. As soon as we had confirmation, that our crew was on the way to Massachusetts with Captain Cocaine and over 2000 kilos, congratulations were in order.

While Jimmy and I drove to the Massachusetts State Police Aviation Unit office at Norwood Airport, we received periodic updates from C3I. In between receiving and relaying messages, we were able to relax and joke around, especially since we knew that the undercover plane and crew was safe and being escorted to Massachusetts by U.S. government aircraft.

The trip to Norwood, Massachusetts didn't take long to make. After picking up a dozen cups of Dunkin Donuts coffee and two dozen donuts, we gathered in the state police air unit office to conduct our briefing. Present were a contingent of U.S. Customs and DEA agents, two INS Special Agents, along with some Massachusetts State Troopers, a few local police detectives, Codfish and Assistant U.S. Attorney Jeff L. (Jeff left before the plane landed)

The purpose of this briefing was to prepare for the covert offloading of the undercover aircraft and the subsequent surveillance of Captain Cocaine. Since I was going undercover as the smuggler in charge of transportation, which included directing the offload crew and managing the storage facility for the coke load, my mission was to work closely with Codfish until the controlled delivery was completed. Assisting me with the off load would be INS Special Agent Frank D., a colorful federal agent, who spoke fluent Spanish and was definitely Blade Runner material.

As our undercover aircraft flew closer to the northeast coast of the United States, I made some fast calculations and told Jimmy S. that the G2 would land at Norwood Airport at 2:15 AM. Just about that time, U.S. Customs Pilot Brooks B. relayed the news to us that our undercover aircraft was about to enter the airspace over Rhode Island. (Throughout this 5.5 hour estimated flight time, Brooks B. served alongside the twenty six man crew of the U.S. Air Force E3 AWAC aircraft and acted like an air traffic controller, as he helped guide our undercover plane through crowded airspace toward Massachusetts.)

TOUCHDOWN

As the undercover plane began to make its decent, Codfish, Undercover INS Agent Frank D. and I were in position at the extreme end of the runway, while our offload crew headed by U.S. Customs Agent Don L. was waiting out of sight by a hangar. In the woods around us, a number of law enforcement officers were in position to cover us should anything go wrong. Moments later the runway lights came on. This signaled us that the undercover aircraft was close enough to use the specified FAA frequency to radio activate the landing lights at the Norwood Airport. (Norwood Airport officially closed at 11 PM.)

While I waited for our plane to touch down, I couldn't help but think about how much we had been able to accomplish in the past few years. Too many good things had happened for this experience to be a coincidence or a fluke. If anything, it felt as if it was all meant to be.

"There she is," I said as I pointed to a flashing light overhead. The blinking light then executed a tight turn and descended lower and lower in the sky.

"That's her," remarked Codfish in a confident tone when he spotted the undercover aircraft as it came in for a landing.

With the runway in sight, Top Gun came in V minus 10, which basically means that his landing speed would be 10% less than normal, in order to compensate for the fact that he was putting the undercover plane into a relatively short field. With the landing gear down and the flaps extended, our undercover plane came in light on fuel with a crew of two, one passenger and over 2000 kilos of cocaine on board. As soon as the undercover aircraft touched down at 2:15 A.M., it immediately went into a hard breaking procedure. The noise at that hour in the morning was deafening but never sounded sweeter.

As the rented Gulfstream G2 slowed down, I looked up into the night's sky and thanked God for protecting our plane and crew and blessing us with success. Once again, the drug cartels were no match for us, when the full might of the U.S. Government was brought into the fight and the powers to be in Washington backed our play.

As the undercover plane taxied over to where we were standing, I asked Frank D. to flash the high beams in our UC car, while I jumped into the vehicle on the passenger side. "OK, Frank, nice and easy," I said as we escorted our plane around the unfamiliar airport in Norwood, Massachusetts to the spot we picked to conduct the off load. Once we were in position, Frank moved the UC car over to a nearby FBO (Fixed Base Operation) office to get it out of the way.

As the plane slowly approached, I used a small flashlight to guide my crew over to the place where the Boston agents wanted to conduct the off load. Once the G2 came to a stop, The Gambler extended the gangway stairs. Just as I promised our contract crew, Codfish and I were there to greet them.

Captain Cocaine was all smiles as he stood in the doorway of the under-cover aircraft and looked around as if he didn't have a care in the world. As our Colombian passenger walked down the stairs, he smiled and shook my hand as Codfish introduced me as El Chefe de la transportation.

"Welcome to America, Captain," came rolling off my lips and out of my smiling face with all the sincerity that I could muster. Just as we had rehearsed, Codfish jumped in and asked Captain Cocaine to join him, while I took care of the off load. As soon as Top Gun and The Gambler joined us at the bottom of the stairs, we said goodbye to Captain Cocaine.

While the Colombian pilot left with Codfish, I signaled Agent Don L. to bring in the off load crew and the truck. As our off load crew moved into position, Jimmy S. joined me by the bottom of the gangway stairs and congratulated Top Gun and The Gambler, before we entered the aircraft to inspect the load. The sight of 4690 pounds of cocaine stacked up like cord wood inside such a plush and well appointed executive class jet aircraft was truly an amazing sight.

Since I was scheduled to get another MRI scan due to my persistent and worsening back problems, I was supposed to be careful and not pick up anything heavy. Naturally, in the excitement of the moment, I started to help the Boston Agents carry the packages of cocaine off the plane. After picking up and passing a few cocaine laden flower boxes to other agents, I was reminded by Agent Don L. to take it easy. Don was right. If I wasn't real careful I would be put flat on my back and out of commission. (It was no secret that my line if duty injuries were getting worse. In fact, there were times when I was using a cane to walk, that some of my fellow agents who met me at an airport carried my luggage for me.)

While I joined Jimmy Scott, Top Gun and The Gambler on the tarmac by the plane, we gave our contract pilots a quick debriefing, while the other agents finished off loading 82 flower boxes that contained approximately 26 kilos of cocaine in each package from the plane. As soon as we were ready to go, we secured the aircraft and took our brave crew to a nearby hotel to get some well deserved sleep. While our crew checked into their rooms, the Boston Agents transported the 4690 pounds of cocaine to a very secure U.S. Customs storage facility. The Blade Runner Squadron had done it again!

CHAPTER 22

COCAINE! COCAINE! COCAINE!

Immediately after The Gambler and Top Gun returned to South Florida in the Gulfstream G2, I returned to Boston to work on the final phase of the controlled delivery. As usual, the fun was about to begin, now that it was time for us to receive payment for services rendered.

Once the game plan was finalized, Codfish, Frank D. and I drove our UC car to a 7 PM meeting with Captain Cocaine. Our first meeting went well as far as I was concerned, except for the fact that the Colombians only agreed to provide us with $300,000 as an initial payment. Then I remembered a piece of advice I received from a highly experienced federal prosecutor in South Florida by the name of Bill S. According to Assistant U.S. Attorney Bill S., during his service as a federal and state prosecutor, he observed a reluctance by undercover agents to use words such as heroin, cocaine, marijuana, etc. when they had discussions with violators/criminals. Instead, many undercover agents who feared being exposed as a law enforcement officer used words like "the stuff," "the merchandise," "the goods," "the product" and the you-know-what," when they referred to different kinds of illegal contraband.

To strengthen the position of the prosecution, it paid to have a clear tape recording where the undercover agent and the violator used the proper terminology and not the street slang to describe the kind of contraband involved in the transaction. As far as I was concerned, this was excellent advice.

While keeping Bill's advice in mind, I waited patiently until the right moment came for me to use the proper terminology without being obvious. Doing so, would further solidify the fact, that Captain Cocaine knew that he just helped to smuggle over 2000 kilograms of cocaine into the U.S. Fortunately, three quarters of the way through our first meeting, Captain Cocaine opened the door and asked me the right question.

As usual, the negotiations were typically rocky, with Captain Cocaine doing his best to whine and moan about his organization's money problems. Captain Cocaine and Fast Freddie wanted us to front them the entire load, with a promise that our payments would come in drips and drabs on a daily basis. That, of course, was absolutely out of the question. Even their offer of $300,000 was out of the question, considering the size of the load and all we did to safely "smuggle" their shipment from Colombia to Massachusetts.

As soon as Captain Cocaine finished making his case, I leaned closer to him and slapped my pack of cigarettes and my Cricket lighter on the bed in his hotel room and said, "The cigarettes are the cocaine, the lighter is the money. When you hand me $1.5 million dollars I'll release the cocaine." All this was said as I quickly passed the hand with the lighter over the hand with the pack of cigarettes, to emphasize the simultaneous exchange of cash for cocaine.

Even though Captain Cocaine knew exactly what I meant, we took no chances and had Undercover INS Special Agent Frank D. slowly repeat word for word of what I said in Spanish so there would be no misunderstanding. While the tape recorder was turning, Captain Cocaine acknowledged that he understood me perfectly. Best yet, he never once jumped up and said that he didn't know that he was smuggling cocaine into the U.S. When this happened, I knew the day would come, when AUSA Jeff L. would have to thank Assistant U.S. Attorney Bill S. for helping to put the finishing touches to this case.

With this first undercover meeting out of the way, we bid the Captain good night after he placed a flurry of phone calls to several of his people, including to Fast Freddie. During these phone calls, Captain Cocaine explained the situation and relayed our demand that we receive a substantial payment before we would deliver any COCAINE!

On day two we had more and more of the same. It was both typical and predictable to listen to the Colombians whine over and over to us about their money problems. In order to maintain our operational security, we changed hotel rooms and moved from payphone to payphone whenever we placed our recorded telephone calls.

The weekend was quiet for those of us in Boston, because Captain Cocaine traveled by commercial plane to Miami to meet some of his cronies in South Florida. While Pat and I laid low in Boston, Group 7 Supervisor Rob K. arranged for some of our Miami Group 7 Agents to help the Boston Agents, who traveled to South Florida to keep an eye on Captain Cocaine and the violators he met with in Dade County (Miami).

On Saturday August 10th, Codfish was contacted and asked if he could pick up Captain Cocaine and his associate when they landed at Boston Logan Airport. He was also told that the Colombians would pay us on Monday and that they wanted us to have ten boxes of merchandise ready for delivery. Naturally, he agreed. After moving to a new hotel on Sunday, I drove out to Cape Cod for some R&R. (One of my best friends who I went to college with was a police officer on the Cape.)

On Monday morning August 12, 1991, we had a quick briefing session before we went to Logan Airport to pick up Captain Cocaine and an associate of his called Mr. Tony. As soon as Codfish, Special Agent Frank D. and I picked up the two bad guys, I could tell who was in charge.

Mr. Tony was the most streetwise and dangerous member of the group that we were dealing with. In addition to being young and in good shape, Mr. Tony spoke perfect English and was very well groomed. Because he appeared to be as sharp as a tack, I also believed that he had the capability of seeing right through us if we weren't careful. As a fully Americanized drug trafficker, the highly polished Colombian emissary from Miami was under direct orders from the Colombians in Cali to see this deal through.

After making some small talk, we arrived at a hotel in Danvers, Massachusetts.

I knew Tony would be a royal pain in the ass to deal with when he refused to discuss business in his hotel room. Here was a guy, who just rode from Boston to Danvers, Massachusetts in our undercover car, but he was hinky (concerned) about speaking to us in his hotel room. Rather than argue with Mr. Tony, we headed down to the hotel coffee shop to get something to eat and talk about the business at hand.

During this meeting, Codfish became a full fledged Blade Runner, when things didn't go our way and he told Tony where to go and how to get there. Besides having a commanding presence because of his size and demeanor, Codfish was one tough son of a bitch who didn't take crap from anyone. As a result, he looked twice as angry when he stood towering over the table and he reiterated our demands. The moment I stood up and backed his play, Codfish handed me my hat and off we went with undercover INS Special Agent Frank D. by our side.

As we drove away from the hotel, I knew we made the right decision. I also knew that we could deal from a position of strength, because before the pickup was made, Codfish was told that he would be paid for providing his transportation services, even though he was never promised a specific amount. When their idea of a realistic amount wasn't close to what we had in mind, we headed back to the negotiating table to come up with a figure that was acceptable.

As usual, the drug traffickers were hoping to wear us down and get us to start delivering cocaine in drips and drabs, so they could generate capital from the sale of the contraband that we smuggled into the states for them. By demanding that our "clients" live up to the terms of our arrangement, as undefined and unclear as it may have been, we forced them to use money that was the profits from previously successful drug transactions to pay us for services rendered. This means, that we gave them the "double wammy" every time we seized a huge load of drug contraband and relieved them of a big bag of money, before we arrested as many violators as possible.

For over two weeks we listened to the Colombians whine, before we started hearing numbers thrown around that made sense. At one point we were even accused of being the American police. After being told by the main violator in Colombia, that we were doing business the way the American police conduct business, I told Codfish to act as if he was highly offended and slam the phone down which he did. Once our "clients" calmed down, they paged us back and started negotiating again. This was the ultimate game of chicken to see who was going to flinch first. We had their cocaine and they had two choices. They could let us keep the 4,690 pounds of cocaine, or they could pay us a reasonable amount of money to deliver it to their stateside receivers.

In the end, the bad guys were forced to admit that they agreed to pay the transportation people COD. Several hours later, Mr. Tony contacted us and said he was willing to pay us a half a million dollars. Our response was something to affect you'll have to do better than that. While we waited for our clients to raise more money, we took a badly needed break and enjoyed some R&R.

ON THE ROAD AGAIN

After a brief trip back home to South Florida, I returned to Boston on Wednesday, August 26, 1991. Eight months after being initially briefed by Jimmy Scott, I was in Boston to complete my fourth controlled delivery in New England since our operation began.

As soon as Pat R. and I picked up our luggage, we met Agent Dave M. and Agent Bob C. and headed over to the Boston SAC office on Causeway Street. When we arrived at the Group 4 office we found Jimmy S. sitting behind his cluttered desk doing paper work. After discussing the case at hand and joking around about the job, we prepared to wrap up the final phase of this controlled delivery.

CLOSING THE DEAL

All total, we had around thirty law enforcement officers geared up to cover me and Codfish when we went undercover. From what we were told the night before, the Colombians were expected to show up sometime before noon on Friday, August 28, 1991 to make the exchange. As usual, we agreed to meet at 9:30 AM at the command post in Peabody, Massachusetts.

With a whopping four hours of miserable sleep under our belts, Pat R. and I left the Sheraton Hotel in Danvers, Massachusetts and drove over to the hotel where the command post was located. After being introduced as the undercover agent, Jimmy S. presided over the rest of the meeting and began to turn teams loose so they could take up their positions. For the rest of the day we waited to be contacted by the Colombians so we could meet and make the exchange. During the down time, I tried to get some sleep but I was unable to do so. I guess I had a lot on my mind.

By late afternoon, Codfish and I were calling the Colombians who were camped out in a nearby Hilton Hotel. Our surveillance teams had the three Colombians under surveillance. Every suspicious person or car was logged in a surveillance diary and every observation that was made by the surveillance agents was passed on to the command post.

By the end of the day, we had no idea when the mystery guests from New York would show up. The Colombians at the local Hilton Hotel kept telling us that everything was fine and that the cars that carried our money would be in Boston at any time. As usual, the Colombians were behind schedule. Nobody liked the delays, but we collectively made good use of the extra time, by gathering valuable intelligence information on the subjects of our investigation, who were staying at the Hilton Hotel in Wakefield, Massachusetts. (At this time, our surveillance teams had Captain Cocaine and two stateside receivers called Jimmy and Mr. P. under surveillance at the Wakefield Hilton.)

Our first break came after 5:30 PM, when I called Tony's hotel room after one of our surveillance teams reported to Group Supervisor Jimmy S., that Tony just entered the Hilton after being dropped off by a young Colombia kid driving a four door European sedan. According to Tony, he had $750,000 ready for us to pick up with more on the way. All we had to do was meet him at his hotel and wait for the drivers from New York to show up, so we could get paid and take possession of the load vehicles as they arrived.

As the conversation ended, Tony asked me for a phone number so he could call Codfish and me direct rather than page us. "No way, Slick, but nice try," I said to myself. While thinking fast, I told Tony that we were waiting all day for him and his crew and hadn't had lunch or dinner, so we were going out and wouldn't be by the phone. If he needed us, he could contact us on our pagers. Tony was smart and didn't press the issue. Instead, he told me to enjoy my dinner and to meet him at the Hilton Hotel in Wakefield, Massachusetts with Codfish once we were finished eating. Dinner for us was a fast hamburger while we re-grouped at the command post for a late night strategy session before we went back to work.

The closer we got to making the exchange, the more we began to think about the possibility of an undercover operative being taken hostage. We had this concern, because to think otherwise would've been foolish and cavalier. Suppose they didn't have any cash and they wanted to lure us into a trap, by inviting us to their hotel room under the guise of paying us our money? Suppose they handed us our money but held us hostage, until they received a call that the coke load made it safely to New York?

At 9 PM our undercover pager went off. It was Tony. With our hopes up high, we placed the recorded call to the ringleader of the Colombian contingent and were told that the car from New York left at 5 o'clock and was due to arrive in the Boston area soon. Tony's last words before we hung up were, "I'll call you back in ten minutes."

Shortly after we made this call, one of our surveillance teams called in to report, that a guy carrying a large suitcase just arrived at the Hilton. At this point we all knew that we were inching closer and closer to pulling this deal off. Ten minutes turned into forty five while we waited outside a supermarket for our next contact. While we waited, Russ P., Pat R., DEA Agent Ed M., Codfish and I passed the time by discussing a variety of different topics. I also used the time to call home. As soon as I finished talking to my family, we decided to call Tony since his Colombian timetable was an hour off.

"Why don't you come by," was the gist of our conversation with the man in charge of the stateside receivers.

"OK," said Codfish, who was just as curious as I was to see exactly what the Colombians were up to. After racing back to the command post, we had another fast think tank session. The last few taped conversations with Mr. Tony were replayed to give me, Customs Supervisor Jimmy S., AUSA Jeff L., DEA Supervisor Joe G., Pat R. and the other agents in the room a chance to help plan our next move. We played the tapes over and over until we were all in agreement, that Codfish and I had to go over to the Hilton for a face to face meeting with Tony and Captain Cocaine.

Even though we agreed that we had to meet Tony, DEA Group Supervisor Joe G. was very concerned, that once we were allowed into his room the door could be bolted shut. Should this happen and if we were held hostage, our backup team would have a much harder time gaining access to the room. Since the idea of walking into a setup still concerned us, we decided to play it safe and not immediately go to any room that was occupied by a Colombian violator. Instead we decided on Plan B.

When Pat turned to me as I stood next to our undercover car and he asked if I had my gun, I responded as I pulled up my polo shirt, to show him that I was armed with my five shot .38 caliber Smith & Wesson revolver. "Don't leave home without it." (I also carried extra ammunition in my pant's pocket.)

Once Codfish and I were inside the undercover car, I tested the small transmitter to make sure Pat was reading us five by five. With nothing left to do, Codfish and I drove to the Wakefield Hilton, followed closely by a long train of unmarked government cars.

The news of our arrival in the parking lot of the Hilton Hotel was quickly transmitted to all of the surveillance teams in the area. Once we parked our undercover car, Codfish and I headed for the hotel lobby. On the way into the Hilton Hotel Codfish and I looked at each other and rolled our eyes. When Codfish said that things could still end up going bad, I agreed and told him that we should be very careful and take it one step at a time.

By this time in our official relationship, I had gotten to know Codfish and develop a good rapport with him. The fact that he was a career criminal, who became a documented U.S. Customs source of information/confidential informant to save himself, did not prevent me from liking him personally. Had I been in his shoes, I would have probably done the same thing, when Jimmy S. gave him a chance to work off his beef and make some money while working for the feds.

SHOW ME THE MONEY

As soon as Mr. Tony answered the phone in his room, he invited us to join him in his second floor suite. "No, you meet us in the lobby," said Codfish before he hung up the phone. We then found a quiet little corner near the bar area and sat down, leaving a couch available for whoever came out of the room to meet with us. After waiting a few short minutes Mr. Tony and Captain Cocaine walked up to us and shook our hands, then sat down across the table from us.

Mr. Tony wasted no time laying out their idea of how things would go down. So far they had $630,000 ready to turn over to us as soon as the last load car arrived from New York. An additional $150,000 would be forthcoming as soon as we started to make the transactions. They agreed to pay us everything they had, before giving us three load vehicles and showing us where the false compartments were located. Tony also said that he wanted to work the entire weekend and pay us off in full when the last of the shipment was turned over to them.

"Let's not waste time," I said. "Get us the three cars tonight so we can load them and have them ready by morning." When they agreed, we told them that we would have two of our drivers join us at the hotel and be ready to pick up all three cars by 1 AM. The time was 12:15 PM. To kill some time Codfish and I decided to wait in the lounge while Mr. Tony put his end together.

While I waited in the bar, Pat contacted me on my pager. After I looked at the number I glanced over to Codfish and said, "It's the boys. They want to know what's going on." "

As usual, Codfish played along and remarked, "Give 'em a call and tell them to meet us at 1 A.M. out front."

As soon as I excused myself, I was cheering inside that Codfish was really in role now. In the last Boston deal, Codfish broke his cherry as far as doing things our way. Now he was deep undercover again, only this time, he was more in sync with our way of doing business.

When the operator said, "Hilton Hotel, how can I direct your call?" I answered in a low tone of voice, "Room 125 please." While the operator connected me to their room, Pat R. and Russ P. were monitoring my transmission from the bank of payphones near the lounge. When Russ answered the phone in Room 125 I acted like I was talking to one of my drivers. "OK, Danny, you get Bernie and meet us at the Hilton in Wakefield no later than 1."

Russ got the message and said that he would relay the time and place to Don L. and a local task force cop (a state trooper) who were scheduled to portray our drivers in this deal. Then Russ gave me the good news. The transmitter was emitting a strong but broken transmission.

"Can you move it?" asked Pat when he jumped on the phone. By this time I was holding the transmitter up near the phone as I examined the device while Pat remarked, "That's perfect, you're coming in clear."

"No shit," I said, "I'm holding the damn thing up near my frickin mouth." (The bank of phones was away from our meeting location in a private area where no one could see me while I spoke to Russ P. and Pat R.)

Since there was no way that I could walk around holding this device extended out in front of my face like a microphone, I decided to put it back inside my pant's pocket. By the time I finished talking to Pat R., Tony and Captain Cocaine were getting ready to leave. "We'll be here waiting," said Codfish, as the two Colombians said goodbye and walked back to the room that we had gotten for them on Wednesday night.

At 1:15 A.M. Codfish and I headed for the house phone in the lobby. Again the Colombians were late. After placing another call to the Colombian's hotel room, we learned that Mr. Tony and a bad guy named Jimmy just left. As we were told, they were on their way to bring one of the load vehicles over from a nearby hotel. With nothing else to do, Codfish and I camped out in the lobby.

I LOVE IT WHEN A PLAN COMES TOGETHER

Shortly after Tony joined us in the lobby, a young Colombian cowboy type entered the hotel. While acting as if he was waiting for this guy to arrive, Tony stood up and met the young man in the lobby by the house phone. As soon as the mystery guest slapped a set of keys into his hands, Tony returned to where

Codfish and I were sitting.

As Tony handed me the keys, he said they belonged to the red van that was

parked at the end of the parking lot. Once he finished telling us to put six flower

boxes in the van, he caught us by surprise and asked if we would come to his

room to see the Captain, meaning Captain Cocaine. It was moments like this

that you wanted to stop time and walk outside to confer with your fellow agents.

That of course wasn't realistic. Part of being an undercover agent means following

your instincts and making some of the more difficult decisions on your own.

Codfish and I had already discussed the issue of going into a hotel room,

that would likely be occupied by four Colombians during the final phase of the

controlled delivery process. Whatever we discussed didn't mean much now that

we had to make a split second decision about what to do next.

Under the circumstances, we agreed to follow Mr. Tony to his room, even

though we had no way of knowing what to expect. All the way down the hallway

I kept thinking about what DEA Group Supervisor Joe G. said about being

taken hostage. In an effort to alert the backup teams in the area, I called out

room numbers in a casual fashion until we arrived at the Colombian's room. As

I stood in front of the right room, I brushed up against the room across the hall.

I did so to alert our backup team to the fact that we were going in. (I did this for

three reasons. First, I had no idea if our transmitter was functioning properly.

Second, we had agents in the room across the hall from Captain Cocaine's room.

I also knew if anyone asked to search me, we would have a fight on our hands, because I was both armed with a revolver and an undercover transmitter.)

When the door opened Mr. Tony entered the room as if nothing was wrong. As soon as I started to walk into room, Codfish quickly pushed me aside and went in first. He did so to see if it we were walking into a trap. It was moments like this that I wished I had a full pardon signed by the President of the United States in my pocket, so I could make Codfish a free man. What he did that night was above and beyond the call of duty and I made sure to thank him for his unselfish act of bravery when I was able to do so.

As soon as I entered the room, I spotted piles of cash all over both queen size beds. So far so good, I thought. They're not going to rip us off with all this money around. Then, the pessimist in me considered the possibility, that the bad guys could produce guns and force us to remain with them, until the entire shipment of cocaine was delivered and their drivers made it safely to New York.

As I sat down and watched four Colombians counting stacks of 20's and 50's, I turned to my left and noticed that the door to the room was being bolted shut by one of the Colombians. While I sat in a comfortable chair in the corner of the room, I planed what I would do, if any of the bad guys displayed a gun and announced that we had to stay with them, while the load was being delivered to New York. If that happened, I knew exactly what I was going to do. All I will say about my plan, is that when I made my move, I had to make every shot count, because the revolver that I was carrying only contained five rounds of ammunition.

As crazy as this may sound, I was actually quite calm while I sat and waited for the Colombians to make their move. When the money count was complete, a disagreement over the total caused all four Colombians to count the cash two more times, before everyone was happy with the results of the tally. We received more good news, when Jimmy the smuggler left the room and quickly returned to report that the driver of a van arrived and was waiting to show us where to conceal the kilos, that were supposed to be placed in his vehicle. So far we were told to put six boxes containing 26 kilos each in the red van, 38 kilos in the blue van and another 38 kilos in the VW sedan that hadn't arrived yet.

As soon as we were free to go, Codfish picked up our money as we followed Jimmy the smuggler out of the room. On the way out, we were told to keep in touch, because the balance of our money was concealed in a hidden compartment underneath the VW sedan, that was due to arrive at any time. We also agreed to meet Tony and his band of merry men at 8 AM to make the delivery.

Once outside of the hotel room, we met a smuggler called "Blue Van" Willie in the hallway and introduced ourselves. This happy go lucky Colombian had no idea how close he was to being sentenced to a long stretch in federal prison when he shook our hands. As soon as we reached the parking lot, we were taken to a blue van that was parked nearby.

While we stood next to the van, Willie showed us the three hiding places where we had to conceal 38 kilos in the left side interior walls and the right passenger door of the vehicle. In order to accomplish the loading procedure, we were handed a special tool that was needed to pull back the upholstery and vinyl covering on the door of the van. This tool was designed to enable the cocaine to be concealed inside the interior of the vehicle, without leaving any trace that the upholstery or vinyl covering was moved.

Once Willie left, Codfish and I drove the blue van over to where the red van was parked. We then put the cash in the trunk of our undercover car and pulled over to where we had the two load vehicles waiting for our drivers to show up. So far so good I thought, as I talked to myself hoping that Pat R. or Russ P. heard me. Moments later my pager went off with a code that meant I was transmitting clearly.

As soon as Senior Special Agent Don L. and a state police detective arrived in the parking lot, we left the area in a convoy of load vehicles and undercover cars. While I drove the undercover Cadillac, Codfish jumped into the Chevy Caprice, while Don and the state police detective drove the load vehicles. Once we followed the load vehicles to the exit of the hotel, one vehicle went north and one went south followed by each of us in the undercover cars. We were looking for counter-surveillance and anyone trying to follow us back to our stash site.

Once again, a little bit of paranoia goes a long way to keeping you alive. So far we had only been paid a percentage of what we were owed, so we behaved like real bad guys and good undercover agents and did some fancy driving, to prevent from being followed by anyone other than the members of our cover team.

After driving over the rivers and through the dales, we finally arrived at an empty parking lot behind a row of businesses in a shopping mall. It was just past 3 AM when I was greeted by Jimmy S., Pat R. and Robert (Bob) C., the U.S. Customs Service Special Agent in Charge in Boston. Once again, I was impressed beyond belief that the Special Agent in Charge in Boston was out with his troops in the middle of the night. I should also mention, that the Boston SAC was not a micro manager. When the Boston SAC Bob C. was with us in the field, he acted as if he was a regular street agent taking risks like the rest of us.

Congratulations were in order for everyone but no one celebrated yet. Instead we were all pretty serious and down to business when we searched the two load vehicles before moving on. Pat told me that he had gotten some good conversation and that the equipment worked well except for one time when we were near the lounge.

At 5 AM Codfish made a call to find out what happened to the mystery car, that reportedly had our cash hidden in a false compartment. When he was told that it was expected soon, he told the Colombians that we would pick it up in the morning. As a result of our surveillance activities, we had numerous hotel rooms all over the North Boston area. By 5:30 AM Jimmy S. put the word out for everyone except a small surveillance team to find a place to crash until morning. As exhausted and mentally drained as I was, I dreaded trying to sleep. I knew that I was wired and once I hit the pillow I would toss and turn all night.

At 9:30 AM Pat R. and I were heading over to our command post to meet with Codfish and the others. Tony had already paged the hell out of us and was anxious to meet. It never stopped to amaze me how when we were late the Colombians went berserk. They loved to do things their way with their own agenda and timetable. In every deal we did, we put up with all sorts of delays due to their penchant for tardiness. As always, it felt great knowing that we were driving them crazy, because we had their cars, their money, their cocaine and we had the nerve to miss our scheduled 8 AM meeting.

After grabbing a cup of coffee, we all settled down inside the hotel suite, that doubled as our command post, to discuss the take down scenario. So far we did everything possible to cover all of the bases. Even though we were very close to wrapping this deal up, we had to handle things the right way, or risk losing one or more of the subjects of this investigation. Our main concern was having Tony take off, once he knew that we were in the process of delivering the vehicles, that were loaded with the prescribed amounts of cocaine. Since we had all of the evidence that we needed, we decided to have teams of agents move in and arrest every violator we had under surveillance. Doing so, insured that no one would get away.

According to the surveillance units at the Wakefield Hilton Hotel, all of the main players were eating in the hotel restaurant. After making sure that everyone was in place at the Hilton and the nearby Lord Wakefield Motel, U.S. Customs (Boston) Group Supervisor Jimmy S. gave the word for all units to move in and make their arrests.

The last thing that anyone sitting at the table suspected when they sat down to eat, was that they were going to be arrested before they finished their meal. As Tony and the others looked up in amazement, they spotted a handful of special agents approach their table with guns drawn. When Tony ignored the command, "Don't move," the agent who relayed the command drew a bead on his chest and repeated the command, while another agent moved in and grabbed Tony's hands and slapped them on top of the table.

With Captain Cocaine, Mr. Tony, Jimmy the Smuggler and Mr. P. in custody, U.S. Customs Agent Bob C. (not the SAC) and DEA Agent Ed M. went to Room 169 and found Blue Van Willie and the old man, who drove the VW Jetta with the false compartment under the gas tank to the Wakefield Hilton. In a matter of minutes, a total of a nine subjects were arrested at the Wakefield Hilton and at the Lord Wakefield Motel. While we were busy in Massachusetts, Rob K. led a team of U.S. Customs Agents from Group 7 on a raid of a residence in South Florida and took a tenth subject into custody. The Florida connection was the money man and the catch of the day next to Tony and Captain Cocaine.

Later that day at the Boston SAC Office, Jimmy S. asked me to identify myself to Tony. As soon as the handcuffed prisoner was brought into the room where I was standing, I produced my federal credentials and identified myself as Nick Jacobellis, Senior Special Agent U.S. Customs Service. (I should mention that Tony was handcuffed in the front not behind his back.) Being the first class prick that he was, Tony kissed the tip of his right index finger, then placed his "kiss of death" on the photograph that was on my credentials. When Jimmy S. asked our prisoner to explain his actions, Tony decided to remain silent and was led away. Jimmy later thanked me for not bouncing Tony off the walls for the giving me the obvious "kiss of death."

After several months of ups and downs, we managed to put the finishing touches to one of the best cases that we ever worked. While everyone went home to salvage as much of the remainder of the holiday weekend as possible, I volunteered to meet Codfish to place one more recorded call to the main Colombian down south.

As I sat all alone in the empty command post, a place that was bristling with activity in the past few days, I tried to settle down from the adrenaline rush, after working undercover on such a demanding controlled delivery. After Codfish arrived and placed his call we said goodbye and parted company. Rather than go back to my hotel room, I drove out to Cape Cod to stay with a friend, before I returned to Boston for the press conference on Monday morning.

MAN DOWN

The morning of the press conference I felt a sharp stabbing pain in my lower back and collapsed on the floor in my friend's house. I knew I pushed myself too much lately, especially when I tried to carry some of the cocaine off the Gulfsteam G2, after the undercover aircraft landed at Norwood Airport. For all general purposes I was crippled from the waist down.

Even though I could feel my legs and my feet, I was unable to stand up and support my own weight. Whenever I tried to move an inch in any direction I was immediately consumed by excruciating pain. Because this was not the first time that something like this happened, I was deeply concerned that my days as a U.S. Customs Agent were numbered.

After my buddy, who was a cop on Cape Cod, helped me move to a nearby couch, I took some prescription pain medication and remained immobilized. Even then, it would hurt like hell to move. I was in such bad shape, that if my friend's house caught on fire, I would have to be carried out, or I would have to crawl out in order to survive. Four hours later I was taken to the hospital. After being examined by a doctor, who also suffered from a serious back injury, I was given a prescription for more powerful pain medication and advised to take it easy. As a result of the debilitating nature of this medical emergency, I missed the press conference.

AN UNEXPECTED PAT ON THE BACK

After recuperating on Cape Cod, I returned to Boston to drop off my undercover car before I caught a flight back to Florida. On the way to Boston I got pulled over for speeding by a veteran Massachusetts State Trooper. Because I looked like a dirt bag and I was armed, I identified myself to the trooper and explained that I was a Miami based U.S. Customs Agent working on a case in Boston and I had no idea where the registration to my undercover car was located.

After asking for my badge and credentials the trooper returned to his car. When I looked in the rear view mirror, I saw the trooper use his radio before he examined the newspaper that he had in his vehicle. It took a while, but eventually, the state trooper got out of his marked police car and returned to the driver's side of my undercover car.

After the trooper handed me my badge and ID, he patted me on the back of my left shoulder before he sent me on my way. Having that state trooper pat me on the back was one of the best compliments I ever received in my entire law enforcement career. I have no idea if this trooper confirmed who I was, or if he simply assumed that I was involved in the case that was a front page news story. Regardless, getting a pat on the back from that state trooper meant a lot more to me than not getting cited for speeding.

THE OUTCOME

After being convicted in federal court, Tony escaped from a federal prison. Immediately after his escape, Jimmy S. called to warn me that Tony might be on the loose in South Florida. We later learned that Tony managed to flee the country and was shot dead on a street in Colombia. I guess the kiss of death that Tony gave me backfired.

BACK IN THE SUNSHINE STATE

Shortly after I returned home, I was notified that I was finally being sent to undercover school. The U.S. Customs Service was finally going to teach me how to be an undercover agent.

AUTHOR'S NOTE:

For various reasons, I will not be discussing specific details about a transportation case that we worked with an office in another part of the country. All I will say, is that when I went undercover on this case, one of the Colombian violators confirmed that the aircraft under my control would be transporting several thousand of kilos of cocaine into the United States. As usual, this conversation was recorded and witnessed by members of my backup team. Shortly after the Colombian violators turned over a respectable amount of front money, this case was compromised and had to be shut down. As much as I would love to say more, I will jump ahead to the summer of 1992.

CHAPTER 23

HURRICANE ANDREW

When Hurricane Andrew hit South Florida, it cut a swath of destruction all the way to Homestead and Florida City. Homestead Air Force Base was so devastated, it looked more like ground zero during a nuclear attack, than an area that was the victim of a major natural disaster.

Since I lived in northern Broward County, my home was not affected by the impact of the hurricane. Even though all federal employees were given the day off, I decided to head south to salvage what I could from our office and check on the agents in my group who lived in the hardest hit areas. Rather than do this alone, I picked up Eddie C. and a visiting agent from our New Jersey SAC Office.

After driving to Homestead, Florida, which is just north of the Florida Keys, we headed straight for the U.S. Air Force Base where the Miami Air Branch and the Group 7 office complex was located. In addition to the buildings that were heavily damaged and destroyed, the smell of aviation fuel permeated the air, because some of the fuel tanks on base were leaking.

As soon as I approached the main gate, I was greeted by the base commander and a small contingent of U.S. Air Force Security Police Officers who stayed behind and were holding the fort by themselves. Since I had no idea where Rob

K. was, I assumed command of Group 7.

After presenting my credentials to the base commander, I asked for permission to inspect the damage at the Customs Air Branch and the Group 7 trailer complex. I made this request because we had all sorts of case files, information relating to our undercover operation, radios and other government property that had to be recovered. Initially, no one was being permitted to enter the base for any reason. Somehow, I managed to persuade the base commander to let me enter, to see if there was anything left to recover. Unfortunately, I had to enter alone and was only permitted to load one car at a time with anything of value that I found.

While I rummaged through the remains of our completely destroyed office complex, I noticed that most of our files looked as if they had been taken out to the firing range and used for target practice. What wasn't torn to bits or shredded was water damaged and looked as if a metal scraper or an eraser removed the words right off the paper.

As I continued looking through the remains of the Group 7 office, I couldn't believe my eyes, when I found the one and only complete copy of the undercover books and records for the Group 7 certified undercover operation. (It's amazing how some items can survive such destruction and others do not.) After filling my car with as many items of value and importance as possible, including the undercover books and records, I headed back to the main gate. Once I parked outside the entrance to the base, I briefed Eddie C. and the visiting agent about the damage to the Air Branch facilities and the Group 7 trailer complex. (On another trip I recovered thousands of dollars in undercover funds from the small safe in the remains of Rob K's office.)

Clearly, had I, or any of the agents that I worked with, stole, or misused any trafficker funds, we could have easily taken advantage of the opportunity to destroy the only complete copy of the undercover books and records that existed. Without these books and records, it would have been difficult to impossible to thoroughly audit the Miami Group 7 certified undercover operation. This was the case, because bean counters need receipts, vouchers and ledger books to check facts and make sure that every penny was properly accounted for. This included documenting the exact amounts of undercover funds that were used by specific special agents to pay authorized expenses on specific occasions.

Since I knew that my colleagues and I never misused any undercover funds, I recovered these records and shared the responsibility to safeguarded these financial records with Rob K. Pat R. and Eddie C. Once operations began to normalize, these records, along with money that was recovered from the office safe, were turned over to an Assistant Special Agent in Charge.

As a result of Hurricane Andrew, several sections of South Florida were sent back to the stone age, as far as living conditions were concerned. Those of us who lived in the unaffected areas traveled into the hardest hit areas on a daily basis, to provide assistance as required.

My wife was so affected by what she saw on the news, she took money out of our family food budget and had me go to the supermarket to buy food for my fellow agents and their families. The items that I purchased and delivered to these grateful agents were normally considered basic staples of life, but during a disaster they were considered luxury items. In addition to transporting ice, fuel and bottled water into the affected areas, items like fresh bagels, milk, loaves of bread and food that could be cooked on an outdoor grill were greatly appreciated.

While putting in fourteen to sixteen hour days, we did what we could to assist the agents who had damaged homes. In addition, we traveled to Homestead Air Force Base to take carloads of anything that wasn't destroyed from the remains of the Group 7 office complex.

For well over a month, those of us who were able to provide assistance, navigated the roads that were jammed with cars and trucks heading into the most devastated areas. Special lanes were made in the breakdown lanes, or on the grassy medium along the highway for law enforcement officers and other first responders to use, to expedite their travel into and out of the most devastated areas. Once it got dark, the roadblocks went up and the good people were told to get off the street. The only way past a checkpoint, was if you possessed the appropriate credentials and were driving a car with a police light on the roof.

SHOTS FIRED

One night, Eddie C., Dave T. and I were asked if we could secure a mobile field hospital until the Metro Dade Police could respond to relieve us. Based on what we were told, this particular MASH type medical unit had been attacked by local drug dealers. These attacks took place, so drug dealers could get their hands on the pharmaceuticals that were stored in this field hospital to care for patients.

Shortly after we arrived, it started raining so hard you could barely see the hand in front of your face. To make things worse, we were smack in the middle of one of the hardest hit areas, not to mention, a high crime section of Homestead, Florida. The more it rained and the darker it got, the more I felt as I was in a war zone, especially since we were surrounded by destroyed buildings. Needless to say, the medical staff at the field hospital was happy to have us present to protect them, while we waited to be relieved. In the meantime, the medical staff offered us hot coffee and Twinkies (my favorite).

The only security this mobile field hospital had, was an old former Marine who was armed with a .410 shotgun and a pocketful of shells. After showing us the layout and telling us how the local druggies tried breaking into this field hospital's makeshift compound, we assumed the best defensive positions possible and prepared to repel any attack that came our way.

All three of us were wearing U.S. Customs raid jackets and were heavily armed with our 9mm pistols, extra ammunition, a .12 gauge Remington pump shotgun, a 9mm Walther MPK submachine gun and a select fire .5.56 NATO caliber Steyr Aug assault rifle. While Eddie and Dave waited outside, I entered the field hospital to pick up a supply of first aid supplies that would come in handy in case of emergency.

The second I stepped into the makeshift supply room, that had an exposed view of the parking lot, and the former Marine turned on the light to retrieve some supplies, a sniper opened fire. At the time, I heard two bullets wiz by. Special Agent Dave T. later told me that he heard four shots fired.

As the former Marine instinctively shut off the light and took the best cover available, I ran outside to join my fellow agents. By the time I got outside, I found Eddie and Dave taking cover behind our government cars. As I joined them, I gripped my 9mm submachine gun, but held my fire, because we were in a residential area and I had no clear shot of the person who fired at us.

While I waited for the sniper to open fire again, all I could think about was the scene in the World War II movie, The Longest Day, when Major John Howard of the British 6th Airborne kept repeating his orders to, "Hold until relieved." Then, with headlights blaring, a Miami Metro Dade Police car drove into the parking lot behind us. After being illuminated by high beams, while we took cover from the sniper, I called out to the cops to kill the headlights. Fortunately, they got the message before anyone got hurt and called for backup.

When help arrived, Eddie, Dave and I volunteered to assist the mixed bag of South Florida police officers search the abandoned building, that seemed to be the most logical hiding spot for the sniper. After leapfrogging our way to the right building, we made our way inside the run down apartment house in search of the shooter.

As soon as we entered the pitch black building, the only noise you could hear was the rain dripping down from the ceiling and the squishing sound our shoes made, as we sloshed through ankle deep muck on the floor. While I had no concerns about engaging the sniper, I felt more and more uncomfortable as we walked deeper and deeper into the pitch black building. By the time we reached what seemed to be the top floor, I could barely breath as I felt the walls closing in on me.

Throughout my entire law enforcement career I always felt very comfortable and in complete control whenever I went in harm's way. Even when I heard gunshots wiz by, my first reaction after hearing the sniper open fire was to run outside to be with my fellow agents. Unfortunately, the situation changed after we started searching for the sniper, inside a pitch black abandoned building that was damaged during a Category 5 hurricane. (At the time, I believed I was suffering from a bad case of claustrophobia as a result of the plane crash landing in New Mexico.)

Somehow I managed to hold it together and was extremely grateful, when a police officer illuminated the area in front of us with the flashlight that was attached to his rifle. In fact, as soon as the light went on, I was able to breathe again and felt completely normal. During our search, we found a wooden ladder leading up to the roof but no sniper. Whoever shot at us must have escaped out the back, when the cavalry arrived and we searched the building.

Once we got outside, I was grateful that my colleagues and I survived another adventure. This disaster relief stuff was dangerous business and I couldn't wait to get back to the safer duties of working undercover. I should also mention

that after the hurricane, the U.S. Customs Service handed out a number of

commendations to various special agents who participated in the Hurricane

Andrew disaster relief effort. For some reason, Eddie C., Dave T. and I were

overlooked. I guess we didn't do enough.

CHAPTER 24

THE END OF AN ERA

B y 1992, I wasn't the only member of our undercover operation who wondered if we were pushing our luck, by continuing to participate in high risk transportation cases. The fact that we already survived a few close calls was making some of us think about our own mortality. Clearly, there was a price to pay, in order to enjoy "the free wielding nature" and the creative aspects of our duties. Once again, I had to ask myself, "if the juice was worth the squeeze?" For some crazy reason the answer was yes. As a result, I stayed in the game. Fortunately, I had plenty of company.

As you know from CD Book I, Major Tom was one the first contract pilots that I recruited. In addition to being the only African American member of our group, Major Tom was a highly decorated combat aviator who served during The Vietnam War. As far as his personality was concerned, Major Tom was an easy going guy who had a somewhat dry but great sense of humor. He proved this, when I told my core group of sources of information that I was just given permission to activate our undercover air operation. After hearing me tell everyone present that we had the green light to go operational, Major Tom cracked a smile, then remarked something to the affect of, "What a country. They just put a GS12 Special Agent with an expired student pilot's license in charge of his own undercover air unit."

The only thing that bothered Major Tom, was that he was unable to have a personal relationship with me and the other special agents. Even though he knew why we had to keep things on a professional basis, he didn't have to like it. The main reason this barrier existed was due to money. Once a special agent paid sources of information and contract personnel large sums of money for services rendered, it was too easy for people who were "friends" to cross the line. Like it or not, we had to keep things on a friendly but professional basis.

One day Major Tom dropped by the undercover office to introduce us to someone who he believed would be an asset to our operation. During this meeting, Pat R. and I were actually very surprised when this individual made certain admissions about his previous involvement with drug smugglers. In fact, based on what our new recruit had to say, it certainly sounded like he was lucky that he was never arrested. Even though it took some doing to get our new recruit to do things our way, this particular documented source of information provided a very valuable service. I wish I could say more, but I can't.

Toward the end of our operation, Senior Special Agent Eddie C. conducted two undercover operations that utilized the services of various undercover agents, contract pilots and sources of information. On a personal note, all I can say, is that the operation that I was involved in was expertly planned and involved the use of an undercover seaplane, an executive class jet aircraft, an undercover vessel and two "stash" houses that had access to the ocean. Again, I wish I could say more, but I can't.

THE KOREAN CONNECTION

Even though our undercover operation was initiated to execute controlled deliveries involving drug contraband, I initiated a very interesting case that involved the smuggling of counterfeit designer women's handbags into the U.S. from Korea. While working with a former FBI Agent, who was now employed as a private investigator, I went undercover to facilitate the "smuggling" of a shipping container that was filled with counterfeit products.

The day I went to meet the violator in this case for the second time I could barely walk. After being dropped off by my cover team, I limped along with the aid of a cane, as I made my way to the small hotel were I was expected to meet the subject of this investigation. This was another one of those instances, when being in such obvious pain and barely being able to walk bolstered my cover story as a drug smuggler who survived a plane crash.

As soon as I got closer to the small hotel, I spotted some young Asian males who looked like they were providing security for nefarious activities in the area. I was convinced that no one suspected that I was a law enforcement officer, when one of these young Asian males opened the door for me as I approached the entrance to the hotel.

After meeting with the main violator in this counterfeit case, this investigation was turned over to U.S. Customs Agents in another city. I included a brief description of this case in this book, to let people know that investigating the smuggling of counterfeit goods is just as important as investigating other crimes. I say that, because the smuggling of counterfeit products can have a negative impact on legitimate commerce and the economy of the United States.

Before I end this book, I feel compelled to mention that a bit of pessimistic attitude was developing in the early 1990s. This attitude promoted the feeling that nobody really cares, so why bother working hard. Another negative attitude that was expressed at the time, was the more you did, the more scrutiny you came under. This was also the beginning of the age of political correctness and we all know how well that pathetic policy has worked out for our country.

I also couldn't believe how afraid some people seemed to be of the Special Agent in Charge in Miami. In fact, I got the distinct impression that some of his subordinates liked it better when the SAC was away from the office, so they could get various official papers signed by the Acting SAC, who was easier to deal with. Again, this in my opinion, but the Special Agent in Charge at the time had the disposition of a god with a small g one minute and a regular guy the next. Allow me to explain.

On one occasion, a high ranking manager actually stepped on my foot to get me not to raise a certain issue, while I was meeting with this particular Special

Agent in Charge. While I assume this particular Customs manager thought he was protecting me, I was never concerned about talking to the SAC. Neither was my partner Pat R., or my Group Supervisor Rob K. Senior Special Agent Eddie C. also had balls of steel and would stand up to anyone, including a boss, when it was right to do so. After all, our SAC put his pants on one leg at a time just like we did. In fact, so did everyone else in our chain of command.

On another occasion, this same Customs manager gave Pat R. and I the distinct impression, that he didn't want us to push the issue of asking to see the SAC, about a specific course of action that we wanted to take on one of our cases. By the way some people reacted, you would think that going to see the Special Agent in Charge, was the equivalent of Dorothy and the Cowardly Lion being in the presence of the Wizard of Oz.

When Pat R. and I felt that we really needed to see the SAC, we managed to coax one of our superiors into getting us an audience with his eminence. Trust me when I tell you, that we had to pester the shit out of this particular manager, in order to motivate him to ask the SAC to see us.

Before we entered his office, we could hear the SAC (The Wizard of Oz) using a raised voice to explain that no matter what "those agents" (meaning me and Pat R.) had to say, he wasn't going to change his position. Regardless, the grand high exalted mystic ruler of the U.S. Customs Service in Miami at that time, permitted my partner and I to enter his royal chamber.

The way the manager who arranged this meeting acted, I expected to walk into the SAC's office and find a little man (The Wizard) standing on a stool

behind a curtain, while hitting noise-makers and speaking into a public address

system, that amplified his voice and made him sound like a terrifying supreme

being. Instead of the Special Agent in Charge being a first class prick, the SAC

was actually very polite, while he listened to what Pat and I had to say. In fact, it

took no time at all, for my partner and I to explain what we had in mind and for

the SAC to let us handle things the way we planned to do so. No screaming, no

yelling, he just agreed with our logic and was actually quite personable during

this exchange. Who knows, maybe the Special Agent in Charge of Miami in 1992

was impressed, that some of his special agents actually had the fucking balls to

approach him, after he used a raised voice to let others in the office know, that

he was set in his ways and was not about to change his mind.

On another occasion, a high ranking Customs manager tried to give me advice

that made absolutely no sense, before I left to work undercover in another city.

As soon as I rejected this "advice," the SAC once again acted like a regular guy

and went as far as disagreeing with this particular manager in front of everyone

who was in his office at the time. Quite frankly, seeing the SAC react the way

he did impressed me to no end.

As a result of these interactions, I became convinced that our SAC would

have enjoyed his job a lot more, if he spent more time hanging out with his

hardest working special agents in the field, instead of going to the office everyday.

Again, this is just my opinion.

CLIPPING MY WINGS

The day that my ASAC called me into his office to tell me that my wings were being clipped and that I was being reeled in from my undercover duties, I got the impression that this manager expected me to object to being reassigned. Instead, I was grateful that our undercover operation was being shut down. I was finally free. I felt this way, because I accomplished everything that I originally set out to do, when I asked for permission to form a Group 7 undercover air operation.

After several long years of working in Group 7, I left my ASAC's Office relieved that I would not have to work undercover, or execute another controlled delivery by plane or boat. (It is important to note, that U.S. Customs Agents could not be compelled to work undercover. As a result, working in an undercover capacity was strictly voluntary.) To celebrate my new orders, I went home and cut my long hair and shaved my beard.

When Group 7 was disbanded in May of 1993, I was assigned to the Fraud Group. Once again, I was lucky to have a group supervisor who proved to be a truly decent human being. Kathy S. quickly earned my respect, when she told me to lay on the floor in the back of the office, whenever my line of duty injuries were acting up and I needed to get off my feet.

After a brief stint in the Fraud Group, I was transferred with Rob K., Pat R. and Eddie C. to the C31 Air Intelligence Center at Homestead Air Force Base. We were back among our friends in Air Operations and that suited all of us just fine.

The day eventually came when I received a transfer to a duty station that was located in a rugged but picturesque part of the country. Once again, I got lucky and I ended up working for Ron, I., an outstanding supervisor who previously served as a hard charging Senior Special Agent in Miami. Relocating provided the opportunity to make a new life for myself and my family while I worked as a so-called "regular agent." It was time to put the past behind me and move as far away from "the flagpole" as possible.

CHAPTER 25

JUST ONE MORE TIME

S hortly after I arrived at my new duty station, I was introduced to a Colombian informant and was asked to participate in a controlled delivery involving a large quantity of cocaine. I couldn't believe it. Here I was trying to lay low and rebuild my personal life and I was being thrust back into a world that I wanted no part of.

Once this cargo case fizzled out, I was kept busy enough to be entertained, even though my new duties were nothing like what I did when I was assigned to Miami Group 7. Working in a drug task force with a group of local police officers was also like being a cop again, which suited me just fine. I also participated in the longest mobile and stationary surveillance of my entire law enforcement career, when I worked in the wide open spaces of this particular duty station. Best yet, I was generally home every night for dinner and spent the weekends with my wife and two sons. I had completely turned my life around and it felt great. In the process, I also had the opportunity to become familiar with a completely different part of the country. In many respects, it was like being on a paid vacation.

Even though I swore that I would never work undercover again, I agreed to do so to help Ron I. conduct an investigation that had tremendous potential. To make a long story short, Ron I. had a machine gun trafficking case that was dead in the water, because his informant took off and went to work for DEA. Rather than see a case with tremendous potential go down the drain, I told my supervisor to pull over and park next to a pay phone that was near our office. With the authorization to record conversations on this case still active, I hooked up a tape recorder and contacted the target of this investigation.

The cover story for this case was simple. The individual who originally contacted the subject of this investigation was looking to purchase machine guns and other firearms, that could be taken to Colombia for use by drug smugglers. As soon as I made contact with the illegal gun runner, I introduced myself as Nick Franco, a friend of the individual that he was dealing with before. (With the informant gone and the individual that the illegal gun runner was dealing with out of the country, I had nothing to lose by contacting the subject of this otherwise dead in the water investigation.)

I couldn't believe my ears, when the subject of this investigation said that he still had the weapons and ammunition that he was previously willing to sell. Even though I reluctantly agreed to work undercover on this case as a favor for a friend, it felt great to know that I hadn't lost my touch.

After making several recorded telephone calls and successfully completing one face to face meeting, we were ready to do business. Rather than work alone on this deal, I asked if a female undercover agent could play the roll of my girlfriend and accompany me when I purchased the AK47s. Once again I lucked out, when a very capable and attractive female U.S. Customs Air Officer volunteered to work as my undercover partner on this case. Simply put, this particular female Air Officer possessed all of the attributes that made her well suited for undercover work.

As soon as we arrived in the small town near the Mexican Border, I parked my undercover car in front of the location where the meeting was scheduled to take place. I did so, to insure that our back up team would know exactly where we would be, if they needed to come to our rescue.

The second I walked into the building and came face to face with the main violator and his associate, I immediately felt the presence of evil in the room. I experienced this same eerie feeling on other occasions, including when I met with Mr. Rogers.

The good news was, my female partner did an OUTSTANDING job and put on a command performance. This was actually quite a feat, when you consider that we never met before and we planned what we were going to say and how we needed to act on the car ride down to this meeting.

Just when things were going smoothly, the main violator asked to speak to me privately. One of the longest walks I ever made when I worked undercover, took place when I followed the main violator into a dimly lit room in the back of the building. In addition to being concerned about my female partner, I knew enough about the main subject of this investigation to be especially concerned about my personal safety. As I sucked it up and prepared to do battle, I was pleasantly surprised when all went well.

Shortly after this private meeting took place, I pulled the UC car around back with my "girlfriend" by my side and watched as the main subject of this investigation loaded two fully automatic AK47s and 4000 rounds of Chinese 7.62x39 caliber ammunition into the trunk of our car. Once the bad guy was paid, we headed north to the closest major city. (On another occasion I purchased a .22 caliber Ruger pistol with a removable suppressor (silencer) from the same violator).

After the illegal gun dealer was arrested and prosecuted, he received three years probation and no jail time. Whenever I think about the outcome of this case, I remember the famous words of Alfred Lord Tennyson who wrote, "Ours is not to reason why, ours is just to do or die."

CHAPTER 26

PULLING THE PIN

Unfortunately, the undercover car that I used during the illegal weapons trafficking case was totaled in a serious accident, when my vehicle was struck from the side. This collision was so severe, I was knocked unconscious when the air bags deployed and my head ended up impacting the driver's side window. In fact, the second I lost consciousness I had a broad daylight flashback of the plane crash landing incident. I also assume that I sustained a concussion, by the symptoms that I experienced after surviving this serious motor vehicle accident, that totaled my rented undercover car.

As a result of this very serious motor vehicle accident, I re-injured my lower back and neck again. It was also after this accident, that my family and I relocated to another duty station; one that proved to be an even nicer place to live. Unfortunately, I lasted long enough to participate in one arrest, before my line of duty physical injuries flared up so bad, that my doctor requested that I be placed on permanent light duty.

As I expected for some time, the day finally came when I was told that I was physically unfit to be a U.S. Customs Agent. In fact, I was specifically told that I would not be accommodated or permitted to work in a light duty capacity. When my attempt to plead my case fell on deaf ears, I was sent for a medical fitness for duty examination, which I failed. According to my retirement papers, "Senior Special Agent Nick Jacobellis is unable to perform the full range of duties of a GS 1811 Criminal Investigator because of physical injuries sustained in the line of duty."

Despite the fact that there were times when I was physically unfit for full duty, various supervisors accommodated me and allowed me to use a cane when necessary. Even when certain agency officials asked if I was taking prescription medication and I showed them the medication that I took on a when needed basis, I was allowed to remain on the job. Working in various undercover offices and on the Air Force Base where Group 7 was located, also made it possible for me to remain out of sight when my injuries were acting up.

Even when I didn't hide the fact that my injuries were acting up, I was never taken out of service. A perfect example of what I am referring to, took place when I had to go to the Miami SAC Office and I had to use my cane to walk because I was in a great deal of pain.

While meeting with my ASAC, another high ranking Customs manager stopped by and inquired about my medical condition. I was actually quite surprised, when my ASAC turned to this other supervisor and said, "Nick crashed a plane with his drunken contract pilots and can retire any time he wants." In other words, the choice was mine to stay or go. In fact, many of my fellow agents had no idea, that I was actually offered the opportunity to receive full disability pay and medically retire, after I was injured in the plane crash landing incident and I was re-injured while serving on an undercover vessel.

Instead of accepting the opportunity to medically retire in the early 1990s, I decided to remain on the job for as long as possible. Even though I didn't believe that I would last long enough to qualify for a regular retirement, I wasn't ready to voluntarily walk away from the job that I wanted ever since I was a kid. All that changed when I was injured for a third time in the line of duty.

In the summer of 1997, I left the U.S. Customs Service with my Special Agent's credentials stamped RETIRED, a paycheck every month for the rest of my life and written permission to tell this true story. On a personal note, my faith was strengthened by all that I witnessed and experienced during my law enforcement career, especially during my service in our nation's Drug War.

I also want you to know, that even though I was forced to medically retire, I can honestly say that "the juice was worth the squeeze." I feel this way, because what I gained from my experience as a U.S. Customs Agent, is significantly greater than what I lost as a result of being physically disabled in the line of duty. I should also mention, that by the time I retired I stopped having nightmares about undercover operations. Clearly, there was life after Customs.

Over the years, my physical injuries got progressively worse and became more painful and debilitating. Walking with a cane and an impaired gait since the early 1990s, also contributed to the need for me to undergo a very painful total left hip replacement. Years after I retired, a second government medical doctor documented that I have a total of eight line of duty permanent physical injuries, including six spine injuries and two hip injuries. Sustaining two line of duty companion hip injuries made a bad situation worse and has added to the level of pain and discomfort that I experience on a regular basis.

The cervical injury that I sustained also causes moderate to severe headaches that can last for days on end. For several years prior to July of 2017, these spine pain induced headaches increased in intensity and would last from two to thirteen days in a row. From July 15, 2017 until March 21,, 2018 (the day I finished the final edit for CD II), I have been experiencing varying degrees of headaches due to spine pain on almost a daily basis. This is due to a condition known as bilateral occipital neuralgia.

So far, the Botox injections that I am currently receiving in my head, neck and upper shoulders have provided varying degrees of partial relief. Unfortunately, these injections wear off and have to be administered every 90 days. Even modest forms of physical activity can also detract from the benefits of these injections. The fact that my hip replacement did not produce all of the desired results, has also caused me to limit my activities.

I mention all this to let you know, that if I could go back in time I wouldn't change much if anything, as far as remaining involved in high risk undercover operations. The simple fact is, that people who serve in certain professions get injured, permanently disabled and killed in the line of duty. Clearly, in my case,

I was truly fortunate that things didn't turn out worse than they did.

In closing, I leave you with this two part journal as a lasting tribute to those who sacrificed so much, for so many, in a conflict that never offered much hope of a final victory. The fact that The Drug War is still being waged to this day, proves that this conflict is deeply rooted in the eternal struggle between good and evil. Just as in other conflicts, "big picture" politics are also involved in deciding how The Drug War is fought.

To those who are currently engaged as combatants in this ongoing conflict, I say good luck and be safe. To those who are addicted to drugs of any kind, I pray that you will get the help that you need to recover. I also express my condolences to those who lost loved ones and friends to the illegal use of drugs. In addition, I ask you to take a moment to remember the law enforcement officers who were killed in the line of duty during drug enforcement operations. To those who continue to produce, smuggle and sell illegal narcotics and dangerous drugs I say go to hell, because that is exactly where you belong.

THE END

93054387R00212

Made in the USA
Columbia, SC
03 April 2018